An American Paramedic's Account of Life Inside the Mysterious World of the Kingdom of Saudi Arabia

Paramedic
to the Prince

Patrick (Tom) Notestine

D0818575

ISBN: 1-4392-4581-9
ISBN-13: 9781439245811

Visit www.booksurge.com to order additional copies.

Paramedic to the Prince

———

"As a journalist and observer of the human condition, Notestine is highly perceptive. Some Saudis will not be particularly flattered by the way their country comes across, but this warts and all account is never ever dull."

Daniel Bardsley, *Gulf Times*

"Tom literally grabs you by the throat in the opening chapter. A fascinating look at contract EMS in a foreign land. An insightful look at Western Middle Eastern society and mindset. A fascinating autobiographical tale."

Norm Rooker, *EMS Responder*

"This is one of the best books of its kind. An insight into Saudi life that most westerners would overlook."

Sandy A. Mitchell (Author), *Saudi Babylon*

"This book is a must read and should be placed in American school libraries. So fascinating, that I got up at 3:00 am to finish it. It is raw, interesting and the emotions it stirs are intense. Made me both laugh and cry."

Theodocia Mclean, *Ghost Writer Reviews*

"In short, it is a really interesting book and I highly recommend it."

The Anonymous Arabist

About the Author

_____

Patrick Thomas Notestine was born in Yuba City, California. Growing up in this rural farm community, he drifted from job to job after leaving high school, working as a gas station attendant, auto-mechanic and farm laborer amongst other things. At the age of twenty-three, he took a long hard look at the direction his life was going.

At the back of his mind was a keen interest in science and medicine. Becoming an Emergency Medical Technician (EMT) seemed a good option, so he enrolled on an EMT course at his local community college. Graduating in March 1983, he found work on an ambulance in Sacramento, California. It was there working alongside a seasoned paramedic, that he found his calling in life.

He attended UCLA School for Pre-hospital Care, and in 1986, graduated as a paramedic. Living on his sailboat, he found work in the San Francisco Bay area. He started out on primary 911 response ambulances and eventually moved on to helicopter and air medical evacuation.

In 1993, the author answered an advertisement to work at a military hospital in Saudi Arabia. This is where his story begins. Working on the private medical staff of King Abdullah, he enjoyed unprecedented access to the "House of Saud".

The Middle East is never far from the author's heart. He has recently taken yet another assignment working as the

Emergency Medical Coordinator for a major oil company in the Persian Gulf.

Tom enjoys exploring the desert with his wife in his beat up 1985 Range Rover. His hobbies include scuba diving, rock climbing and caving.

Authors Message: I consider myself an ordinary person, who was fortunate enough to have some extra-ordinary opportunities. I hope whoever reads this book enjoys it as much as I enjoyed writing it. I believe everyone has a story to tell.

This just happens to be mine.

Patrick Thomas Notestine

This book is dedicated to:

———

The many healthcare professionals I have had the honor to work with over the course of my career. These professionals work selflessly to preserve and save lives. They have mentored me and taught me the true meaning of compassion and empathy.

And

My wife Pamela without her belief, encouragement and support this book would never have been published.

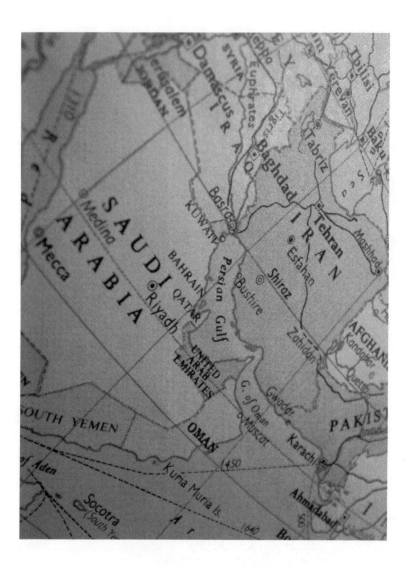

Contents

Saudi Arabia – September 11ᵗʰ 2001

I was working in Jeddah, Saudi Arabia, in my office at the King Faisal Hospital, where I managed the ambulance service. It was late afternoon, on a Tuesday, in September 2001. I got a call from a South African guy who works in the military hospital there. He told me one of the World Trade Center towers caved in, and they blew up the Pentagon.

"Huh, *ri-ight*."

"No," he said, "I swear to God."

I put down the phone, and ran into the office of the Assistant Director of the hospital, right across the corridor.

"What's going on? What's the matter?" Short fellow, dyed black hair, a real slime-ball. I correctly suspect that his job is way beyond him.

I told him "Something bad's happening."

I ran to his TV.

"You got CNN? Turn on CNN."

We sit close and watch it, I'm from California and he's from Little Rock, Arkansas. Guys start filtering in behind us through the open door. All the Saudi management, a few in western suits, but mostly in long white *thobe* and red checkered *ghutra*. On the screen there's the New York skyline, sparkling white and blue and sunny, with a vast dark cloud rising from

Lower Manhattan. They're leaning against filing cabinets, and hunched over the backs of chairs, riveted, silent.

I look up at them, the Head of Personnel, several men from the finance department, and the rest of them, and the second plane is coming in. Live. You have never seen such broad smiles. They were joyous. It was wow, man, HIT IT. Nobody said anything.

Well the aftershock lasted a couple of hours, with everybody shaking their heads and bemoaning the carnage, and then nearly all of them left. I have a habit of saying what's on my mind.

"Salman," I said to my friend, his name's Salman Al Dubair, "do you realize, when that second plane hit the tower, how you and Ali Bougesh were standing there grinning? It means you're happy."

"Oh no," he said. "We are always smiling. It's a terrible thing."

Not long afterwards Prince Naif[1], the Minister of the Interior and Information, explained publicly that this dreadful event had been a Jewish-American conspiracy. To single out the Saudi passengers on those planes at such short notice, as the FBI had done, was ludicrous; every one of them had been a harmless student or tourist. In the Jewish section of New York on that day, on the other hand, the Jewish community had been dancing in the streets. Not a single Jew had been killed in the World Trade Center, because they had all been warned to stay away. Four hundred Muslims had died in this conspiracy to incite hatred of Islam.

George Bush talking about a crusade really pissed them off. After that most Saudis believed that the CIA, or the FBI, or

---

1   Prince Naif bin Abdulaziz is one of the six surviving sons of the Kingdom's first king, Abdulaziz Al Saud. Third in line for the throne, he has held the position of Second Deputy Prime Minister since March 2009.

George Bush personally in collusion with Israel, was responsible for 9/11. It is the conventional wisdom among Saudis to this day, even highly educated ones.

I was talking to a smart, rich Saudi I know, who was complaining that religious education in Saudi Arabia puts a brake on scientific development. You couldn't get the students to think, he said, because they'd been taught to view the world from a religious perspective and never to ask awkward questions. The people in charge didn't want people to think they wanted a continuance of the status quo. Then 9/11 came up, as it always did for a few weeks afterwards, and he went on to tell me how exultant he'd felt. He and his friends had watched the whole thing and cheered.

"Because we hate Americans," he said complacently.

"But not the people, of course," I said. "It's like us in the Gulf, we were against the regime, we didn't hate the people."

"No, the people too," he said. "We hate all Americans."

He looked right into my wide blue eyes as he said it.

I've been here for the best part of a decade, I speak Arabic okay (with a Riyadh accent), and for two years I was part of the entourage around Crown Prince Abdullah, now the reigning king, the ruler of the Kingdom. I have been served with a plateful of fried mice (it isn't a misprint) and presented with a gold Rolex, and I have been arrested with alcohol 200 proof. I know, like and respect Saudis rich and poor, and in some ways I am as mystified as the day I came.

It's like the jihad. At the hospital there is an ambulance driver, Mustafa, who is studying Islam and Sharia law at university, with a view to becoming a judge (the kind that decides whether people will lose a hand for stealing). He is a kind, gentle fellow, a little holy man or *ulema*, and since he's totally bought into the system, I want to explore this idea of the jihad with him.

"Let's say," I suggest to him, "that it's like in Afghanistan when you were fighting the Russians, and you run up and fight and you're killed, and it was a jihad, so you go to heaven, like the best place, the *best* level of heaven?"

"Right," he says, "yes."

"And," I say, "you get 72 virgins."

"Yes."

"You really believe that?"

"Of course," he says, "if it is in the Quran, it is so."

"So what do the girls get?"

"What?" He looks bewildered.

"Just last week, that 28-year-old Palestinian girl[2] blew herself up in Nablus, on the west bank of Israel. What will she get? Will she get the best place?"

"I suppose so."

"What about the virgins? Does she get 72 husbands?"

"No!"

"Well she's getting ripped off, then."

He looks mutinous. This is heresy and he should cover his ears or get me arrested, but he wouldn't do that, he likes me. I hate reductionist arguments too, but how can I get through to him except with irony? I drive right on.

"Do you really believe that if you die in a jihad, God will give you 72 virgins?"

"Of course. It is in the holy Quran."

---

2   On January 27, 2002, 28 year old, Wafa Idriss walked into a shopping district in Jerusalem and detonated a bomb killing herself, an Israeli, and injuring 150 others.

"And you don't believe some man made that up, some very horny man who wanted to entice other men into battle, and make them fight like crazy and not fear death?"

"It is in the Quran which came from God."

"Do you think it came from God that you can have four wives, but Mohamed, peace be upon him, could have as many wives as he wanted because he was the Prophet? Like I just talked to God yesterday and he said Mohamed, you just go have sex with as many of those young girls as you want as long as you are *married*. So he had eleven. Do you think God really said that to him?"

"Of course! It is in the holy Quran."

A lot of western staff at the hospital resigned after 9/11 because they were scared. Rocks were thrown at the bus full of nurses on their way to work. A group of young Saudis drove by a New Zealand couple and pointed a gun at them and laughed. A young Saudi man gunned his engine right out of the parking lot in the gas station and came at me, real fast. I jumped, Jeez! and he loved that. Locked his brakes and slid sideways, laughing. 9/11 briefly gave the Saudis a sense of pride and empowerment. Out there on the streets was triumph, sheer delight. We just laid low, stayed home in the compound.

A few months later, I made the penultimate sacrifice. I am not easily intimidated, but I do have some common sense, so I sold my BMW Z3. Now this was a very, very, nice, shiny black two-seater, with a great stereo. You have the top down all the time in Jeddah with the heat, and you're blasting your American rock n'roll music, and you very much draw attention to yourself. There is, at a guess, fifty percent unemployment among young Saudis, and I look at it through their eyes; even without seeing myself as an infidel, I see a sonofabitch American, over here taking money out of our pockets.

So I sold the Z3 and got a Jeep that blends in. There is of course a limit – I won't cower – but it was a very nice little car and I'd have hated to see it get blown up. With me in it.

Much of this book may read like a long whinge of frustration. *Why can't the whole world be just like us?* That's George Bush's position. I don't share it. I don't claim to understand Saudi thinking, but in America we have corruption, social exclusion, institutionalized cruelty, and ignorance to match a great deal of what you find here.

Hold tight to that thought.

2

Paramedic to the Front

In January 1993, I turned up to work at the King Fahd Hospital in Riyadh, Saudi Arabia, for the first time. I'd been a paramedic for seven years: three with the air ambulance service in Tulsa, Oklahoma (road accidents, heart attacks), and four years before that I'd trained in LA, in Watts, and then worked in the Bay area of San Francisco (drive-by shootings, stabbings, substance abuse). I knew my job.

I'd been briefed; the King Fahd Hospital is familiarly known as the National Guard Hospital, and the 250,000 strong National Guard is the major military force in Saudi Arabia. Its dedicated hospital caters for everyone, from general to foot-soldier and their families, who live in subsidized housing in Riyadh. Plus it receives stray road accidents because of its location near a major highway, and any emergencies from Naseem the nearby slum.

It is quietish, good for my induction. It's my first time out of the States, and I've only been in this country a few days. I'm still tired and not fully acclimatized to the blazing sun of a Saudi winter. I've got an impression of Riyadh, a huge modern city, dotted with minarets, sprawling across flat desert. I've got accommodation with a couple of other guys in a Westerners' compound, and I come to see the hospital. It's like any good general hospital, white and grey everywhere, well equipped and busy. Right outside, traffic is roaring to and from the city center along the King Fahd Highway which runs from the airport east into Riyadh.

The lead paramedic, John from Alabama, is in the emergency room. All is reassuring white, clean, up to date, prepared for anything, and divided into five or six areas: triage, fast track (runny noses), examination (medical but not critical), the dome which is for minor injuries, a preparatory area for admissions, and a thirteen-bed trauma bay which is to be my workstation. Nurses get rotated through trauma, but paramedics don't. We are always there.

"You ever wanted to be a doctor?" John says.

"Y'know, I've thought about it. Maybe someday I'll go to medical school."

"I got news, Tom," he says, "You're a doctor now."

"What do you mean?"

"You'll see."

By the end of that first day, I did. In the North American emergency room paramedics work with doctors, who tell them: "Get me an IV here," "Intubate there," "Get me some drugs, I'm gonna push some Lasix," – this wasn't like that.

As a paramedic in this hospital in Riyadh you are relied upon to make diagnoses, intervene and treat, all on your own. You have to make instant decisions: who needs admitting, who gets transferred. You do a lot of triage. You decide who can be treated and who is beyond help. There are so many critical patients, and so many people around them, that you've got to take control. The doctors don't have time to monitor each one.

Saudis are concerned citizens. They see a freeway pile-up, and they don't expect a public ambulance to deal with it.

The Red Crescent ambulance will head for a public hospital, and nobody would wish that on a fellow citizen. Instead they swerve across the highway in their little white Toyota pick-ups, and pile six or seven bodies into the back, and roar off to the National Guard Hospital.

Beep, Beep, Beep. PARAMEDIC TO THE FRONT, growls the intercom. You run out of the emergency doors and into the heat, even at night it can be hot, and you start doing triage right there. There are endless multiple pile-ups, and most involve children. In 1993 Saudis did not – would not – would literally rather die than – wear seat-belts. There's a law now, but then they just didn't think about it; the highway accident death rate was twenty five times higher than it was in the States. Life and death were God's will. Seat-belts were for sissies, and probably un-Islamic, and you cut them out of your car with a knife.

Kids – and this is still true today because the new seat-belt rule doesn't apply to them – travel standing between their parents and any other children in the family car, which is driven at maximum speed immediately behind the vehicle ahead. Western medical staff call all small children Saudi Airbags.

A lot of pediatric injuries happen at night. In Saudi Arabia, in summer, the daytime temperature can reach 120°F. Bedouin families stay indoors most of the day and socialize at night, when it's cooler, so the kids play out then too. That's when the action is. Children will be playing in the street at two or three in the morning and get hit by a car. It's easy to recognize these injuries; there's always a broken femur on one side, and a head injury bleeding into the brain on the other. If the car hits them from the right, the head injury where they smash into the tarmac will be on the left. You get good at diagnosing this.

There is a traction splint we use on the femur, and we regularly ran out of them since demand was so high. So we would improvise. We would take a child-size crutch, run it out past the end of the foot, tie the ankle with a sling, and then pull the leg straight and tie it off on the end of the crutch. If we had down-time we'd spend it making pediatric arm splints, because we got through those by the case as well. We got good at making them out of old cardboard boxes and gauze. Paramedics are practical people.

The first or second day I was there, there's been a beaten woman housemaid, and several road accidents one after another, and I'm in a state best described as startled. A small Toyota sedan drives up, honk, honk, PARAMEDIC TO THE FRONT. Two guys are prone on the back seat. Obviously their faces have gone through a windshield, because they have ghastly gashes and their skin and their white *thobes* are red with blood.

We maneuver both out on backboards, stabilize them, and run them into the ER. The guy who's brought them in, having picked them up off the street, has grabbed me and he's saying, "No, No, Come on there's more" – of course in Arabic, but there's a Saudi student interpreting for me. I resist this guy. I've seen there are no more, and no room for any. But he pulls me out onto the apron and opens the trunk. Inside is a folded body soaked in blood, a skull fracture, half the brains hanging out. This guy's jabbering at me in Arabic. I just stare.

"Yeah, he is dead," I agree.

I can't believe I'm here.

We go back, sort out the two live ones, and go for tea in the tea-room. My hand is shaking as I lift the cup.

"John, this is too wild. I dunno if I can...."

"Oh," he says, "you'll get used to it after a while."

After a while, I did get used to it, eventually becoming lead paramedic in the trauma bay. I had been a paramedic for years before I arrived in Saudi, Watts included, but I'd seen nothing like this plethora of injuries. In the States we might see something that gory once a week, or once a month, but this was one after another, disasters coming at you like they were swinging down a helter skelter, in the course of everyday. Often outside the Emergency Room doors there would be a pickup full of bodies, anywhere from two to eight people in the back, and you'd come out into broiling sun, feel pulses, lift eyelids, and stare into pupils.

"Dead, Dead, Alive, Walking, Head injury, Over here, Over there."

You make your decision within forty seconds. One of my biggest nightmares was saying Dead! – Because you have to do it so quickly – and then thinking somebody might not be. I had a nightmare about it once.

Around that time I asked John about what I fastidiously called "My Role". I'd been used to working with North American physicians, expecting their decisions, but the Saudi doctors were always busy, or absent, or indecisive. I explained my uneasiness about taking control.

"I bin here three years," he said gloomily. "These dumb motherfuckers gonna kill these people, you just gotta go in there and do what you gotta do."

Triage must be fast. The biggest accident I ever triaged was a bus rollover involving 38 people and I did it in ten minutes. By this time I'd been at the National Guard Hospital for a while and was kind of inured. As they were driven in some of the injured couldn't move, some of them couldn't stand, and about 25 of the 38 couldn't walk.

"Every one of you that's walking, sit over there."

They were Pakistani laborers on this bus, and Pakistanis, that is to say the ones that survive in Saudi Arabia, are subservient people. Most of them staggered to a seat, so I could ignore them. Then I had to sort out the dead, and I identified them fairly quickly. That left me with nine for the trauma bay. You check the airway first, and if they're breathing that's good. If they have some kind of compromise, blood or vomit in their mouth, or some other breathing problem they go to the top of the list. Next thing, you stop obvious bleeding. Of the nine, about six were in a life-threatening state and had to be treated fast. It is overwhelming until you have done it repeatedly. You have to distance yourself, especially from the pediatric trauma. That is how you get out after your shift without going crazy; you keep your emotional guard up while you're working so you can deal with all this.

The housing compound was about a mile from the ER, and on a day off, I went up to the hospital to fill out the sheet for my pay. I rode my little Honda dirt bike up there. There was a white car parked in front of ER, with the doors open, which isn't unusual, and the red streaks down one side of it were blood.

I remember thinking, "What the Heck happened here?"

The passenger seat was soaked with blood, and the door was open, and on the ground was a white blob. I walked by. It didn't fully register.

I walked into the trauma bay. There was a sheet over a small shape.

I said, "What's going on?"

A paramedic said, "Yawanna see something really gross?"

And I hadn't even said yes or no, and he pulled back the sheet, and I would have told him NO. There was a 4-year-old kid who'd been hit by a car. It flashed in my head, the driver had hit the kid, put him in the passenger seat, and when he pulled him out that was his brain I saw on the ground. Because his head looked like a broken eggshell. You could see the whole cavity inside, within one second I had put it together –

"You *sonofabitch. I do not need to see this on my day off.*"

I hadn't got my emotional guard up. I wasn't prepared. It really traumatized me. I still find it hard even to think about it to this day.

That paramedic was not re-contracted after his first year; he got sent back to California. I heard he is now a self-proclaimed expert on international travel for medical workers. He even wrote a book about it.

Expatriate workers generally go through predictable stages of culture shock: exaggerated enthusiasm for the new place is followed, after a few months, by deep disillusion, then resignation, fascination and a kind of loyalty. Because of my job, and the hours I was working, and the social segregation that all Westerners suffer, I jumped off the high board already dismayed and dove straight down to disillusion. It was only after about a year, when I was making some progress with the language, that I started to enjoy the company of Saudi friends, and understand what separates us, and why. But I had plenty to learn at the National Guard Hospital first.

3

Dying Saudi Soldier Syndrome!

———

The National Guard are the Wahhabi Muslim, Bedouin descendants of the tribesmen who helped King Abdul Aziz, of the House of Saud, to unify (i.e. conquer the rest of) Arabia in the 1920s. Every male member of these tribes is entitled to a job for life in the National Guard, in which Crown Prince Abdullah has taken a personal interest since he took command in 1962.

In theory, this is an army responsible for civil order. In practice, it's two hundred and fifty thousand people in a welfare system. Once you join, every member of your family is covered for health insurance. Since Saudis don't do nuclear families, this means your wife and children, parents, grandparents, brothers and sisters and cousins and in-laws will be looked after. You also get nice housing and a monthly salary which, for someone who cannot read or write (and most Bedouin are functionally illiterate), is an attractive offer.

Should the opportunity arise to fight in defense of the nation, enthusiasm is pretty pallid. John told me that during the first Gulf War twenty per cent of the National Guard went AWOL. How he came up with that figure is a mystery, since indicators of low morale generally remain unrecorded, and certainly unreported, but it wouldn't surprise me.

Several mornings a month serious cases of DSSS, or Dying Saudi Soldier Syndrome, would be brought in. When I first started to work at the hospital, I did wonder why nearly everyday when I came in, there would be a young soldier lying rigid on the emergency room floor, surrounded by an agitated group of his friends screaming for help. But there was a lot of other stuff going on at the time.

The cadets' training ground was right behind our hospital. At six-thirty every morning, a car, or a jeep, or a military ambulance would pull up and four or five anxious young soldiers would come in carrying some comrade, stiff as a board with his eyes tight shut. Touch, shake, yell at him, he would stay like that (Remember, training starts at seven). His friends would be fussing around him.

"We found him like this – we can't wake him up! He needs help!"

As a paramedic, I'd always have a stethoscope around my neck, but at the National Guard Hospital I quickly learned to tape two ammonia capsules to it against DSSS. I'd produce the caps and crunch them under his face, and he'd hold his breath until he could hold it no longer, then with one huge inhalation he would get a huge hit of pungent gas, and having to fight for breath he would magically come to life.

That's when I slap him gently around the face. Oh, he's fine now.

For the longest time I said to myself, are these soldiers so stupid as to think their friends are not malingering? John enlightened me. Not only does the Dying Saudi Soldier get out of training for a day, they all do. They take turns. Who's gonna be the DSS today, and who's gonna be the concerned friends?

In this military hospital nothing happens to the DSS, he just gets the rest of the day free.

They are Bedouin. The uniform is uncomfy. It's a furnace out there, they need to wear thin white cotton neck-to-ankle to catch a draught up the backside. Nowhere else in the world do you see a regular army with their boots without laces, hats on backwards, shirt untucked. Military discipline is pretty much absent.

A new paramedic, Kurt, had just arrived from New York, and we were outside the hospital near a soldier on guard.

I nudged him, "Watch this."

I said in Arabic, "Abdullah, let me see your gun."

He just slung over his machine-gun, no worries. There were no bullets in it, anyway. They accidentally shot a window out of the hospital once, so they're not allowed bullets.

This is not to say Saudis are not warlike people. On the contrary, they are extremely fierce in defense of tribal honor and family values. They don't go in for fisticuffs, they'll back off rather than engage in a brawl, but there is swift recourse to dagger, pistol, or occasionally sword.

One evening I was working with Dr Razak, an Egyptian doctor, a very experienced trauma surgeon, when a man with a sword wound was carried in. A single sword cut had sliced open one side of his chest and lacerated his heart. There was blood pouring out. Usually, with trauma to the heart, we'd have to seize rib spreaders, make an incision and pull the ribs apart, but this time it had been done for us; it looked like a neat sword-cut diagonally across each rib. Despite our best efforts the patient died.

The Royal Guard, the elite force that works for the Crown Prince, carry ceremonial swords. Most are descendants of the original soldiers who fought with Abdul Aziz, and some of their swords are historic, perfectly crafted artifacts worth tens of thousands of dollars. They take great pride in them.

And you can get swords in the markets.

I was working with a fine paramedic, Dave from Florida, and one evening a private car skidded up. A young Saudi man lay still on the back seat, *thobe* covered with blood, face parchment white. I took a look, and was pretty sure this was a corpse. We kept a gurney by the front door and they wheeled that out and flopped him on it.

Dave was standing by the door.

He said, "I see blood around his neck."

The corpse was motionless, so I pulled the head back to see the injury. Somebody had just slit his throat right across and cut his trachea in half. I could look down it and see the vocal chords. But as I pulled his head back he drew breath inward; I had opened his airway.

I'm holding his head back, we're standing there at the emergency entrance.

"*Damn*, Dave, you ever seen anything like that?"

"No Tom, I never did."

We stand there, frozen, wondering how to secure the airway. We had our ET (endotracheal tubes) for intubation; they go down the throat, and through the vocal cords, and they're long – but this was no ordinary throat obstruction.

Dave says, "You know those trach tubes we got?"

These are little tubes, curved, with a balloon on the end that blows up to seal the airway. Dave had correctly identified the problem. This guy had had a tracheotomy of sorts anyway, except cut across instead of in. So we waited until he took a breath, his vocal chords opened up and Dave just popped that tube in there, filled it full of air, and put four-by-four bandages on each side.

So now he starts waking up because he's breathing. The oxygen is getting to his brain and he's starting to fight us. Maybe he's only been out cold four minutes tops. But the more he fights, the more he's bleeding, and the more agitated he gets, the more likely it is that something will give way. He has both carotid arteries cut anyway. When you get a clean cut across an artery it won't bleed. There is an extra layer of muscle around an artery, though not in a vein, and it clamps shut. A jagged cut to an artery spurts a lot. Veins have no clamp and they ooze. But this was a surgical cut the guy had, with a razor or a very sharp knife.

We gave him a shot of Pavulon to effect temporary paralysis, put him on a ventilator to breathe for him, and got him into the operating room. He made a full recovery.

Blood feuds between the Bedouin go on and on; the Al Utaibis have some long-running argument with the Al Anazis, and so on. If tribes that have resented each other for years meet in a social situation, and offence is caused, somebody will probably get attacked with a knife or a gun.

One night there was an uproar around the emergency room, which was unusual, even for Riyadh. Half a dozen cars roar up, and about thirty Saudis pour in to the ER. They're all talking at once and they bring in two injured friends; one guy gets carried in, and one walks. Both are wearing the now familiar blood-stained *thobe*. The carried one has a stab wound to the chest, and the other has two knife slices right across his upper arm. They're brothers apparently.

Meanwhile, more people are turning up, even black-shrouded women. There's been some confrontation at a wedding, and all the guests are following on, shouting across each other. The chest wound has no pulse and he's not breathing. We start CPR, cardio-pulmonary resuscitation, wheel him fast into the emergency room, and slam the doors to the trauma bay closed. Outside people are hammering and screaming to get in. They want to see our guy with the chest wound. His stab wound goes deep through the ribcage into the left ventricle of his heart. We can't keep the mob out of here much longer. Somebody calls out the National Guard.

Our guy's bleeding out somewhere. Dr Razak cracks his chest and we start two lines in the internal jugular vein, then we start running blood and breathing for this guy. The racket outside is tremendous. The Guard have turned up, there's a guy with a machine gun every two feet outside the emergency room, and more armed men outside the entrance.

And those hundreds of people out there are his family. Outside, the one with the cuts to the arm keeps demanding, "How's my brother?"

Inside, in the emergency room, Dr Razak reaches in, finds the hole in the ventricle and sutures up the heart where the knife has gone in. We're still doing CPR, but the guy's been dead too long; he's bled to death on the way to hospital.

We are told not to leave. It's getting on for an hour since this started, and now a third wedding guest has turned up, dumped on the tarmac out of a car, and raced into the emergency room protected by the soldiers. This guy's had the living shit beaten out of him. A crowd of men has hit him in the head with rocks, they've taken off their *arghals*, the black cord circles that keep the red checkered *ghutra* on, and used them as whips and left nasty welts all over him.

We're told what happened. Nearly all Saudis are Wahhabis, hard-line Islamists. At their weddings, men and women do not mix. They celebrate apart, in different rooms. A man from the groom's family peeked at the girls. The two brothers caught him. There was an argument. He pulled a knife and stabbed both of them. Their friends brought the brothers to hospital, while the men of the bride's family turned their attention to the culprit.

We've got three hundred wedding guests screaming outside our room. The only reason they haven't killed this beaten guy yet, is that they don't know the chest case is dead. We start treating the murderer. Meanwhile the National Guard, who know their own kind only too well, are bringing a small motorcade of three Chevy Suburbans as close as they can get to the emergency entrance. There are six armed men in the first car and the last car, the middle one is bristling with machine guns, and about a hundred soldiers form a path through which they hustle the guy we've patched up. They push him into the middle vehicle and race off, sirens wailing.

The frustrated crowd now has nobody to yell at except us, inside the hospital. At last one of the senior soldiers goes out and tells them that their friend has died, and that the police will take their enemy before the Sharia court. They disperse soon afterwards, disappointed.

They knew that learned men would deliberate before announcing that, according to God's law, the culprit should be executed in public at Chop-Chop Square, down town, on Friday. But the bride's family had been cheated out of killing him with their bare hands. He did, after all, look at their women. He may even have seen their faces or their hair. He had behaved without respect! He had boldly gazed upon their women as though they were common prostitutes. The entire family's honor was besmirched, and the men folk remained unsatisfied.

4

God Willing

———

There are three things I thought I knew about Saudi Arabia when I went. One, Saudis are rich from oil. Two, they decapitate adulterers. Three, no woman dare be seen in public unless she is robed in a black *abayah* that covers her from head to toe.

The first two are based on fact, but need a lot of qualifying. The third, about women, doesn't even begin to describe the strangeness of Saudi women's lives.

I had not been working at the National Guard Hospital more than two months, when I heard the now familiar call, PARAMEDIC TO THE FRONT, and people screaming *wallada, wallada* (labor) – there was a woman in the final stages of labor out in the parking lot. This happened all the time (my record was three parking-lot deliveries in one night), so we kept a delivery tray at the front desk beside the emergency entrance, with cord clamps and drapes and so on.

So I run out, and the lady's lying in the pickup. I can't of course see her face, because she is covered in black, but her knees are splayed and I can see the child's legs. It's a breech birth.

By now I know enough Arabic to say, *"lazam anna ashouf"* – It's important I look.

She hears me, sees me, and somehow clamps her legs together. She is squishing the baby. I can see her eyes glaring at me through a slit in the black cloth, but I force her knees apart and can see the baby is about three quarters of the way presented, and the cord is looped twice around the neck. I can't let go of her knees without her clamping them shut again.

She's suffocating the baby, but God forbid I, a man, an infidel, should see her private parts. She's yelling at me and Dr Razak comes out.

"What is the matter?"

"She's fucking killing this kid."

I am so frustrated. I can't do my job. What else does she think I want with her? She's in labor for Chrissake. He yells at her in Arabic. I get my finger around the little shoulders and cut the cord, but of course the child is not breathing. We have to do CPR; the heart-rate is very slow, we have to intubate and rush him to neo-natal intensive care.

I never found out what happened to the baby, but I asked Dr Razak what he thought. He said as the child had been deprived of oxygen for well over 6 minutes, and thanks to her it had, it would probably suffer irreversible brain damage.

I couldn't stop talking. I was really distressed. I didn't understand these people.

I said, "She'd rather keep her legs shut and kill her own child than let me look!"

"She was right in what she did," Wahleed, the Saudi EOD (Executive on Duty), told me.

"Whaddya mean, she was right?"

"Absolutely. She did the right thing. A woman's honor is beyond any other consideration."

I knew that a country where women are literally swathed in black from head to toe must have a few hang-ups, but until that moment I didn't appreciate that the hang-ups could be so very different from ours. Within weeks of the parking lot incident I was starting an IV on a tiny baby which was screaming and crying, its mother was jiggling keys to try and keep him entertained. I'm crouched over the cot and trying to fix this tiny arm, and suddenly a huge breast lands against my cheek, and the nipple's being shoved into the child's mouth. I look up frantically for the interpreter.

"Can you tell her to get that thing outta my face?"

But God forbid I see her face or her hair. You'll see women on trolleys in a corridor, the *abayah* pulled up around the waist, but if a nurse removes the cloth covering the face, they'll scream.

After I'd been in Saudi Arabia for a year things began to make sense, in a crazy kind of way. But at the start, it was like standing at the bottom of a well getting pelted with offal. I'd no idea why these people appeared to be acting according to values I didn't understand, and I was too far removed from anybody in control to find out.

I'd come to Saudi on a two-year contract expecting nothing more than to save up some money, and travel, and go home richer than when I came. As a paramedic I was in the trauma bay treating critical cases all the time. We never got rotated out. Our burnout rate was high, but I liked stashing the money in the bank. The basic week was 44 hours before overtime, but my record was 28 twelve-hour night shifts in a row. In the States I would routinely work three twelve-hour shifts in a week, whereas in Saudi I always did four or five. And at night, which is the busy time in Riyadh.

Maybe it wasn't the sweetest introduction to the customs and culture of a foreign land.

Inevitably, after a few months nothing surprised me. I began to sort out sets of behavior, and look for some consistency. I looked around the country, I talked to Westerners, I nagged the student interpreters to teach me some Arabic. I'd hardly been out of America until I came here, so like most western medical people I assumed, without even thinking about it, frank confrontation of medical problems and a belief that science afforded us a measure of control over events. These ideas were fundamental to the way I did my job.

Neither cut any ice here, because neither takes Allah into account.

First, I learned about frank talking.

If a cancer patient, say, was dying and his family asked whether he would be okay, the Saudi doctor would answer, "*Inshallah*." If God wills it.

This would amaze me. I think I know when someone extremely old and sick is about to expire.

"He's got no chance," I'd say to the doctor. "Why don't you say?"

"But who am I to tell the family that he is dying?"

"But they will hold on to that hope."

"It would be cruel to say."

One family wheeled in their ancient father day after day. He had had a severe stroke which permanently affected his left side. Everyday they were told, *Inshallah*, he will improve, and the next day they'd bundle him into the car and drag him up to the hospital, and into the emergency room again. Finally I gently told them, through the interpreter, that he was probably not going to improve. When they had gone the interpreter looked dismayed.

"Why did you say this? Why did you say he does not get better?"

"It's true. Now they can plan their lives. Now they know."

He shook his head.

"It is not for you to say. It is for God."

Terminal patients were brought into the emergency room who would, in the States, have been coded DNR: Do Not Resuscitate. But there was no such thing as DNR here. If their heart had stopped, we had to try to start it even if this person had zero chance of returning to life, far less recovering. It was not for us to assume that God did not have a plan for that person. The western medics developed slow codes, a way of giving the impression that we were compressing chests and giving drugs, without getting at all aggressive with the therapy.

We had a head injury, a bad one. We take him to CT scan. His brain is full of blood. There is no way this guy, about 19 years old, is going to live. I intubate him, bag him to breathe for him, and all the consultants and a surgeon come down to check him out. He has hardly any blood pressure, and I'm thinking he'd make a good organ donor, but they're not really into that here. And everybody drifts away. Nobody says what is going to happen next. Maybe they don't like to. But they've gone, and I'm still sitting there covered in blood, with an ambu-bag. He's not on the ventilator, there's a tube into his lungs. He still has a heartbeat, beep, beep, beep. Still has a blood pressure, and everybody's gone. After a while a nurse comes in.

"What are you doing?"

"I'm breathing for him."

"There's nothing you can do for him, he's brain dead."

"I know that and you know that. If I stop, then he'll go hypoxic, his heart rate will slow down and stop, and he will be dead. But get the doctor's ass down here, because I don't have authority to let the boy die."

She shrugged and went to get a doctor, but I could see she was of that state of mind – it's only Saudi, nothing's as serious as it would be in the West. But to my mind they're all patients, and all get my best effort, irrespective of where we are. The Pakistani street sweeper will get the same treatment as the prince. And anyway, it's up to the doctor to make a decision about death and I am getting the feeling that Saudi doctors have an almost superstitious reluctance to do that.

Finally the doctor comes.

"You can stop, why are you even going on?"

I try to explain that my release from responsibility must be expressed, not just delicately ignored. Later, I wrapped up the boy's body in a clean white sheet and took him to the morgue. It was stressful.

Liver transplants began at the National Guard Hospital and I was sent out to meet a medivac plane. On board was a canary-yellow, 82-year-old gentleman, in a hepatic coma. His liver had shut down, but they'd brought him in for a transplant anyway. They wasted a perfectly good liver on him, because of course he died. But the family felt better because nobody had said death was inevitable, and they'd insisted on every kind of medical intervention that God might, if God was some kind of obsessive compulsive, have wanted.

The other taboo was talking about anything political. Right off the freeway, hidden from businessmen speeding by from the airport into central Riyadh, is the ghetto called Naseem.

As paramedics we got called out in the ambulance to treat people in National Guard housing, so I'd been driven through Naseem; great anonymous concrete blocks of despair in the burning sun, set in a sea of dust and broken things, and mangy dogs.

On three occasions we had children aged between four and eight brought into the emergency room; they'd been abducted off the street down there, sodomized and tossed back out of the car. Once we'd done what we could, we were duty bound to transfer them to Shimaisi, the third-world public hospital, for further treatment.

One came in with his father and insisted it had been a *metawah* that took him. He was a bright lucid kid, and his father believed him. The father was standing there wanting to kill somebody, and we called the police. You don't stay long in Saudi without learning to recognize a *metawah*. The serious ones are official members of the Commission for the Promotion of Virtue and the Eradication of Vice, which comes under the Interior Ministry, run by Prince Naïf (he of the Jewish-American conspiracy theory). They wear the usual *thobe*, only short and hoicked up to show the ankles, sandals, often a white *ghutra* without an *arghal* round it, and their beards spring out from below the chin, giving them a square-faced look like Bluto in the Popeye cartoons. The dangerous ones – the real fundamentalists that enforce public decency – are accompanied by policemen and carry a big stick. I had no doubt, and nor did anybody who heard the boy and his father, that a Saudi four-year-old would know a *metawah* if he saw one, but the police played it down.

"He's a child, he is most likely mistaken."

They couldn't do anything; if they'd been able to find this man, and charge him with the offence, which carried the death sentence, he would simply have counter-charged the family with heresy. They would have made an accusation that flew in the face of God, because the *metawah*, at any rate the members of the Commission, have a direct line to Allah. I could not help but think of the correlation between this and the Catholic priests on trial back home.

I also learned in the first few months the importance of *Inshallah* generally. I did not meet a Saudi for whom God's will was not the impenetrable meaning of life, and end to all arguments. It came up in every conversation. Let's say I wanted something.

"Can I get it now?"

"Five minutes, *Inshallah*." God willing.

I hear: *Maybe*. I try again.

"Will it be here by the end of the day?"

"*Inshallah*."

I smell an avoidance strategy. Struggle with my Arabic.

"Westerners do not like it when you say, *inshallah*."

"Why?"

"Because to us *inshallah* means, maybe. I want you to say, *akeed*." It is certain.

"To us it is the same."

But they never do say *akeed*, because God has already decided what will happen, and to predict God's will would be presumptuous and heretical.

Or say I was horrified by something. Anything: maids jumping out of windows to get away from abusive employers, cruelty to children – and I was told that maids had no rights and parents were allowed to beat their own offspring – Both of which were in fact the case.

I'd say, "Why doesn't the government do something?"

But Saudis would think that bizarre. Gently they would explain.

"The laws are Sharia laws. They come from God. There is nothing in Sharia law specifically to protect a maid or a child, so nothing can be done. With God's will it won't happen again."

We had a child of twelve whose leg and arm had been broken, on different occasions, by her father. Eventually she ran away from him, but she had injuries and had to be brought to the emergency room. The father caught up with her. The police were called. Of course they could do nothing. The father was within his rights to beat her. If he killed her, then he would himself be put to the sword, because that is the penalty for murder under Sharia law, but there was no way to protect her. *Inshallah*, the police said, it would not happen again.

Hence the seat-belt issue. I would watch a Saudi colleague drive into the hospital grounds.

"Why don't you wear a seat belt?"

"You know Tom, God has a time and place where you are going to die. Nothing we do can change that."

"You mean to say I can smoke as much as I want, drive crazy with no seat belt, eat any kind of food I like, and it doesn't matter?"

"Nothing we do can make a difference. Our lives are God's, to take from us or not. The Quran tells us so."

After a few months at the National Guard Hospital I got a car. At first I drove defensively, cautiously. I got trashed. I'd be in the slow lane and the guy in the fast lane would swerve right across me, VROOM, a right-angled turn, I'd be braking to avoid him and nothing behind me would even slow down.

I learned. When you drive in Saudi Arabia and something cuts you off, you do not alter your speed, you do not slow down, and if necessary you hit him. It's his problem; he didn't get out of your way.

"Stop for me or hit me, it's up to you. *Inshallah,* you'll stop for me."

Every once in a while you'll get a guy who's stubborn, and you'll ram him. I had a Chevy Blazer, a 1982, the Tank was its nickname; it had huge tires high off the ground and it was the size of a small bus. Anybody touched me in that thing, I'd just keep going. I got bumped and sideswiped and rear-ended on a daily basis. I had a guy turn left in front of me and I clipped his back bumper and he spun round like a top, and I just kept on truckin. Oh, Saudi.

5

Becoming an Urban Legend

———

After a month at the National Guard Hospital I was claustrophobic. I'm a Californian; I need ozone. Fortunately, Saudi Arabia's one railway line goes to and from the Persian Gulf. With three days off, I left the Westerners' compound, got to the railway station and bought a ticket east to Dammam. I rode the train across flat sand for two or three hours. I took a hotel room, swam and did some snorkeling; I saw a livelier, more relaxed version of Riyadh beside the deep blue sea. Two days later, I returned to the station to buy a ticket back.

I knew that in theory, as a non-Saudi going more than fifty kilometers beyond my place of employment, I should have asked my employer (my "sponsor") for a travel letter saying why I needed to go. But I didn't have one.

"Travel letter?" the clerk said. "Where's your travel letter?"

There are soldiers with machine guns in the station. Idle. There are men, women in *abayahs* with bundles, and impatient children behind me in the queue.

"Well, I think I left it at the hotel. I had it, but I lost it."

The queue is getting fractious. Soldiers are gathering round. At last, an event. What are we gonna do with him? Finally, they get a guy who speaks English. Up he comes, talking importantly, clearing a path through. Everybody's got something to say about me now. I can't understand any of it.

"Where do you work?"

"The National Guard Hospital in Riyadh."

He looks at my passport and my face. Gives it back to me. Looks disgusted, barks at the clerk.

"Why did you even call me? Give him a ticket, let him go." He leaves.

As far as I could make out from facial expressions, body language, and tone of voice, this is what was said. I got given a ticket.

I get on the train and everybody's been watching this, there are fifteen sullen soldiers round me, hovering outside until the train pulls out. At last we move off.

I'm sitting next to a small dark man, who turns out to be an Egyptian schoolteacher. He speaks good English.

"What was happening?"

"Well," I said "I didn't get a travel letter."

"You are American?"

"Yup."

"If you are Indian, Asian, Egyptian, you go to prison."

He was right. I could go to jail for moving around Saudi Arabia without permission. Americans get away with a lot more than other nationalities, because the Saudi authorities make a political judgment on whose embassy will, or will not, bring pressure. There are seven million expatriate workers here, and two million of the seven are from North America, Europe, or predominantly white ex-colonies like Australia. The Saudis need western workers and technology, but we have a secondary, political value as well; Western individuals can also be scapegoats. Thus, Prince Naif (Minister of the Interior) can trundle out mini-versions of his 9/11 conspiracy theory whenever an opponent of the ruling class blows something up. A bomb goes off around an Englishman or a Dutchman, and he says it's all about turf wars between western alcohol barons.

"There are no religious extremists or terrorists in Saudi Arabia," he announces.

So it follows, that the only way a Westerner can get blown up in his country, is to get involved in the illegal alcohol trade. Westerners, Sandy Mitchell and William Sampson, spent thirty two months in a Riyadh prison, after being tortured into confessing to the car bombing murder of a British engineer, in November 2000. Some accused Al Qaida, but Prince Naif boldly claimed, "There are no Al Qaida in Saudi Arabia."

After Al Qaida claimed responsibility for a 2003 suicide attack in Riyadh, which killed thirty five people and left two hundred injured, Prince Naif was forced to eat his words. It was soon after this that Sandy Mitchell and William Sampson were quietly released. It was no coincidence that five Saudis held in Guantanamo Bay were released at the same time.

To understand Prince Naif's way of thinking, you need a ten-point guide to Saudi politics before 9/11 and for a few years afterwards. Here it is.

1. The Royal Family, the House of Saud, controls the oil revenues of Saudi Arabia, which is sitting on top of a quarter of the world's capacity.

2. There are thirty thousand members of the House of Saud. The ones that matter are seven old men. They are seven of thirty seven sons born to King Abdul Aziz, who died November 9th 1953. They and their families are mind-bogglingly rich.

3. Prince Naïf is one of the seven. The Crown Prince, Abdullah, is essentially Regent. King Fahd, the oldest and most senior of them all, is too sick to deal with affairs of state.

4. The annual income of the ordinary Saudi man is around six hundred dollars per month.

5. There is no political structure through which any discussion about wealth redistribution can be channeled.

6. There isn't even a mental structure for it. This is a pre-enlightenment society. If you're sick and poor, that's God's will.

7. Religious men, who like the people, are poor, have the confidence of the people. (That is, the masses. They don't boil you alive for heresy, as they did in Europe in the Middle Ages. They don't have to, religious dissent of any kind is unthinkable. It is not only blasphemous, but indicates derangement.)

8. Religious men oppose the House of Saud's friendly stance towards America, and by association Israel.

9. Religious fanatics sometimes feel so strongly about this that they try to blow up Westerners.

10. The House of Saud lives in mortal terror of being next on the list, but nobody likes to acknowledge that fear.

Confrontation of uncomfortable reality is not a Saudi thing. There are two reasons for this. One is cultural: it's the thinking behind that refusal to talk about imminent death – a kind of squirming away, a notion that pre-empting, or assuming, God's will before the event may be blasphemy.

The other reason why Saudi royals prefer to think of theirs as a trouble-free social system is that if they acknowledge its problems, the communication dam may burst. Everybody'll want some. Before they know where they are, they'll end up like the Iranian ruling class, hounded out of their own country, forced to flee forever to London or Geneva.

At 9/11 the American administration woke up to the fragility of American influence in Saudi Arabia and they have begun, as I write this, to seek control over a different bunch of oil wells[3].

I came to Saudi Arabia in January '93 having taken the advice of my recruiter to wear a lightweight suit and a tie, and thereby create a good impression. I flew from Tulsa to Chicago, Chicago to New York. Waited for the plane and got a beer at the bar, knowing it would be my last for a couple of years, and pretty soon I was drinking with a couple of Saudis wearing western clothes. We got along fine.

"Your first time in our country?"

"Yeah."

"You'll like it there, don't worry. It's a good life."

Regular guys in tee-shirts and jeans. Students.

I'd never been out of the United States, except to Mexico, and certainly I'd never taken a twelve-hour flight before. The plane was like a cattle car, just packed. On the last leg there were long queues down the aisles. Every Arab gets up carrying a big wash-bag, takes a long time in the bathroom. I'd watch a pretty girl go in, she'd take forever, and out would come this Ninja, clad head to toe in black, her eyes barely visible between

3   On March 20, 2003, The United States of America spearheaded the invasion of Iraq. According to then president George W. Bush the reason for the invasion was to disarm Iraq of its "weapons of mass destruction." To date no such weapons have been found.

folds in the cloth. I couldn't believe it. The men went in like accountants on a dress-down Friday, and strode out in snowy floor-length robes with checkered head-dresses.

Pretty soon all the passengers were wearing the uniform of their team: the men's team or the women's. Small children looked more or less normal. Only American adults were conspicuous. It was as though everybody, by mutual tacit consent, had decided to exclude us from their club.

We landed. We waded slowly out through garbage: a sea of old newspapers, wrappers and rubbish. They'd just trashed that plane. I was shocked. I had wrapped my discarded paper, kept my area tidy, and behaved like a good citizen. This is not the Saudi way. In Saudi Arabia if they have something empty they just throw it out the window, or onto the ground. There are teams of little Bangladeshi men in green coveralls who go round and pick up your trash. If you're following a car in front, things fly out of it. But I didn't know that.

Outside the plane it was mid-afternoon. Hot wind in my face; hot wind against my light-weight tailoring, the shirt and tie that I'd worn from Tulsa to Chicago to New York, and now to Riyadh. The airport was air-conditioned, which was a good thing as I was destined to spend the next six and a half hours there. I could see blazing yellow and white outside, pearly blue sky, white buses, and cars. Crowds came and went, but my recruiter had omitted to tell the National Guard Hospital the exact day I was coming, so they had no accommodation ready for me. It took that long to sort out the mess.

As I waited, I was mystified to see, twice, that every white-robed man in the airport stopped what he was doing, knelt on the floor facing in a particular direction, bowed his nose to the ground and prayed. This surprised me. I had seen a few men doing this at JFK, but I had thought they were the members of a strange sect. I had not yet realized that here everyone prays, five times a day.

Around ten or eleven at night (I'm now 32 hours from Tulsa), in the dark, a little Filipino man from the hospital's housing department arrives in a beat-up Toyota pickup. He collects me. He speaks English. We turn onto the highway that crosses flat desert with billboards in Arabic. Not far ahead is the big city, light blazing from high buildings, and off in the dirt at the side of the road next to the traffic there are mats thrown out and people are sleeping beside parked cars. There is often a little brazier going, and some of the guys have their portable TV hooked up to their car batteries and they're sitting in their *thobes* watching TV.

"I thought Saudis were rich! They're all living out here in the dirt."

"No," said the driver, "that's what they like to do."

I was mystified. He was right though. I know that now. At the end of the day, the average Saudi man in Riyadh will drive out with the family, park wherever he can find a clear space, have a picnic and watch TV. The Bedouin don't like sleeping inside. Often they're overcrowded at home. I like to camp myself. Out in the desert you can see the stars.

The next day I woke up in the empty dormitory where Housing, having had no notice of my arrival, had given me a bed for the night. I showered, and strolled outside for a look at the compound. Inside its high walls, pale villas and apartment blocks sprawled in every direction, with proper streets and parked cars, and I could see a playground, but it was like a ghost town. And always this yellow sun, beating down on concrete, and a huge blue sky. I went back indoors, figuring somebody must eventually call me and let me know what to do.

John, the paramedic from Alabama, found out I was there. He shared a villa in the same compound, and he and Bob, a big blond paramedic from Oregon, came and picked me up. Driving over to his villa John told me when to report to the hospital, and that I'd have two weeks orientation.

We pulled up outside his home. It was nice, cool marble floors inside, but he'd made every room dark and put in spinning disco lights. This was a guy who'd never had any money and suddenly he had a lot, so there's a beautiful stereo with lights, and the apartment is all fixed up; it's like being inside a particularly well-equipped trailer.

"Nahss, isn't it? Got it fixed up with ahl mah stuff. Yew wannah drink?"

"Yeah." I recalled the information sheet issued by my recruiter. *There is no alcohol at all in the whole of Saudi Arabia.* "I'll take a glass of water."

"Oh, we got *beer*, here."

They brewed their own beer. There is hardly a Westerner in Saudi who does not know how this is done, and I was about to be initiated. You buy non-alcoholic beer and put it in a five gallon tub with a kilo of sugar and activated brewers' yeast, you let it cook and bubble, and then bottle it. You buy those lovely juice bottles with self-sealable wired caps, and use those for storage and distribution purposes.

It happens fairly often that bottles explode. You have to make sure it's not still bubbling when you cap it, as John points out. Once it clears, after about three weeks, you have beer that's 10% alcohol, so then you need to cut it 50/50 with non-alcoholic beer again.

Westerners in Saudi are artists in winemaking, beer making, and distilling. I was to find more alcohol, and more drinking in that country, than I've ever seen in my whole life in California. It's almost like you tell a Westerner they can't do something, they're gonna go to great lengths to do it.

It got hotter. In the day, people don't go out. Summer came, and I had never lived before week after week in temperatures way above 110°F. When it hits 120°F, there is supposed to be an announcement telling people they should get inside in the cool, but you never hear that. The radio will say it's 118°F, so that the little Bangladeshi in the green coverall will stay right out there, sweeping the streets. In summer you go from air conditioning indoors, to air conditioning in your car.

They eventually moved me into a two-story villa with marble floors and marble staircases, television and video, and a fully equipped kitchen. Every single room had a wall air-con unit. There was no central air conditioning, and you'd see the same thing in office buildings. They were designed that way, with zero concern for energy efficiency. In the villa which I shared with another paramedic, we had nine wall air conditioners and they broke constantly.

I learned not to give it a thought. If anything broke, I just picked up the phone. If a light bulb blew, a little man with a ladder from Pakistan or Somalia came round and changed it. Every week a maid from Malaysia or the Philippines came in and scrubbed my bathtub and cleaned my toilet. For twenty dollars a month another little man came and washed my car everyday. I had no concerns. Phone calls were put through, cable TV was on tap, laundry was done, I had no utility bills to pay. Transport to work arrived promptly before my shift, and unauthorized entry to the compound where I lived with three thousand other Westerners, was prevented by the National Guard.

Outside my work, I was banking a good salary tax-free, making friends, shopping in the *souq* and partying. I had been seduced.

I even became an urban legend.

Dr Brewerton was a North American doctor on the Crown Prince's personal medical team. He was a Mormon from Utah, married, with half a dozen children to put through college. By working for Crown Prince Abdullah, he'd be able to do it. I thought he was a decent fellow, and when he arrived within six months of me, and moved into accommodation in the National Guard Hospital compound, I showed him around Riyadh.

We went down to the animal *souq*. You need to steel yourself for a visit like this. Saudis don't respect animals or treat them with kindness. Some of us had only recently rescued a kitten that had been tied to a bush with wire around its neck, and left to die. I'd seen dogs stoned, and kicked, and dragged behind cars.

In a parrot cage in the market, cramped up miserably, is a baboon, a female. I reach my hand out and the poor thing grasps my fingers.

"That might make a nice pet," says Dr Brewerton. She's holding on tight.

"How much do you want for this?"

The man wanted 1,000 riyals, $300. Eventually we got him down to 400 riyals.

I bought the baboon, and brought her back to the villa I was sharing with another paramedic. Whatever she wanted, she would take. I had fruit on the counter. She leapt on it, stuffed it in both cheeks, and if you tried to pull her away she would bite you. Quite hard. But as long as she got lots of food she was fine. She slept in my room the first night, and kept trying to groom me. If I left the room she would shriek. There is no sound like it, it's half way between a scream and a croak. When I came back she was peaceful.

There was a van for when the paramedics were on call, a beat-up thing for driving around the compound, and up to the store. The baboon loved driving around in the van. She would sit on the passenger seat.

My room-mate Kurt looked after her the second night I went to work – but this baboon was driving me wild; I was on night shift and getting no sleep. She wanted to sit and groom me all the time. My bedroom upstairs had a balcony. Fronting the balcony and providing shade we had a concrete façade, ornate Arabic style, and she enjoyed climbing around on that. The wall of the apartment block is straight, flat, up and down. There is no way she could get off. It was twenty feet down.

So it's late in the afternoon, 120°F, and I shut her out there, so I can have one hour of sleep before I have to go to for work. I have been dozing for about fifteen minutes when my friend calls me from the hospital. Bear in mind this is over a mile away.

"Tom, your monkey's down here at the hospital."

"That's impossible. The sidewalks are too hot, and anyway how could she have got that far?"

I fly to the balcony – she's gone.

I run down, and drive to the hospital. Round the back beside the kitchens, where the bus lets the employees off before their shift, there are about thirty people peering into a dumpster. I shove my way through. There she is, stuffing leftovers into her little face, both cheeks bulging. She has a collar and I lean in to clip the leash onto it, but she's trying to bite me, and I'm just falling in all over bits of half-eaten kebab, and plastic cups of orange juice going sticky in the heat.

I'm thinking Security is going to hate this. Everybody's scattered. She's pulling one way and I'm pulling the other. Finally I get her out, and get her back to the villa in my car.

Everything is fine, but I realize I can't take care of her. This is going to get worse. Baboons are wild animals and don't belong in villas.

And I am supposed to be at work in 30 minutes.

Not long before all this we'd had a lecture at the hospital, an Englishman, who came with a colleague to give a talk. He was Dr Nigel Browne who was running the King Khaled Wildlife Center. They were trying to re-introduce the Saudi desert gazelle after the Bedouin had killed them all. They had the gazelle in an enclosure (two or three acres around) in the desert, but the Bedouin were dining off those as well – they came through the fence – so his program was failing.

Other zoologists out there were studying baboons. I remembered the talk, and I had his card if ever I wanted to visit. It was way out and they'd said – bring some nurses.

I empty my wallet, find the card. I call Dr Browne and explain.

"I just can't control her. Can you take her?"

"We'll be happy to. Be there in an hour."

The baboon is jumping around the living room, watching while I telephone, chattering, and looking for more to eat. I call work and tell them I'll be late.

Here comes Dr Browne, he gets out of a pickup, in the back there's a huge cage. He pulls on leather gauntlets to the elbow, seizes a long pole with a noose on the end. Like he's coming to collect a wild animal. I go downstairs to meet him.

"You won't need that," I say, "this thing follows you around like a dog."

"Uh-uh. Tom, I've dealt with baboons – I take no chances."

He's hauling the cage out, lays it on the front porch. I go up and collect her.

She's walking behind me as usual, she walks out on the porch, she takes one look at Dr Browne and one look at the cage and she shins up the corner of the villa in three seconds. About forty feet up. I spend the next hour on the flat roof chasing around. There is no edge to this roof. I coax, I cajole, I throw water at her – finally I grab her, my uniform is covered in sweat, I get the leash on her, she is kicking and screaming and biting and off she goes in the pickup. To a happier life, I hope.

I still had no idea how she got to the hospital, but when I got to work, there were plenty of people waiting to tell me. There is a bus that circulates through the compound picking up employees, and during a shift change it circles about every fifteen minutes. Well the bus came and stopped at the corner near my villa, and when the driver opened the door she just jumped on with everyone else and sat on the seat. Everyone was terrified of her since they'd never seen a baboon before.

She just rode up to the hospital. She didn't get off at any of the interim stops, she just waited till all the rest of the people alighted, and then got off too. And then jumped into the dumpster.

Emails went out all over the world, about the baboon that rode the bus. About a year later I was flying back from Bombay with a planeload of Indians and one other Westerner. We started talking. He was an engineer, worked in Jeddah. I introduced myself – Tom, National Guard Hospital, I work in the emergency room. He said – Tom with the baboon? He had heard the story eleven hundred kilometers away. When I had been there a few more years, people used to tell me the story like it would all be new to me.

"Did the guy pay you for that baboon?" my flat-mate asked, afterwards.

I would have paid Dr Browne any amount to take her away. She was probably around a year old, an adolescent, he said. They do not make pets. They bite too hard. And they hate to be alone.

6

Wassta (connections and influence)

In the first thirty years of the twentieth century, when Abdul Aziz and the Bedouin tribes that fought with him captured the vast land of Saudi Arabia, nobody at first understood the importance of the oil beneath the sand. Riyadh was a small walled city, and the only desert town of note, excepting Mecca. Mecca has been a source of income from pilgrims for over one thousand five hundred years. Jeddah is the natural cultural capital, an old fortified port on the Red Sea, the home of merchants and immigrants. Jeddah is historic, confident, less threatened by new ideas. Riyadh today is bible-belt fierce, and brash. Both towns were insignificant enough when Abdul Aziz came to power.

The Bedouin were nomads, not city folk. They understood camels, hunting, dates and fishing, a few handicrafts, and trade. They had one rare skill; they knew how to thrive in the desert.

When the House of Saud started selling oil, and money came flowing in, an infrastructure was bought: potable water, roads, hospitals, television, consumer goods, and of course defense. All these were part of life in Saudi Arabia by the 1970s and all had to be got from the people who paid for the oil. European and American contractors built the infrastructure and sold the arms, and the Japanese provided the video players.

The House of Saud seemed to have a never-ending supply of money. It was just gushing out of the ground. Drive through Riyadh, you're on smooth American-built freeways and underpasses and overpasses, or tree-shaded boulevards like King Abdul Aziz Road, where you see the huge Ministry of Petroleum (bright blue, designed to look like oil pipelines) and the saucer-shaped Ministry of the Interior, which is supposed to look like the ripples of the sand in the desert.

On the Mecca Road you pass King Fahd Medical City. This is the biggest medical complex in Riyadh. King Fahd, with more money pouring in than he knew what to do with went to Houston Medical Center and bought the blueprints. He came back and had the whole thing built, an exact replica of Houston, and filled it with brand-new equipment.

That was in 1984. In 1993 when you went past, you'd think you were looking at a functioning hospital, but it was abandoned and empty. It was never opened. Grounds men attended to the grass and cleaned the windows. Every once in a while we heard that the Ministry of Health were going to hire staff and open the hospital. The hospital was designed with accommodation for three thousand staff in various apartments and villas. There were X-ray machines, CT scanners in there – never used and now over a decade out of date. From time to time somebody works out a way of getting the billions of riyals required to re-equip it, and then they don't[4].

When I first came to Saudi, we had a man come to the National Guard Hospital trying to recruit staff for the Medical City. It was going to be a public resource, but most people still have to go to Shimaisi.

---

4   King Fahd Medical City was finally inaugurated by Crown Prince Abdullah on October 5, 2004, twenty years after it was first built.

With all this cash flowing in pretty soon there were a hell of a lot of healthy, well fed Saudis, with nothing much to do. They could cope with desk jobs, the bureaucratic, organizational jobs, but when it came to hands-on action, all the new resources were staffed and maintained by foreigners. Publicly, everyone agreed that this had got to change.

"Saudization" was very much in fashion when I came in '93. Within five years there were going to be no Westerners left in the country at all. Sure, the Indian scaffolders and Pakistani mechanics would remain, because Bedouin are too proud to lower themselves to dirty trades, but there would be Saudi pilots, doctors, nurses, paramedics, teachers, computer programmers, water engineers, architects, and surveyors.

These days Riyadh is a city of several million people, and Jeddah of well over a million. There are plenty of Saudi professionals, but because they are not selected on merit, they may be excellent at what they do, or useless. As a result, there are still plenty of jobs for Westerners, and Saudis themselves often trust western professionals better.

I knew a Saudi university student, who was a translator at the National Guard Hospital. He wanted to be a pilot with Saudia, the national airline. He studied hard. If he passed their exam, they would provide excellent training, first on small planes, then on bigger ones, until from a standing start after ten years he would be a Captain flying internationally. Most of his training would take place in Florida. It's glamorous, it's well paid; it's a job with great status and even a measure of political freedom.

This student, who was single-minded and clever, not only passed Saudia's exam; he came third in the whole country. But they didn't give him a chance. The people who got onto the training course were, let's say, numbers seven, twenty, and sixty. Not him.

"I have no *wassta*," he told me sadly. *Wassta,* is influence or contacts.

"Don't you know anybody?"

"Nobody. And my family knows nobody."

I felt angry for him. What had been the point of working so hard? He was disheartened. Advancement by merit is a sham in Saudi Arabia. The structure is there, but the reality is *wassta*: jobs for the boys. The obvious conclusion for a young man like that is that there's a class above his which is blocking his advancement. Hmm, what to do?

The same thing prevails throughout every profession, the armed services and the National Guard included. Al Tweijry, Jamjun, Bin Mahfouz —certain rich loyal families will be favored. In Kamis, a town in the north-east, I heard there was a general with Down's syndrome. He was a high-functioning Down's person, certainly, but from an important family, so of course he would be preferred. Like any other incompetent with *wassta*. There would be no room at the top for a smart Bedouin wishing to work his way up through the ranks.

So ambition is discouraged. For those whose families do have *wassta*, there is just as little incentive to be conscientious. The plums will fall into their lap in any case, so why worry? The trouble with this is that most professions carry a certain amount of responsibility. Architects and engineers can't be incompetent, or houses will fall down and kill people. Paramedics should kind of understand how to save lives, otherwise – *et cetera*.

When I'd been in the country a while, I was given twenty National Guard soldiers to train. They were just back from the States. What had happened was this. In America there is a basic EMT – emergency medical technician – course that takes

150 hours of tuition and practice, over four weeks. The National Guard had sent a group of 18 to 21-year-old Saudi boys to the States to do this course. Out of this uptight, segregated society, they had picked ten young men with *wassta* to go to Atlanta and ten to go to Chicago.

The course wasn't going to take four weeks though. It took three years. They got one year of English language training, well okay – but an EMT program stretched out over the next two years? Even then they couldn't complete it, because they were not allowed to do hands-on patient care – just theory. The program was run by an American university, so I don't know whether that restriction had been approved by the university for liability purposes, or by the Saudi government. Ordinarily, students on the course work with patients. They have to buy public liability insurance in case they do any harm, and they are supervised.

The fees of these privileged young men had been paid for three years, and free accommodation was provided during their stay, and they'd received $1,000 a month, per head, as pocket money. Oh yeah, and field trips to Las Vegas and New York. Well would you believe it; they didn't want to go home? They petitioned (unsuccessfully) the Saudi government to extend their time in the States.

I know all this, because I received all their paperwork. I evaluated it and it was meaningless. I stood in that air-conditioned classroom and looked at them, twenty young men, slouching in their olive drab National Guard uniform and *ghutra* for the first time in three years. I tested them, I gave them the same exam they would have taken in Atlanta or Chicago, and every one of them failed miserably.

I called them all together again.

"Come on, you guys. What did you do for three years? You just partied your asses off, didn't you?"

They looked sheepish. Much later, when I got to know them better, I ran an informal test on one of the twenty who was a friend: Night-clubs of New York. He did very well at that.

In the meantime, we had to do something, because the National Guard had spent a whole lot of money on this particular Saudization exercise. We set up a two-month refresher course. This was essentially the four-week EMT course that they should have done, only taken slowly. Practical experience, skills practice, classroom time. It was the second time around so you'd think they'd have sailed through, but I could see that most were unmotivated, and often squeamish.

We were training them in IV therapy. I put a canula in the bag for the intravenous fluid to run, and showed them how the needle goes into the patient, and how it all works.

"Now I want you to get into pairs, and practice on each other."

They exchanged astonished glances.

"What?" they said. "Stick needles in each other?"

"Yup. That's how I learned in the States, that's how you'll learn here."

There was muttering. One of the young Saudis spoke up.

"There are many people in the hospital, sick people. We'll practice on them."

"No—ooo."

Mentally I reviewed the possible alternatives. There are mannequins you can use that have veins, but we didn't have those. The best way to learn is on another person, because you know how much pain you are inflicting; you learn to be gentle. I had to insist.

"You pair up and practice on each other. It's normal and it's the best way."

They refused.

"You will do this. It is part of your training."

"We won't do it. We can use the sick people."

"Okay, I'll get Colonel Tweijry, he'll tell you."

"Go ahead."

Colonel Tweijry was their CO – commanding officer. I called him down from his office and he went into the classroom to talk to them. I could hear laughter. He came out.

"You know they really don't want to do this. Can't they just skip this bit of the training?"

"IV therapy is very important. It saves lives."

He shrugged. I try another tack,

"You know when I told them I was going to call you, you know what they said? They said go ahead and call him, he's nobody, he can't do anything."

His face darkened under his *ghutra*.

"They said that?"

"They said that."

He stormed back into the classroom and yelled at them.

"I want you all outside, at attention, NOW!"

They trooped out and stood to attention in the sunshine. It was mid-afternoon, about 115°F, and they were in uniform. I got the impression that it was the first time they'd been stood to attention in their lives. After ten minutes a bus came and they all got on. Off they went, towards the military prison.

Fifteen minutes later they were back, having agreed to do the exercise. It took months, after they'd qualified, for most of them to become competent at starting an IV, or taking blood pressure without supervision. They were not stupid; they just didn't see why this should be their responsibility.

I didn't see how I was going to get them through the exam at the end of the course, and I said so to Colonel Tweijry.

"Oh no," he said. "They'll all pass."

Saudi exams always yield a 100% pass rate. We were not allowed to fail our students.

"But if they all pass, then some will not be fully competent."

"Where they work," he explained, "will be a matter of how well they do."

In other words, the real duds would go to patrol the dust at some military clinic on the Yemeni border, where any harm they did would go unreported. They would never be heard of again. Those who were useless, but unlikely actually to kill anyone that mattered would go to a clinic somewhere in the National Guard housing complex in Riyadh. The guys capable of improvement would work in the ER at the hospital. And the competent 15%, who genuinely passed the exam, would be eligible for responsible positions with the Crown Prince, who heads the National Guard.

In the event, it didn't work out quite like that. I know because later on, two of the best students ended up working where I did, for the Crown Prince, and a third showed up with them who had been bottom of the class. But he had *wassta*.

Education is free for Saudis, but it is heavily religious and unscientific, and encourages a certain arrogance (implicit in the instruction that all who are not Muslims will burn in hell). A Bedouin cannot easily see himself as a mechanic, or a computer programmer, or an employee in a shop. Those jobs are done by foreigners. He wouldn't want their lives. He doesn't have a work ethic: all that is too tame. He is above all a Bedouin, and proud, because he can impregnate his wife and produce sons and the will of God has helped him along so far. Being fiercely defensive of his brothers and sisters in the tribe, that's pretty much it as far as ambition goes.

King Faisal, who went head to head with the West over some deal or other, famously said "We came from the desert; we can go back to the desert."

Like hell they can.

There are over twenty million Saudis now (or so the government says). They lack skills and they live in cities. They watch DVDs and drive Chevy Suburbans. When their sons marry, they bring their brides home, and the whole family lives together. Some of the sons will stay jobless, and the ones who are working will have to support the rest. Unofficial figures put unemployment as high as 50%. All figures are unreliable – there isn't even a proper census – and if they assessed unemployment among women, it would be 99% (women are pretty well invisible). The Bedouin in the street doesn't have much of an income, and even if he works as a cab driver, or sells vegetables in the market, he will probably live in ramshackle public housing, and be mortified by the wealth of others which is constantly visible. He's got a feeling of inferiority, underlying his pride of identity.

Saudi society is a simmering pot.

Somewhere near the top are those sons of rich families who have managed to get an education. Some of them get to be doctors. Four years out of school, aged 22, they can be qualified to treat you. It's too quick. Even if they develop excellent competence through practice, you often come across a lack of responsibility in these guys. Maybe a lack of human fellow-feeling, or an arrogance, I don't know what it is, but I give you just one example from my experience at the National Guard Hospital.

A guy gets brought into the emergency room, a Pakistani laborer, his leg is sliced open from one end to the other, and is full of dirt. He's been brought here because it's the nearest place, and it's my job to tidy him up and send him on to Shimaisi the public hospital. But it's two o'clock in the morning and they won't work on him for hours, by which time his leg is going to be septic. So I call the young surgical resident and explain the case.

"Is he a Saudi?"

"No," I say. "He's a human being. Come down and see him."

Reluctantly he comes down, and takes a look. The Pakistani lies patiently on the bed, his leg red, and black, and brown, and rigid.

"Wrap it up, and send him over to Shimaisi."

"Let me tell you," I say, patiently "what will happen to him in Shimaisi. His leg will not get cleaned properly, and it will get infected. In the end, they'll lop it off. Or they'll lop it off right away and save themselves the trouble. There's no way they're going to take him into the operating room and debride his leg and fix it like you can."

"I've had five hours sleep since the night before last."

"I know, I know, and it'll take you four hours to fix his leg. But if you don't do it, he will lose that leg over at Shimaisi, we both know that. For the rest of his life, he will have only one leg and he won't be able to work. Now what do you want to do? Save his leg, save his working life for the next thirty years? Or go back to sleep?"

"Oh, Tom you are a bastard. You put it that way, I must fix the leg."

This sense of duty was something I had just introduced him to. He was a nice young man, probably 25 years old, but in his four years of medical training there had been no time for discussions about duty. In the States he would have had to do four years of pre-med and take M-cat (the medical school test) before training began, and then put in four years of medical school followed by at least two years as a resident. Here, you get a religious education and your four years in medical school, and then you've got a residency. If you have an ethical problem, I guess you consult a *metawah*.

Western paramedics can arrive with ten years experience in the ER; they have to be careful not to offend these guys, and to treat them with respect. The Saudis doctors are proud. Only they have learned medicine as a trade, rather than a calling.

When Ramadan comes, if you've got two or three critical patients waiting to be seen at the end of the day, they're out of luck. Like everyone else the doctors will have been fasting since sunrise, and when dusk falls and the prayer for *Iftah* (break fast) is called, the doctors are outta there – phwitt! Off to eat. For a lot of these guys Ramadan is no longer the modest duty that it is supposed to be. Instead, a lot of doctors fast all day and at night it's party time. The critical patients just have to wait. Their fate is up to God, anyway.

7

Funny-Looking Kids

———

We got a lot of FLKs in Riyadh.

FLKs are Funny-Looking Kids. Traditionally Saudis marry their first cousins, so that wealth does not leave the tribe. This results in one of the highest pediatric genetic defect rates in the world. At one time, nine of the top ten geneticists in the world were working in Saudi Arabia because of the plethora of mutations.

It is not that Saudis don't know why it happens. Sophisticated Saudis shun first cousin marriage the same way they shun camping in tents and driving a Suburban. They think it's a Bedouin thing, and to proclaim yourself Bedouin is somehow low class. But for a lot of traditional families, *Inshallah,* it won't happen. So there are a lot of Downs babies, congenital heart defects, babies with their heart vessels twisted round, or internal organs somehow wrong, and FLKs.

I was assessing a baby who'd come in with breathing difficulty, congestion in the lungs, and of course he had an odd-shaped head – it's normal for us to see such defects.

The doctor asked, "What did you notice?"

I told him.

"Did you listen to his chest?"

"Yeah."

"Well go back there and listen again."

I did. This time I noticed. He had no nipples.

The doctor said, "You'll never see that again in your life. You'll see four, six, eight nipples, before you see a chest with none."

The child is six months old, and the stack of charts is two feet high. It is his medical history. *This child fits into no known genetic syndrome*, I read. I think it would be a good study for a thesis. Maybe I will call it Notestine syndrome...

Another time, we were doing a lumbar puncture on a child, from the look of him about twelve. He seemed retarded. He had pubic hair.

The doctor said, "How old d'you think he is?"

"Twelve?"

"Younger."

"Nine?"

"Younger."

"Wow. Well..." I thought, how young he could possibly be according to any textbook I have ever read.

I tried again, "Seven."

"He's three", said the doctor.

"He has gigantism. He is going to be huge."

There is an IVF unit at the hospital. Wealthy Saudi families seized on IVF as soon as the technology existed, because a woman's value is gauged by her fertility. Women come in their fifties. They try IVF and we get a lot of strange births.

There was a set of twins being medivaced from Jeddah to Riyadh. I was told they were conjoined, so out of interest, I volunteered to collect them from the airport. It was pitiful: one large misshaped head, with a face on each side. One face had a cleft palate, and a body with two legs and two arms. The other side had two arms and then one long fin-like body, and out of the bottom of the spine, came a necrosed – black, dead – tail of tissue. It was like one huge skull with a misshapen body, and there was no way it was going to survive. Yet, surgeons repaired the cleft palate. Then they tried to separate the bits and of course it died[5]. The brains were interconnected. The mother was fifty four and on fertility drugs.

We had a cute little fellow on the wards, he lived there, looked after by the nurses. His name was Ahmed. There is a syndrome where babies are born with a recessed jaw. The tongue usually occludes the airways, and they have to have a tracheotomy. The surgeons have to wait until the child is older to build up the jaw. Ahmed had this syndrome. He was born in the hospital, and his parents went home and never came back to collect him. He became the little pet of everyone; some of the nurses would take him home at weekends, and buy him little presents at Christmas. He would wander around the hospital and play – he spoke English, Tagalog, but no Arabic at all.

The Saudi doctors got very frustrated by this. One day – Ahmed was close to five by then – he came along, clutching the hand of a male nurse. They were waiting for a car.

"Where's he going?" I asked.

They were taking him to some kind of orphanage. He'd been at the hospital all his life, but they were telling him he was going for a day trip, a little ride in the car. The doctors had kept him there as long as they could, but now he was going where they spoke only Arabic.

In Riyadh traditional first cousin weddings prevail, but less so in Jeddah. There is no point in arguing about

---

5   King Abdulaziz Medical City in Riyadh has become a world leader in the separation of conjoined twins. As of March 1, 2009, the hospital has successfully separated 14 pairs of conjoined twins.

cousin marriage, no chance of a sudden reversal in the habit of generations, because so many Saudis believe it would be irreverent to assume control of the future, as God might – who knows? – have intended a person with two faces and a tail to survive.

I know a doctor who was about to marry his first cousin. I queried the wisdom of this and he said, "If it happens it is God's will."

Nobody seems to take God's response for an answer though. They can see God's will made flesh – like this person is stone cold dead, this person was never intended to live – and then they start negotiating.

One day in 1994, I was glancing through the *Arab News,* when I read that the Ministry of Health had reported 122 cases of AIDS, in the Kingdom of Saudi Arabia. All the cases, of course, were expatriate workers who had been deported.

What a relief, they were all foreigners, and they'd gone home.

I asked a Saudi doctor what he thought. He shook his head, puzzled.

"I've got two patients with AIDS, and they're both Saudis."

The first time I took a weekend break to Bahrain, on the Gulf, I went with a French-Canadian nurse and another girl from Arizona. Just about everyone else on the plane was a Saudi man. We got there, showered and changed, and got ready to go clubbing at the Sheraton. Everything starts late, after midnight mostly, because of the daytime heat, but we were drinking in the bar by about nine o'clock. I noticed many young, pretty blonde girls in western clothes, and felt a nice glow, because whenever my eye happened to catch theirs they would smile invitingly. I liked being so popular.

It got crowded and the dancing started. The *thobes* and *ghutras* were coming in, and pairing off with the blonde East European prostitutes. Now these guys don't have the word "condom" in their vocabulary. Sex to a Saudi means unprotected sex. Anything else would be an affront to their manhood.

They do therefore, occasionally, return and give AIDS to their wives. We had a child born with AIDS in the hospital, and the family refused all tests on the mother or father. A Saudi doctor told them the child had probably caught the disease from the western nurses. I challenged him about this. He knew it wasn't true, but there was no way he'd confront the husband. Discussing taboo subjects, as I already knew, is just not what happens, and now I could add sexually transmitted diseases to the list of unmentionables.

You might wonder how Saudis receive sex education. I wondered the same myself, when a young couple, the girl seventeen and the man in his twenties, came in after a year of marriage. The husband complained that she could not conceive. What was the matter with her? There was a full examination, and the lady doctor asked the girl about her sex life. Gradually the truth became clear. Sodomy was the only method of intercourse the young man knew about. As for the girl, nobody had told her anything. She was still technically a virgin, her hymen was intact.

Saudi men appear, to a Westerner, oddly cavalier about anal intercourse. I have seen a fifteen-year-old brought in with a rectal bleed the day of her wedding to a 57-year-old man. The tears in her rectum were so severe that they had to take her to the operating theatre, and suture her up. He wasn't ashamed; he was merely exercising his right as a husband.

Homosexuality is punishable by decapitation, yet it is rampant. I have been hit on by more men than I have women in Saudi. It is probably the most male-oriented, male-dominated society in the world, and when I learned Arabic well enough to hang out with Saudi men, I understood that it's socially acceptable to boast about having cruised down in the sleazier parts of town, picked up a Filipino transvestite, and sodomized him. As long as a Saudi is the initiator (God forbid he should be the recipient) he is regarded as a regular guy.

In contrast, thousands upon thousands of censors are gainfully employed policing images of women. Every single copy of every magazine, and newspaper, and book coming into the country is scrutinized by the lascivious eyes and perverse prejudices of these people, wielding scissors and a big black marker pen. Either an entire page is ripped out, or a modestly revealing neckline, or a bare arm or thigh, is laboriously blacked over with felt-tip.

Wealthy Saudi women are extremely fashionable, but *Elle* or *Vogue* would come to them in shreds. Instead there is a magazine called *Arab Woman*, which carries pictures of girls in high-necked long-sleeved tops.

Girls are expected to marry, preferably in their teens; the younger the girl, the better[6]. The Prophet Mohamed married his third wife Aisha when she was seven years old, although

6   On April 29, 2009, after an international outcry, the marriage of an eight-year old Saudi girl to a man in his 50s was annulled. Her father had arranged the marriage to settle a financial debt. It had been stipulated that the groom could not have sex with her until she reached puberty.

she lived with her family until the age of nine, when the marriage was finally consummated. She remained a favorite wife of Mohamed until his death, and is much revered amongst Muslims to this day.

Saudi men and women are forced to resort to their own sex for companionship. From the age of about seven, girls and boys are segregated. This segregation can have terrifying results. One day, a fourteen-year-old boy was brought into the emergency room. He had lost a lot of blood, and his penis had been severed. He would die unless we acted fast. The father said the boy had been peeing into a broken bottle, and there had been an accident.

There was an emergency operation to reattach it, but it didn't take. So he lost his penis. While he was recovering, the real story came out. The child had been having sex with his eleven-year- old sister, when his father caught him, and took a knife and cut off the boy's penis.

When I got some vacation time I visited Thailand, and amongst the other amusements, I got myself a tattoo. The tattooist was Chinese, but had lived in Bangkok for years. He told me that Saudis used to come to Thailand by the plane-load, until diplomatic relations broke off over a jewel theft. In Jeddah, one of the royal families noticed that some valuable jewelry was missing. Oddly, this had disappeared at the same time as their Thai houseboy went home for his holiday. So they contacted the police in Bangkok, who arrested him, but when the jewels were returned some had been replaced by fakes.

As the guy had become a local hero, and Thai policemen are not the most high-minded in the world, collusion was suspected. Then three Saudi diplomats were shot on the streets of Bangkok, and that was never solved either. The Saudi government was livid, and broke off relations. Saudis were no longer allowed to travel to Thailand. The Chinese guy said he was glad the Saudis didn't come any more.

"When they did come, they were not like normal tourists. First thing off the plane – they want whisky, and a woman, but not really a woman. They want little girls of ten, eleven, twelve, years old."

It is true that they are proud to say they have a child bride. Sometimes, in the National Guard Hospital, I would see a Saudi girl of about thirteen waiting for treatment alongside a man in his fifties.

"Is this your grandfather?"

"No. This is my husband."

I quickly learned not to ask that question.

Mohamed, I was told, decreed that a man should marry a girl half his age plus seven years. So if you are forty, you marry a girl of twenty seven. Up to a point, it makes sense.

The bride price of young, pretty girls is high. With the high rate of unemployment, few men are able to afford to marry their first choice. In my time at the National Guard Hospital, if young soldiers wanted a cheap wife they used to go to India. There was a huge trade, which lasted until about 1998, when the government finally ended it. Men would buy a twelve-year-old Indian girl, bring her back and keep her for two or three years, then divorce her and send her back. If she had children they would of course remain with the father, in Saudi Arabia.

Nowadays poorer men go to Yemen for wives. In the eyes of a Saudi man, Yemeni women are almost as racially superior as Saudi women, but their bride price is cheaper. Who knows what kind of life they will have? Some Saudis genuinely love their wives. But I would go out with the ambulance into the National Guard housing complex, and when the men were out working, you'd pass along streets where every third or fourth villa showed no sign of life. Concrete walls soared alongside the dusty roadway, nine feet high, and behind them, you could see the shutters behind the second floor windows. No-one can see in.

No-one can get out either. There is no escape from fire because there are bars on those windows. The house door is locked from the outside, and so is the iron gate in the wall. The men have locked in their women, and taken the key.

One day, I was asked to take a discharged Malaysian woman to the airport. She was flying home, paralyzed from the waist down, to Kuala Lumpur. At least, she was if she got her passport back.

"Her sponsor will meet you both at the airport and give back her passport," the Executive on Duty told me.

There was no further explanation, so I went up to the ward to collect her. She was a woman in her twenties, who spoke English. A Canadian nurse took me aside. It seemed this woman had been in Saudi Arabia for three months, and had been repeatedly raped by her sponsor and his two sons since she arrived. The sponsor, a wealthy Saudi – teaching his boys how to be men – had kept her locked in on the second floor of the villa, and had threatened to kill her. One day, desperate and with nothing left to lose, she had forced the window and jumped. This was MJS, Maid Jumping Syndrome. I would see several more cases before I left the country.

So we arrive at the King Fahd Airport, and I wheel her from the ambulance into the lounge, and the guy comes over. He produces the passport. She has closed her eyes and turned her head away, so I take it from him, as if to give it to her.

"You may go now," he says, dismissing me.

"No," I say, "you may go now. I take the passport, and I take the patient."

He stood, nonplussed. He wouldn't leave.

I got her into the departure lounge, but I didn't trust him. Even now it was within his power to make some accusation that would delay her departure, and probably restore her to his tender care. She was shaking.

She whispered, "He wants to take me to the desert and kill me. He says the wild animals will eat me, nobody will know."

He sat in a separate area and glowered at us from under his *ghutra*. I telephoned the Head Nurse and told her the girl was terrified of him. I couldn't see anything that would stop him from getting her out of the airport if he was determined enough.

"I'm going to physically put her on the plane myself."

The Head Nurse agreed, so we get to wait an hour and a half for the plane, with this guy looking mean across the lounge. She has come out to help her family, now she's returning a paraplegic.

In my wallet I had about eighty dollars in riyals, and I gave it to her. When I got back to the hospital the nurses were shocked that she'd gone; she had left suddenly and they'd planned on setting up a collection for her. When they finally took up a collection for her they got a total of seven or eight hundred dollars, and sent it to her in Malaysia.

Some of the nurses regularly visited the jail in Riyadh, to take food and clothes. There were Filipino maids in there, who had children by their sponsors and were never likely to get out, because their Embassy could not bring any pressure to bear.

They were in jail, of course, because they had been single and pregnant. It naturally followed that they were sinners.

One day an Indonesian maid was brought into the National Guard Hospital. I had never seen a human being so severely beaten. Literally not one inch of her body was without a bruise. She had rope burns around both wrists where they'd been tied, and marks where they'd burned her.

"What bastard did this....?"

"No, no, it was the women of the house who did it."

A doctor told me that some of the most brutal beatings and tortures I would ever see, were inflicted by women in frustration and unhappiness. They are not empowered in their own right. Even their own children, especially the male ones, treat their mothers with disrespect, so those who are wealthy enough to have a maid, take it all out on her.

One day, I found a family group waiting outside the ER; a woman in an *abayah,* clutching a six-month-old baby, accompanied by a twelve-year-old boy. He was kicking her, hard, and sniggering, and kicking her again. She did not respond. I told him to stop it. He looked derisively at me. Like, *What are you gonna do about it?*, I grabbed him by the collar and hauled him out of the building. He was cussing me in Arabic, and the men in the waiting room were looking on, kind of admiring him for his nerve.

In Arabic I snarled, "I understand what you are saying. And don't you tell me to eat shit."

I told the guard outside not to let him back inside the hospital, gave the kid a shove towards the car park, and left him there. The look on his face – nobody had ever laid a hand on him before.

When I went outside later for a cigarette he was jabbering on a phone to his father, creating a hell of a fuss. I got away with it because his family was Bedouin. I didn't recognize their surname. They were without *wassta*. If they'd had influence, I'd have been on the next plane out.

8

Moonshine

———

I used to walk into the National Guard Hospital and say, jeez this is a madhouse. But if I'd never worked in the States, and you put me in a compound next to the Martin Luther King Hospital in Watts, and I stayed there for two years, and treated the drug overdoses, and shootings, and stabbings, and car crashes, and hardly ever went out of my compound, then I'd have some very strange ideas about America. I would have a terrible impression, and I would think the country was full of crazy people.

That's what happens to a lot of people from America and Europe, who only see one side of life in Saudi Arabia. Especially the ones who work at the National Guard Hospital, which happens to be right next to Naseem, the big slum. They have western friends, and poor-screwed up Bedouin patients, and they come away with a very skewed view of Saudi society.

In my second year at the National Guard Hospital, John the lead paramedic went home, and I got his job. He had been in Saudi for three years. He got paid, he spent it. He went to Thailand, he went to Europe, he spent $25,000 on holidays in one year. When he went home he had only his final paycheck. He had not saved a dime, and had never wanted to. He tended to drink quite a bit as well.

In the Gulf War anyone who stayed to work got double pay. He stayed. The National Guard Hospital was closed to civilians for three months, only combat casualties could be accepted. American military staff came in to supplement the usual complement of doctors and nurses.

There are ten hospitals closer to the center of Riyadh than ours, and the National Guard were never in the front line anyway, so the patient census was zero. The hospital staff did a lot of partying.

The Colonel in charge called John into his office and said, "Son, I'd appreciate it if you didn't give my soldiers any more of that *sidiqi*."

Sidiqi means my friend in Arabic; it is moonshine, 200 proof. Guaranteed to make the night go with a swing.

"I hear you had a party at your place last night?"

"Yessir."

"Well nine of my men have reported sick."

There were Scud attacks on Riyadh. At 8.40 pm, February 25, 1991, a hit on a US barracks killed 29 and wounded 99 of the 475th Quarter Master Group. The insignificant total of Scud hits that Schwarzkopf was reporting on CNN everyday was a lie. He said there were two or three hits in and around Riyadh, when there had been more like two dozen, at least one of which resulted in many civilian fatalities. US propaganda minimized the damage. I once had a military map of the area showing the hits, and I counted twenty-four, and that figure was backed up by eye-witnesses. There were no shelters, no bunkers, so there must have been a lot of people hurt.

They told me some Scud debris fell in our compound. Everybody was supposed to wear a gasmask and dive for cover, and they all did at first, but after a while they would just sit on the roofs of the villas on lounge chairs and watch. Forget the gasmasks.

There are photos of two Patriots intercepting a Scud, which were taken from one of the roofs of our hospital compound by a nurse. She sold that photo all over the world and made a lot of money.

In those days, in the early nineties, Westerners like John used to buy real booze – branded beer and spirits and wine – from the American military where he had connections. Five hundred riyals was about $100, and that's what it cost for a case of beer, twenty-four cans, or one bottle of vodka, or Gordon's gin, or Johnny Walker.

So most people made their own. One and a half liters of *sid* cost 150 riyals, about $35, but with that you could fix a small garbage can of fruit punch – enough for twenty people. And in Riyadh, where there is desert in all directions, no mountains or seaside and no cinemas, partying is what you do. In our compound, which was one of the few mixed ones (although, in theory, our housing was segregated within it) it was a lot like college dorm life. Everybody knew everyone else, and most of us worked together, or at least saw each other around the hospital.

One day I'm in the Emergency Room, busy but kind of aware that a casualty is getting brought in through the doors, and from all the way across the other side I hear a booming voice.

"HEY! How y'all doin? You guys all cracked many chests in this Emergency Room?"

This means splitting the ribs open to get inside, to deal with trauma. It's only done in really bad cases.

We go over, help with the patient, and when it's all over this skinny American paramedic, he's the owner of the voice, holds out his hand.

"Hallo Tom. Mah nayum's Ed and this here's mah wife Miz Lily."

Ed and Lil were from Shrieveport, Louisiana. Miss Lily was a rodeo queen in her youth, a big woman, a bull rider. She had a jagged scar across her face where she got gored by the bull. They were proud members of the Ugly Motherfuckers' Biker Club and oh, Miss Lily she was a wonderful cook. Jambalaya, shrimp, all the Louisiana dishes – and they hadn't been there a month before they were expert wine-makers. If Ed wasn't at work he was drunk.

I'm sharing a villa with this other guy, and they come knocking on our door about eleven o'clock one night. Lily's got this shoebox in her hand.

"D'y'all wanna ride out with us into the desert? We're going out there."

"What for?"

"Well you know that kitten we found? Well that kitten it died. And I got it right here in this box – I bathed it and I cleaned it and it smells real pretty, and I put a li'l bow round its neck – and we're gonna bury it."

We stayed home.

"How did it go?" I asked next day.

"Oh," Lily said, with a faraway look "you should'a went. We went out there, we buried the cat, very quiet, all the stars, and said a prayer over it, and drank some wine. I just took off all mah clothes out in the desert and was totally nekkid, and I just stood up under the stars and I yelled, FUCK YOU SAUDI ARABIA."

For Christmas she made a turducken. Turkey, duck and chicken all deboned and stuffed one inside the other, and Ed cut slices right through.

She'd been married four times, Ed three times, and they had a tribe of different children from these different marriages. All the kids lived in the trailer park in Shreveport, right across from Ed and Lily's trailer, with the big ones looking after the small ones. I think there may have been some dysfunction in this family. Anyhow, they were going to be in Saudi ten years, that was the plan, then go home and retire. But they didn't make it.

They'd been working at the hospital about a year when Ed said, "We gotta go home on emergency leave, Lily's daughter's knocked up. We gotta take care of things."

Lily's daughter was sixteen, and another daughter was pregnant too, and I think Lily's father had cancer.

Ed had a bit of a drug problem in his youth, and I'm not sure he was quite over it. There were a few drug errors on his shift. A lot of the staff were happy to see them go. I on the other hand missed them. Cause life just got a little more boring in their absence.

What with all the booze, and no shortage of malls where girls can buy designer clothes and make-up, there is going to be a little flirtation in the compounds. The Saudis know it goes on, and a lot of them are kind of wistful, because it is axiomatic that all western women are pretty much hookers.

Women are not allowed to drive anywhere in Saudi Arabia. They must never get into a private car with a man to whom they are not married or related, and above all they must be covered from head to toe at all times in public. In Riyadh especially, the *metawah* enforce these strict codes of behavior quite ferociously. When I lived there, there was one *metawah*, an active member of the Commission for the Promotion of Virtue and the Eradication of Vice, who was notorious. He was a wild-looking fellow, who haunted the Al- Khrea shopping mall, and never went out without two policemen, and a big swishing cane. All the western women pulled their *hijabs* (head cover) tightly over their hair when they saw him, because they'd seen how he was with the Saudi girls. Five times a day, at prayer time, the wail of the muezzin comes over the tannoy, and if at prayer time anybody in a *thobe* moved off kind of leisurely from a shop that was closing, he'd come and shout behind them, berating them, swinging at their calves with his long stick until they were practically running to get to mosque. Saudi girls told me they couldn't win, there was always something. He was like a sheep-dog herding them towards the exits, and if any young Saudi man was sitting minding his own business finishing a cigarette, he'd get whacked around the shoulders and screamed at.

Usually they are more discreet. It is not proper for a *metawah* to address an accompanied woman directly, so they will speak quietly to the man.

"Your wife's hair is uncovered."

The man should bark, "Cover your hair!"

This is the correct response and tone of voice to use towards a wife.

Ordinary *metawah*, unaccompanied by police, are not frightening; it is their duty to enforce morality. But they are never to be underestimated. The official penalty for a single man and woman caught driving together, or eating together in a restaurant, is jail and lashing followed by deportation.

And anyone caught with the least whiff of alcohol on the breath is sent to jail.

Sharia law lays down these penalties. Sharia means *"The Way that leads to God"*, and this Way is discovered by scholars, who have found it in the Quran and especially the Sunna (the words of Prophet Mohamed himself). It can be redefined as new situations arise.

No Saudi woman I have ever heard of would go out with a western man. I did date a Moroccan Muslim girl in Riyadh. She was over there working. We were only seen together on the compound; it's self-contained, there is a grocery store, gymnasium, restaurant, video store, library, recreation department, swimming pool – a bank – you literally don't have to leave and it is walled in and guarded. They give you a set of rules and pretty much leave you to your own devices. It's mostly Westerners there.

I asked her, "What if your family knew we were dating? Your brothers?"

"They would kill you," she said.

"It would be a big disgrace for my family that I was dating a non-Muslim."

But so far from Morocco, we felt pretty safe.

It was stricter before Dr Fahd Al Jabar took over.

Security went and told him, "They're mingling. Men and women, they're having parties. It is all against the rules."

"Are they causing trouble?" he asked.

"Well no...."

"Well leave them alone. They are Westerners that is what they do."

The *metawah* knew that parties went on in western compounds like ours, and sometimes they would wait outside in cars to trap anyone leaving. None of the guests wanted to leave until these guys had given up and gone home.

One time a Canadian couple was over seeing some friends. Fortunately, they had taken nothing stronger than tea and were married. When they left it was night time and they were followed and boxed in at an intersection by three cars. The husband was hauled out and surrounded by these fanatics, one of them stuck a gun in his ribs (many Saudis have guns and often the *metawah* do). He was bruised; they handled him roughly.

There was a policeman at the intersection and the woman yelled at him, "Help us! Help us!" He turned his head and drove away.

These five or six *metawah* separated the man from his wife, and drove them off in separate cars.

"You were drinking. You are not married."

They took them to a private house, frog-marched the man at gunpoint into a room on his own, and harangued him and interrogated him for an hour and a half, before finally letting them both go. These were not official members of the Committee, just independent religious fanatics, who decided to catch some Westerners doing something really bad, and deal with them.

When the couple were released they contacted the police, and the man wanted these men arrested for kidnapping. He showed them his bruises. He offered to lead them to the house where he and his wife had been held. But the police said the *metawah* had just been trying to uphold the law, and the Canadian Embassy decided to take no action. Politics and oil often took precedence over people.

In my second year at the National Guard Hospital, I knew three Canadian girls who worked there, who were friendly with a group of Lebanese men. These guys happened to be Muslims, but since they had none of the hang-ups of the Wahhabis, they invited their Canadian girl-friends to dinner at their villa. The girls went over there in their *abayahs*, but the neighbors called the Committee for the Promotion of Virtue and Eradication of Vice, and complained of uncovered western women going into a house. Their faces had been visible, so it followed that they must be prostitutes.

That evening, a group of *metawah* gathered outside the villa. They waited until the women came out, and seized them. Then they rushed into the house and beat the living shit out of the guys, before bundling them off to jail. One of the girls fled, and locked herself in her boyfriend's car. They busted out the window to get at her and she got glass in her eye. Later she had eye surgery for corneal abrasions.

The girls were also taken to jail. This time, the Canadian Embassy did make a complaint, and they were allowed to leave after a few days. They all left the country because they were so upset. But before they did, one of them – she worked in our lab – told me that when they were in the prison there were men, not prisoners, but men who were there in some official capacity, who would be there watching them. And the female guard sneered, "I could just give you to these men if I wanted to."

The Lebanese guys spent months in jail before they were deported.

This sort of thing can even happen to Saudis, though it is rare. A Saudi surgical resident at the hospital – Dr Sam, who was a Major in the National Guard – had been to school in the States, and everyone liked him, and he would come to our parties. He was seen with a western woman in his car and spotted taking her to his house. Disapproving neighbors saw this, and reported it to the *metawah*. The two of them were pulled over driving down the street. She went to jail and was almost immediately deported. He was jailed, released, demoted, posted to a clinic in the desert and never seen again.

These things happen, and then are forgotten, and in any case there are so many warm, lovely days when you're off work, and it would be nice just to get out away from the traffic and the noise. One day, I had two nurses in my car and we'd been out in the desert for a picnic and some fossil hunting. There is a checkpoint before you get back to the city, but the *metawah* are rarely there – so if Saudis want to get some privacy with a Saudi girl they know, they drive out for the day. But the *metawah* must have heard rumors that unmarried couples were doing this, because I'm driving along this road and ahead, I can see white *thobes* and *ghutras* bustling around the checkpoint.

"Uh-oh. We're in trouble."

The girls go silent. I drive up and just as I do, the nearest *metawah* sticks his head into another car. A soldier is approaching. I show my papers to him and he catches my eye. He sees the look on my face and in a flash he's taken in the situation and mouthed something at me in Arabic.

"Fine. Just go."

And off we went.

He couldn't care less. Most Saudis are perfectly happy to mind their own business. The way I see it, it's like living among Creationists or other fundamentalist Christians in the States. But, the *metawah* have influence disproportionate to their numbers because they are potentially a political force.

9

Friendship, Loyalty and Generosity

———

At the National Guard Hospital everybody is paid according to their country of origin and Americans irrespective of skin color are at the top. Canadians get slightly less, then Europeans and Australians, then South Africans, Filipinos, Indians and other less developed countries in that order. In the markets downtown, the traders offer an American price, a Filipino price and a Saudi price, in descending order.

Filipino nurses have gone through four years at school. Their nursing training is western based and they have a Bachelor's degree, yet they make a quarter of the salary of an American. As a Westerner you could be working in intensive care with post cardiac-surgery patients – a complex job – alongside people who would be getting a heck of a lot less money.

We had a Filipino intensive care nurse who lost her job thanks to *metawah* in a restaurant in Riyadh. She was having dinner with her boyfriend. They were unmarried and therefore in gross violation of the Wahhabi code. Had they both been Westerners, there would have been a lot of fuss and maybe a few days in jail followed by deportation. As it was she was jailed, and tried by a Sharia court and told she would be lashed forty times before she was deported.

The Saudi hospital management went into overdrive. They tried everything to get her out of this. They told the authorities they'd put her on the next plane out, but no dice. Okay, they said, but can her Charge Nurse come down to the jail to make sure she is all right? (Relatively, that is.) Nobody can come.

She got forty lashes and was deported. It happens to expatriates from third-world countries.

When an American brat vandalized some cars in Singapore and got sentenced to eight whacks with a bamboo cane, Bill Clinton appeared on television begging for mercy, but I had no sympathy. Give him *twenty*, I found myself thinking. He's a juvenile delinquent abroad. I was seeing worse injustices everyday.

Most of the expats in Saudi Arabia are Malaysian, Filipino, Bangladeshi, Pakistani, Indian or from African countries. Besides the problem of *wassta*, Saudization faces another cultural obstacle in that Saudis, no matter how poor they are, are demeaned by most service-oriented employment. There are Saudi taxi-drivers and shopkeepers, but you'll never see a Saudi pumping gas or flipping burgers.

I went to work a few shifts with the Saudi Red Crescent. That's the equivalent of the Red Cross. It's not well paid and has no prestige. I would go out with them in the ambulance and I'd see them bringing in people in full cardiac arrest and they'd be doing nothing. Sometimes they'd have them on oxygen, but if they're not breathing, then the oxygen is not a lot of help. One time a guy was pumping on a patient's chest, but nobody was breathing for him so that wasn't going to work, either.

I was just a little exasperated.

I said to Suleiman, who was in charge of training them in paramedical skills, "Don't these guys *know* CPR? Did you not teach them?"

"Well — we taught them but you know they just don't like to do it. Saudi men...."

Often I would come out of the hospital, hop in the back of the ambulance, and find that the patient had expired. I'd decline admission. The Red Crescent guys hated that. One time, quite early on, I climbed in and found no pulse, no breathing, flat-lining on the monitor, cold. As Ed would say, day-ud.

"Sorry, no."

"You must take him."

"No."

"But where does he go?"

"I don't know. You take him wherever.... But not here."

"He was awake and talking until YOU TOUCHED HIM!"

I was very cross. I got out and walked into the ER and grabbed a Saudi student who was working at the hospital as an interpreter.

"Hey Said, how do you say Lying Dog?"

He said something that sounded like *"Ennta kaathub kelb.* But this is a big big insult Tom."

I muttered it over and over. *"Ennta kaathub kelb. Ennta kaathub kelb. Ennta kaathub kelb"* and I set off back out the door.

"Where are you going?"

"Ennta kaathub kelb. That's what I'm going to call him."

"Wait for me. I'm coming with you. I want to see the fight."

There was no fight. But there was no recognition of incompetence on their part either. Anyhow I know better now. If they're casting around for someone to blame I just explain that if God has decided to take somebody, there is nothing any of us can do to bring that person back. When you live in

Saudi long enough, you recognize the Will of God as closure to any argument.

When I did a shift with the Red Crescent I went into ordinary Saudi homes (though how the ambulance driver could find all the addresses in streets that were not numbered was amazing to me). The calls were of the same kind that paramedics in the States get: shortness of breath, chest pain, cut finger. The houses were mostly the poorer ones because the service is a public resource. These are bare square buildings made of dried mud, where I would find people sitting on the floor on a blanket or cushions, rudimentary cooking facilities, a sink, a television. Lives of the unemployed, regulated by the muezzin's plaintive call and the cooking of food.

Millions of Saudis live like this. Riyadh has wide streets with palm trees and in the main boulevards and shopping malls you can buy imported food in supermarkets: frozen meat, vegetables flown in from Europe and Africa, fancy cakes. You can get Armani suits, and top of the range BMWs, and Bose speakers, and Rolex watches. But most of the women thronging the back streets in their *abayahs* have never been near a supermarket. They get their vegetables in street markets, they don't eat meat everyday, and Rolexes are not high priority. They consider themselves well off if they've got cold running water and a hole-in-the-floor toilet that flushes on demand.

You might wonder how they get by. How whole families can eat fly-blown food, how they survive in this hot humid place without air-con, how men with no jobs can pay hundreds of dollars for electronics. They've learned to survive in the cities the way they did in the desert, by sheer cunning.

I never saw a case of food poisoning at the National Guard Hospital. The women cook at fierce heat because it kills all the bugs. I never saw heatstroke either, because nobody goes out in the heat of the day; shops and offices shut from first prayer at midday until early evening.

And if they need consumer goods, the men go up to Ben Ghasem. That's way up in the north of Riyadh, a *souq* —there's another one like it in Jeddah. On their weekend, that's Thursday and Friday, they bring old televisions and refrigerators and sell them. I went there in the early nineties and there was all our ex-military gear from the Gulf War: US Army uniforms, chemical weapons suits, gasmasks British and American, and the biggest generators.

Bedouin rely on their generators. You'll see a white tent in the middle of the desert with an antenna sticking up out of it, and they'll be inside watching soccer. And in Ben Ghasem there were generators with American and British markings, right from the smallest Honda up to one the size of a trailer, a CAT diesel generator that would light a small city. How they ever hauled it away – American soldiers stationed outside Riyadh told me that during and after the Gulf War, the Bedouin would steal everything that wasn't nailed down.

They still do go on camel trails. Nomadic tribes don't have to travel far. They graze mostly camels and sheep. A very few still travel far down south-west, through the Empty Quarter, where shifting sands can build dunes a thousand feet high.

Outside Riyadh is a camel market, where they hold an auction at the weekends. There's one of these in every city as well, but in Riyadh it's so big it's a tourist attraction, especially watching the Bedouin driving away with their prize. There'll be a crane on the back of a truck, they put a strap round the camel and it goes soaring up in the air looking amazed, with its long legs stuck out straight. Then you'll see this huge camel hunkered down in the back of a little Toyota pickup, hobbled so it can't get up, and off it goes, peering anxiously over the back.

If you want to sit on a camel and have your picture taken there are two guys who'll do that for five riyals, or fifty if you've never been before, and especially if you are a nice new blonde nurse from the National Guard Hospital. They help you up very nicely with their hands groping your breasts, these two dirty old Bedouin men, and you can almost see them sniggering –

Those western women are so dumb! – not only do they pay us many, many riyals but they let us grope them as well.

The new girls are too shocked to say anything.

Bahtaa is where ordinary people shop. It's the old part of Riyadh, down south of today's city and it used to have walls all around it. It's a maze of cobbled alleyways lined with three or four-storey houses built of red-brown straw and mud. It's smelly, a bit drainy; until the 1980s the sewers were open down there. The shops are open-fronted, all the gaily-colored goods on display out front, like a stall with a little convivial area for tea and haggling in the room behind. Beyond the bread shops, and the guys selling spices and dried fruit heaped in wide trays, there are old Bedouin men sitting around on carpets drinking Lipton's tea and sweet Turkish coffee, and there are shops selling *thobes* and *ghutras* and *abayahs* and leather shoes and holsters. Mostly it goes by street, there will be clothes in one place, food in another, junk in another, and then there is a car *souq*, and just outside the city a camel *souq*.

Periodically bits of Bahtaa get knocked down and now there is a new façade on the gold *souq*. But it always fascinates me, especially the animal *souq*, where there are miniature deer from Yemen and birds from Africa. You can get any kind of parrot down there free of import tax or restriction, an African grey, or a huge cockatoo for a few hundred dollars. The shops in the carpet *souq* are hung with everything from old silk Iranian carpets, blue and shimmering like water, to modern Afghan wool rugs with tanks and guns on them. And you will see Maria Theresa *thalers*, the first coin used for international commerce, each one an ounce of pure silver, used as weights by the spice dealers. They were the first coin to have writing round the edge – so there was no point in filing the edge off – and they are still trusted. Lawrence of Arabia paid the tribes with those when they were helping to drive out the Ottoman Turks.

There is one shop piled high with dusty guns and swords. A lot of the guns are American and British military rifles. There are old Henry repeating rifles and the ones the British used against the Turks in the First World War. You can't export them. I have seen ancient British army bayonets and swords modified for Saudi use, and rifles where they have modified the stock by cutting it and weighting it down. The theory was that if a Bedouin could hold the rifle with its weight at the back, he could fire it while riding fast and holding the reins of a camel with one hand.

When the soldiers came during the Gulf War, the market people would ask outrageous prices, because Americans were too dim to haggle. One of the carpet dealers told me he made a fortune. My Dad was an antique dealer, and I have bargained in Mexico, but Arabs are the best. You can haggle for twenty minutes and they'll drop the price a nickel. They just wear you down. They are adamant. If you want whatever it is, you give in, and if you don't, you walk away. In Mexico they won't let you walk away – they'll chase after you.

I wanted an old oak door, intricately carved, of the kind you see on homes and shops with an Arabic prayer carved above it. The dealer would not come down on his price, that door stayed gathering dust for months and months, and he didn't budge an inch. That would never happen in Mexico, or even in Morocco, and I think the difference is the strong tribal culture. The Mexican or Moroccan might go hungry if he can't sell to me. The Saudi's got a huge cushion: his extended family. If they are quietly prosperous they may have lived in the same rambling Bahtaa house for generations. Whatever happens they are not going to throw him out. And then there are his friends.

Friendship to a Bedouin means undying mutual loyalty and generosity. My friend Naif and I have been through a lot together, and if I were penniless, anywhere in the world, he would make sure I got money, with no strings. He's not rich. It's just that friendship, to a Saudi, means a hell of a lot more than it does to a Westerner. If you have a friend you will defend him, never speak ill of him in public, and do anything for him. It took me a while to understand; and it is a two-way street. They don't live in small units, like us; they are constantly surrounded by relations, friends and acquaintances. So they narrow their significant others down to very few, and are loyal.

I am not sure how long the descendants of Abdul Aziz are supposed to go on rewarding the descendants of his supporters with jobs and perks for life. Three quarters of a century has passed since the conquest of Arabia. The Al Rashids, who had seized Riyadh from the Al Sauds at the end of the nineteenth century, have become friends and supporters since Abdul Aziz seized it right back in 1902. The Saudis say, and they are wise, "Keep your friends close but your enemies closer." The Al Rashids are still getting benefits.

The Bin Ladens helped Abdul Aziz too, and whenever the Saudi government wants something built, there are no tenders, no contracts, money is not discussed: the Bin Ladens build it. They are billionaires.

I have heard of members of the National Guard, descendants of the Wahhabi tribes that fought for Abdul Aziz, who never have to live in barracks or appear on parade. They draw an officer's salary and maybe keep a shop, or otherwise amuse themselves. Maybe one of them was the guy who wouldn't budge on the price of the carved door. It wouldn't surprise me. It's all got to do with honor, and brotherhood.

This was a war-mongering, war-torn society until the early thirties. It is said that in the twenties, when Abdul Aziz still had bits of Arabia left to conquer, some American oil men brought a car to show to him. His tribesmen were horrified.

"Surely it must be magic! That a big piece of metal should go with no animals.... Don't get in! You will go in that and never come back."

Abdul Aziz went in it anyway, and they were happy when he came back and got out.

Later when the navy brought a warship into Jeddah harbor the King's men brought eight sheep aboard and set up their tents in the stern. King Abdul Aziz presented all the officers on board with a gift, but they had brought nothing to give him in return, so they presented every one of his tribesmen with a machine gun, and the American officers fired off the back of the deck to show them how they worked.

I was told that at one time the only public telephone in Riyadh was at the Al Bahtaa Hotel. The hotel is still standing, though it looks more than a little run down. And in those days, I guess it was the 1970s, the line for the phone went round the block. Even then, a businessman could not simply come to Saudi Arabia on the off chance of doing some business; he would require contacts to sponsor his admission to the country. You are who you know.

10

"We love you Ameriki!"

Westerners with *wassta*, they are a class in themselves. It is possible for them to make very nice money in Saudi Arabia. When I was at the National Guard Hospital, I sometimes drank at a pub called the Empire Club, ran by a British guy called Gary and his wife. You'd drive over to their house in a residential area, high walls surrounding most of the houses, and there was a security camera and they'd buzz you in the gate. Inside, everybody was there, enjoying a social life. You got to meet people from the construction companies, and the US Army, and other compounds and private villas.

There were drunken people walking in and out all year long. All the Arab neighbors, and thousands of Westerners in Riyadh, knew it was there. But Gary was friendly with a member of the district Governor's family who got a cut of the profits.

When I got to Saudi in '93 there was a pretty relaxed attitude to Americans and Europeans, because they'd assisted the National Guard to liberate Kuwait. You read that right. I'd walk through the shopping centers in downtown Riyadh, and I'd see uniformed American soldiers, and the Saudis would call out,

"Ameriki Number One! We love you Ameriki!"

So nobody interfered with the bar, and Gary was making at least $10,000 a week.

Well this went on for four or five years, but the atmosphere was changing. There were bombings, and foreigners checking for explosives under their cars, and so on. Prince Naïf came up with his story about turf wars between alcohol barons.

So the Empire Club quietly disappeared. I hear Gary is doing very nicely in real estate on a Mediterranean holiday island right now.

Other Westerners will never make it here. This is not because they haven't got *wassta,* or don't take risks, but because they'd be dishonest or incompetent anywhere. The recruiters check your nursing license, but they don't always check out references. If somebody gets sent home within three months the recruiters don't get paid, but I guess they are making high fees on the acceptable ones and just factor in a percentage of failures.

The emergency room is raw and chaotic and problems show up fast. We had a new paramedic come in: short blond guy from Chicago. Polite, helpful, would always volunteer to go and pick up from the pharmacy. Every time you have to get a morphine drip and mix it up in a bag, you call the pharmacy. You have to tell them which patient it's for and they put the patient's stamp and ID number on it. 100 mg of morphine is the dose in 250 ml of saline and they tell you to come and pick it up in ten minutes.

Saudis are very jumpy indeed about drugs. Get caught with opiates and no *wassta*, and it's the death penalty.

So Chicago throws his back-pack on and disappears. On the way back he's stopping in the rest room and he's draining out all that 250 ml of morphine and saline and swapping it for 250 ml of plain saline out of his back-pack. A patient is screaming in pain, and needs an injection of Demerol or Morphine, and he's real concerned.

"I'll do it!" he cries, and caringly administers an intravenous hit of salt water.

Some of the trauma patients, they're intubated, they're on a ventilator, their whole body's busted up so they can't talk, and they are lying there grimacing in pain with tears going down their faces. One of us would give this person another 10 ml of morphine, and five minutes later there'd barely be any change, and you'd think, how *can* he be in pain? If I give him any more he's going to overdose.

When, after about a month, security turned up at his apartment — the short blond guy from Chicago was under drug investigation in the States, and somebody had belatedly told them – he had already left. He must have had a tip-off because he went straight to the American Embassy and they flew him out. Security went through his flat and found used vials of morphine and Demerol, and empty bags of saline.

Then there are the frankly crazy. Sadly, even nurses have issues.

There is one nurse called Louise. She's staying in a four-bed roomed villa with three other girls who work at the hospital. She's very groomed, Louise is, with her hair streaked, always wears lipstick with a dark outliner, and long fingernails. These are fake nails and she tells one of her room-mates they'd look lovely on her.

"I'll put them on for you."

This girl wears them for a day and then she gets a call at work.

"You stole my nails! I want them back. I'm gonna call Security!"

She calls Security and tells them that this girl is a thief. And the girl can't pacify her, so the others intervene. Louise takes umbrage at one of them and starts calling her at work too.

"I'm gonna kill you. I'm gonna *get you*."

All three of them leave. She's living in the villa by herself. She's got just the biggest TV and VCR, charged to her credit card, for company. And I guess the rest of the time she spends grooming herself. At work people notice that she's coming on to Saudi doctors, making sexual advances and touching. The men are appalled. She gets taken aside.

"Louise you don't do that here. You must behave modestly."

"What are you *talking* about?"

She is oblivious. Or makes out she is.

I've been given new nurses to orient, so the Charge Nurse tells her to report to me one night and watch me.

"Okay Louise, you stick with me and I'll show you how this crazy place works."

A private car pulls up with a passenger who has pink frothy sputum bubbling out of his mouth. He's barely breathing. He's in congestive heart failure. I recognize this. I've seen it a hundred times. It's usually secondary to a heart attack, or chronic congestive heart failure. It happens to heart patients on Digoxin who haven't taken their medicine, so fluid is slowly backing up into the lungs. Otherwise it's acute, where a person has had a heart attack and part of the heart is no longer pumping properly, this too means fluid is entering the lungs. This is the worst kind: congestive heart failure secondary to acute myocardial infarction. You have to treat it aggressively because the patient is dying as his lungs fill up.

So we get this guy in, get a tube down to breathe for him, get an IV on him – he has no blood pressure – we're diuresing him with Lasix to get the fluid off his lungs – he's shut down peripherally and it's really hard to get an IV started. I get a small 22-gauge IV and start a dopamine drip to get the blood pressure up and help his heart to beat faster. You really need to give this through a big line and all I have is a small one, but it's life or death, so I don't care.

The Saudi residents have been called and they're on their way.

Louise says, "Can you really do all this treatment without a doctor's orders?"

"See that doctor over there? Reading the chart? Because he's reading the chart to find out why the patient's dying."

"But...."

"If you wait for a doctor, in this hospital, to tell you what to do you'll kill about four people a month."

"Surely though a doctor would...."

"Are you willing to accept that?"

"No but...."

"I'm not willing to accept it either. You just better make sure that whatever treatment you're giving the patient is correct."

Anyway I got his pressure up nicely. I got him ventilated. I got him diuresed and it takes about 20 minutes for the Lasix to start draining fluid out of his lungs. I'm pretty happy at the way things are going.

Louise takes over.

Five minutes later, I look over and his blood pressure's down. I look at the line, make sure my dopamine's still running – the IV is out of his arm.

"Louise what happened to his IV?"

"Oh! I took that out. It was much too small. You know you should really run dopamine through an 18 gauge, not a 22."

It is not a great idea to pull an IV out of a critical patient, especially if it's the only one you can get.

"Don't you ever touch my line again!"

I was seething. I managed to get another line, got the dopamine in again, got the blood pressure back up. I'm going round doing this and that, and I look over. The residents are coming in. Louise is with the patient and my dopamine – the pump is turned off.

"What are you DOING?"

"Well I shut it off. You're trying to run it at 10 mics, right?"

"Yes. 10 mics a minute."

"But I figured it out. If you divide this, and add this up there – that only really adds up to 9.7 mics a minute and not 10. So, I shut it off until I can figure out precisely the calculations to get it to 10 mics."

My teeth are like grinding together. "I have a chart that says 80 kilograms, 10 mics a minute, at 30ccs an hour, it's a *chart*. This is how it works."

"Yes," she says, "In theory. Probably in reality though it is 9.7 mics."

"That chart is an average. The whole world goes by it and don't EVER turn off my line again!" There's a consultant, two resident physicians, me and her standing there and I've humiliated her.

Suddenly she screams, "I'm a fucking NURSE! From America! I know what the fuck I'm doing! I'm not a fucking idiot! You're treating me like I'm fucking stupid."

In the end the patient got transferred to ICU and survived, miraculously. We're all sitting around, it's three in the morning, and she's attending to her face, refreshing her eyeliner. Then she turns to me.

"You know with that patient? You absolutely had no idea what was going on."

"He was in acute congestive heart failure secondary to a myocardial infarction."

"That isn't what was wrong with him."

"What do you think the pink frothy stuff coming out of his mouth was?"

"That was from your intubation. You traumatized his mouth! It was just blood and stuff."

"Did you see the X-ray? His lungs were pure white, full of fluid."

"It was an over-exposure."

I take a deep breath in. Everybody else clears their throat or shuffles their feet on the linoleum. Later the Charge Nurse asked me to write down exactly what happened. My account, along with the death threats on her room-mates, were enough to get her sent home. She had been there less than thirty days.

I was competent, but I didn't have *wassta*, or any immediate desire to do otherwise than be a good paramedic, and towards the end of my contract the relentless head-banging trauma of life in the emergency room had really got to me. I had planned on going home after two years, but you know I liked the *souqs*, I liked the sunshine, I had friends and girl-friends. Most of all

I didn't undervalue the rewards of living here. In the United States I might get paid, say, $40,000 and I'd spend my free time getting my car fixed, paying bills, filling in my tax return, cleaning my house, and looking forward to two weeks paid vacation.

Here, my $40,000 would be worth ninety in lifestyle. There is no tax to pay or errands to run, there's six weeks paid holiday and four unpaid, and two free annual tickets to anywhere I wanted to go in the world, great resorts within reach and the whole world to travel to.

So it was no contest. I was going to stay, but I didn't want to stay in the emergency room.

Then I got an opportunity to join the US army.

Vinnell is a company that works with military personnel and is rumored to be a front company for the CIA. They offered me a job in the military, training Saudi medics. Vinnell trains the Saudi army to shoot, drive tanks, plan campaigns; the company is mostly staffed by retired military personnel from the States. They prefer ex-military people, but I had a lot of experience with training, and by now with training Saudis, so they asked me to join.

I seriously entertained the thought. The pay was higher than I was getting at the National Guard Hospital, but I suspected that might have something to do with the risk. I was by now good friends with Suleiman, a *metawah* who was tolerant of Westerners and had spent time in the States. He had been a jihadi fighter in Afghanistan against the Russians, but as a medic he'd never been on the front line, which disappointed him because if you get killed in a jihad you get no end of great rewards in heaven. He did point out to me, however, that a powerful international brotherhood of jihadists had been forged in that conflict, and incidentally, that they were very well trained by the CIA. Osama bin Laden was amongst that group.

"Tom, we all have guns. I have an AK47. I have a hand gun in my house. You wouldn't believe what we can buy in the grocery store off the shelf to make a bomb. In Afghanistan we learned this and we are just waiting for the time when we have to put it to use. I know you think the *metawah* are nice kind religious men. Don't be fooled. We are waiting to be called! To fight the monarchy, the government, the Americans – whoever." We were to reap the repercussions of this on September 11th 2001.

In considering a future as lackey of the US government, I recalled a social call by suspected Hezbollah terrorists to the Al Khobar Towers, in June 1996. The Khobar bombing killed 19 US servicemen, with another 372 wounded. The towers were being used at the time to house American military personnel from the USAF 4404th wing. Somebody drove a water tanker up to the front of that block and then blew it up. The blast took the whole front off the building.

And I thought my lifestyle would be worse. The base was way out of town, and all male. I'd have to live in something like a barracks, almost. I'd be one of the guys that used to come to our compound by the bus-load for parties, but couldn't anymore, because it provoked ill feeling among the fundamentalists.

On the other hand, I would be an honorary Captain. I wavered.

"You just wanna wear a uniform and drive around in a military truck getting saluted," said my friends.

Yup, I did think that would be pretty cool. Acclaim at last. I could drive around with my sunglasses on like MacArthur. (I'd never been in the military. You *guessed*?)

So I visited the Vinnell offices in the National Guard headquarters in downtown Riyadh, where I'd be working, for the interview. I'd got the job if I wanted it. They said I could call Vinnell when I was in the States, and if I accepted they would change my work visa so that Vinnell would become my sponsor.

At the last minute before I flew to America the girl I was seeing talked me out of it.

She said, "You'd be thirty miles out of town, we'd never get to see each other – you might as well stay where you are."

I went on holiday with my contract at the hospital not yet renewed, but I called the National Guard Hospital from California and said I'd stay.

It turns out my office if I'd worked for Vinnell was gonna be right there in the National Guard offices in Riyadh, and not a week after I got back, on November 13, 1995, a car-bomb blew up that building. In total, five American and civilian personnel, and two Indian soldiers were killed. The injured people were driven away in private cars, but our ambulance picked up dead ones and took them to the Faisal morgue. Later three groups claimed responsibility: Tigers of the Gulf, The Islamic Movement for Change and Fighting Advocates of God. No connection to Osama Bin Laden could be proved. All the groups claimed to draw inspiration from him. Later four people were arrested and publicly beheaded for the bombing.

11

To the Palace

But who would worry about the dark side? I was up for a job as paramedic to Crown Prince Abdullah. It seemed there would soon be a vacancy. The Crown Prince is head of the National Guard, so as lead paramedic at their hospital, I was first in line for the job. He was over seventy, but appeared to be in good health. I had heard there were financial advantages and plenty of days off. And I still wanted a change, because things at the hospital were not getting any quieter.

The Ministry of the Interior initially blamed the car-bomb at the National Guard headquarters on an American soldier with a grudge. As there was no evidence that any such person existed, the authorities set out to find someone. Police stopped every Westerner's car, while Saudi drivers just went about their business as usual. This went on for a few days, and then I kind of forgot about it.

There was a guy called Karl who had a small pub on the compound, and he asked me for a ride over to somebody's villa to pick up some *sid*. I'd been there before, and said yes.

This guy with the villa, he was Irish, and thirty, and wore a gold Rolex sparkling with diamonds. He was employed as manager of a western compound across town, and he ran a huge still in a nearby villa that he kept empty. It supplied pretty much the whole city of Riyadh with spirits. In his own house there was a full bar with real booze in it.

Anyhow he sells Karl a case of Evian (only it isn't, there's *sidiqi* in the bottles) as usual and we set off back to the National Guard Hospital compound. I drive in and flash my ID at the guard and – he stops me.

In two years, I have never before been stopped. In Arabic, he tells me to get out.

"Open the trunk."

I walk round the back of the car. My blood is running cold. It isn't just going to be deportation. A whole case of *sid* means trafficking. I have known an English guy get two years for that.

I mentally kiss goodbye to the new job.

I fumble with the key and lift the lid of the trunk. The case of Evian is sitting there, sweating slightly. The guard hoicks his rifle higher on his shoulder, peers in.

"OK."

He drifts off, and I get back in the car and drive through. Karl and I can barely breathe until we get to his villa.

A near miss with the Saudi legal system makes your stomach turn over. They really do whip prisoners. If you get a lot of lashes it's done in stages, say ten at a time, to give you time to recover before the next assault, and if you've got a few hundred lashes to come you'll be in jail a while until your sentence is carried out.

They also chop off hands for theft, if the offender is persistent. Sharia law is not noted for its flexibility. Around the time of the *sid* incident, I'd read about a man who beat another guy with a rock, nearly killed him – I think he stabbed him as well – and took his money. Stealing is not punishable by death, but the violence used in the theft implied that murder had been the intention.

There isn't a recognized tariff for attempted murder, so the judges were in a quandary. After long deliberation they ordered the executioner to cut off his right arm and his left leg.

I don't see crowds of amputees on the street though. There is leniency. The offence has to be repeated and serious. If you stole food because your family was starving, they would take your situation into account. And although adultery is punishable by death, the sentence is rarely carried out. Conviction would require a group of four Muslims, unusually intent on a couple's destruction, to testify that they had actually witnessed them having intercourse. However if four *metawah* had a grudge, they would probably get together and accuse a person of something, and accusing those guys of lying is heresy in itself.

Despite all this, Saudi youth are increasingly involved in crime, because so many of them are unemployed. There is a thriving trade in stolen cars that get stripped and the parts sold. Drugs, drink, theft – there is every kind of crime here, but to a lesser degree than there is in the West. Certainly less publicized.

Saudis are careful to keep quiet about illegal activities like taking drugs. What a man does inside his own home is his own business. He can beat his children, or rape his maid, but God forbid any allegations by the children or the maid should get repeated. Once a family gets a reputation for anti-social behavior they will be shunned. So out of politeness, others turn a blind eye. Saudi Arabians do not like to be observed and analyzed as individuals, or as a society, and out of courtesy they will avoid exposing the domestic problems of their neighbors.

Like all the other illegal indulgences, hash and heroin are available in certain parts of town, but you'll never hear such things mentioned in polite circles. Drugs come in overland via

Turkey or Syria. One day, a very young-looking Saudi, dressed in regular *thobe* and *ghutra*, was rushed into our emergency room. Within minutes we were inundated with police and it turned out he was an undercover cop aged 21. He'd been shot through the liver with a .9mm. Fifteen minutes later they wheeled in an older guy in shackles, which were kind of redundant, because he'd been shot in both legs. The cops knew he was a drug courier, and they'd followed him all the way down from Syria, because they wanted to know who he was selling to in Riyadh. But he got wise, tried to run, and that's when the two of them shot each other.

They had him chained down to the hospital bed to treat his wounds, and our emergency room was surrounded by police. He had been carrying heroin and hashish.

The young cop ended up dying about twelve hours later.

We'd patched up the courier by then, and a whole caravan of police cars came to take him away. That very Friday they beheaded him in Chop Chop Square, outside the main mosque down in Bahtaa.

The executioner, one of several regular family men who make a living this way, does his job on Fridays at noon prayer, and on Tuesdays as well, if he gets too backed up with people under sentence of decapitation. Executions are carried out in all the main cities. In Riyadh, Chop Chop Square is just a vast expanse of dust, flat as a parade ground, surrounded by high mud walls. You can tell when an execution is going to happen, because there is a bigger police presence in surrounding streets, and they erect barricades to prevent motor traffic. Everyone, men and women, has to walk into the square to see the show.

Some women can have real vicious streak. Our head nurse, one of our x-ray technicians and another nurse were determined to see an execution. They put on their *abayahs* and went down to the square for noon prayers one Friday, but nothing happened. The next week the barricades were up, and they saw two executions and came back and told us about it. They had been sitting modestly on the ground like the rest of the crowd, but when it was finished they got touched and groped as they stood up. This hadn't happened the previous week.

They admitted that they may have been careless about covering their hair or faces. Most western women are. They resent having to cover up, and show their resentment by open defiance whenever they can. They are taking more of a risk than some of them suspect. In general Saudi men, especially in a fundamentalist city like Riyadh, have been told that western women are all sluts and prostitutes. If you want to sleep with them that's fine. They're all willing.

One of the university students asked me, "Tom, in America, are they just out in the *open* having sex? On the *streets?*"

His eyes were like saucers.

"Well not so much on the street."

It seemed a shame to disappoint him.

"Sometimes in cars, though."

His impression of America was of drunken people and acquiescent women, and this had been ingrained in him since he was small, in school and at home. The only Saudis likely to question this stereotyping are those that have lived in the west. And even then you can't count on it.

I'd been in Saudi Arabia nearly two years, and looking back across the long road through routine dysfunction and violence that I'd travelled every working day, I perceived that I'd been recruited to the National Guard Hospital by means of low cunning. Back in California in '92, they had told me on the phone that there were three positions open. Two were in the ER…

"– and one is at the Palace."

"What is the Palace?"

"Oh, you're working out at the palace grounds of Crown Prince Abdullah, in a clinic."

I'd never heard of Crown Prince Abdullah.

"Is it very busy?"

"Oh no, you don't do much work."

"Is there any overtime available?"

Like, that's how paramedics make money.

"No, you just work a regular eight hour shift out there in this little clinic."

"So what's the ER?"

"Now that is quite busy. Unlimited overtime."

So I decided I'd rather work there, keeping my skills up and making extra money, than at this Palace place.

When I got there, I realized the unlimited overtime was at the Palace, but by now they'd changed the system, so you couldn't get a job there straight from the States. They began to recruit directly from our emergency room, because it effectively weeded people out.

Now it was 1995, I still hadn't renewed my contract at the National Guard, which was nearly at an end, and I hadn't been interviewed for the Crown Prince's medical team either. There was an obstacle: a rival with *wassta*. He had not been in Saudi Arabia as long as I had, but he knew people at the Palace, and had been interviewed. So I kept on maneuvering, because I wanted to stay in Saudi.

Just not in the ER.

There is a small clinic at the National Guard housing complex. One night, I've been getting gloomy about my prospects of a promotion to the palace, and thinking of looking for work back in America, when I get a call to attend two Saudis who've been stabbed. I tear up to the clinic in the ambulance, rush in, and find the two chest injuries gasping, and a doctor hopping about in agitation. One guy has a tension pneumothorax, which is where air is escaping from a punctured lung into the chest cavity; this causes pressure that collapses the lung and squashes the heart. I decompress his chest by putting a needle in. The other one has a hemothorax. He is filling up with blood, and I can't do that one in the ambulance.

There is a third man. They hadn't even told me about him. He has been shot in the leg and is on the floor rolling around screaming in pain. I check that he isn't bleeding profusely and take the two chest injuries in the ambulance. They both need chest tubes. I get IVs on them, slam the doors, and tell the driver to move and leave the other guy there. When I get back, I send another ambulance out for him.

They all survived, but I wanted to know the story. It seemed that the two guys got stabbed in the housing complex somewhere, and were taken to the clinic. The brother of one of them immediately found out who'd done it.

He grabs the culprit, holds him at gunpoint, shoves him into his car, and roars round to the clinic. Pushes this guy in through the door, yells for the doctor. The doctor comes out a tad harassed, covered in blood, and sees the hostage with the gun to his head and the guy glaring at him.

"My brother – is he alive?"

"Yes."

"Is his friend alive?"

"Yes."

"They gonna live?"

"Yes yes! The ambulance is coming."

"Okay then."

BANG. Shoots the guy in the leg. If they'd been dead he was gonna shoot him dead. Right there in the clinic.

And yippah-de-DOODAH, I was going to get out of this hell-hole and go to work at the Palace.

12

Paramedic to the Prince

The decision was taken. We'd both go, me and the one with *wassta*.

I got interviewed by Dr Atiq and Dr Kaliq, who have been the Crown Prince's doctors since the early 1970s. The two Pakistani doctors haven't had cause to treat anything much for years. Wisely, long ago, they agreed that in a crisis they would have no idea what to do. So they always have a board-certified North American Emergency doctor and at least two North American paramedics on the team.

We didn't really touch on my medical skills, since I had paid my dues pretty publicly as lead paramedic at the hospital, but they wanted to reassure themselves that my demeanor would be suitable. Does he drink? Is he going to try and seduce anybody? Eyes and ears would have been watching and hearing about what I did out of working hours. The housing compound is close to the hospital, so there is little separation between private and working life. Any misbehavior at home shoots right back up the grapevine to the hospital management and from there to the Crown Prince's medical team (remembering that the Crown Prince runs the National Guard and employs all of us).

There are six paramedics at the Palace, but only two are on duty at any one time. When the Crown Prince leaves Saudi Arabia, two paramedics travel with him. I would continue to live in the hospital's housing compound for six months of the year. The rest of the time, I'd be part of the staff living at the Crown Prince's palaces, or staying abroad. I would spend 24 hours on duty close to the Prince every third day and in between times I'd have 48 hours off. Whenever I traveled to other countries with him I would be on duty 24/7.

Every third day, a car would collect two of us from National Guard housing, and take us to the Palace outside Riyadh. This isn't one rambling building in a large garden as you might expect. It is five palaces, set amid exotic gardens, on a gated estate. Each one is inhabited by one of the four royal wife-and-family units, and one is for the Crown Prince and his house guests.

Surrounding the inner gated estate there's a whole series of other buildings for staff and services. This outer compound encircles the whole complex like a moat.

Within the gardens there is also an old palace, unoccupied since the Crown Prince decided he didn't like it. I was by now used to the Saudi habit of leaving old buildings empty (*djinn*, spirits, fly about inside, so you wouldn't want to live there) but I still thought it would be a great place for us to overnight in on our 24-hour shifts, and said so.

When I saw the accommodation that had been prepared for us, I wished I'd kept my mouth shut. Next to the Crown Prince's imposing palace with its tall white pillars was a smaller building with suites for the medical staff.

Somebody must have told them to build a villa for the medical staff and set a limitless budget. I goggled when I saw it. Everything had been imported. There was French furniture, and chandeliers, and Limoges china, and lead crystal glassware, and the wallpaper matched the pattern in the chairs that matched the pattern in the dishes. And gold taps of course, and marble floors. Outside, miles of white marble path snaked through lush lawns and flowers and hundreds of shady trees. Almost every drop of water in Saudi Arabia comes from a desalination plant on the Gulf or the Red Sea, so the water that made this greenery flourish all year round may have travelled a thousand miles, and was certainly extremely expensive.

There was also a clinic for the Prince's family and servants, permanently staffed with dentist, radiographer, doctor, a couple of nurses and a pharmacist to run the dispensary. That had little to do with us — me, Lofty, Steve, Kurt, the Saudi paramedics — whoever was on duty. We were there primarily for one person.

In the peripheral compound is a warehouse for the royal cars and further warehousing for surplus household equipment. There is also a mosque, a small fire department, a barracks for the fifty-strong Royal Guard, accommodation for ground staff, and a *majlis* building where people come to ask for royal favors. Ancillary staff require a *bataga* (a pass) to get into the outer part of the palace grounds. To get through the next gate into the private paradise where Crown Prince Abdullah lives, you need a special stamp on the back of your *bataga*.

I am introduced to him.

"Come, come, you must meet the Prince."

At his palace a number of men are seated around him. They are all in *thobe* and *ghutra* like him, seated at a low coffee table in a large room, with a television chattering in the corner and tea glasses and bowls of sweetmeats on the table. Servants hover. He is no longer young, but still a handsome man, darkly bearded and six feet four inches tall. His demeanor is modest and friendly. He looks up and smiles, stretches out his hand to shake mine and says a few words of welcome in English.

He looks healthy and at the interview I had been told that he is. I asked what medication he was on, so that I would know what to expect, and was told that he was in fine form but had had a mild heart attack in the 1970s.

None of his paramedics were allowed to know what medicines he was taking. We had no access to his medical records, and therefore no idea what drugs might be contra-indicated, or whether he had any allergies. Anyone who persisted in asking was smoothly told that, *Inshallah*, there would never be a crisis. A wing and a prayer as usual, in other words.

As the weeks went by I did observe my elderly employer at banquets and such, and I thought he slipped out to the bathroom pretty often.

"Does the Crown Prince suffer from, er, prostate problems by any chance?"

This would be pretty normal for a man that age – but no. The doctor looked shifty and sighed.

"His Royal Highness likes to smoke a cigarette."

I imagined the Regent of the Kingdom, with a quarter-share of our planet's most precious mineral resources, hanging out the toilet window furtively puffing and flapping his hands to get rid of the smoke.

His father hated the habit. His doctors have warned him about it, and he conceals his smoking from the Saudi populace, because it sets a bad example. I was told he would be in even better shape were it not for this one small vice. I have read that he chain-smokes, but that is not true, because most of his life is lived in public and he is never seen smoking by ordinary people. Only the innermost of his inner circle would ever see him with a cigarette. And I suppose his wives.... Although it is hard to imagine His Royal Highness indulging in a post-coital Marlboro.

In Riyadh the Crown Prince spends one night of every week with each wife, because according to Islam you have to treat all your wives equally. We would pull up in the motorcade and pick him up outside the relevant palace in the morning. If it's Tuesday, it must be Wife Number One, and so on. Saturday nights are always spent at his own palace.

To us, they were just black-clad figures. I don't of course know what they look like. You will have noticed already that when I mention Saudis, or crowds, unless I specify otherwise I mean men. There may be practical advantages to wearing the veil, and a lot of Muslim women think there are, but the cumulative effect is to make women indistinguishable one from another and therefore to ignore them. They're just there, like paving stones.

When I began to work for the Crown Prince he had recently divorced, and married a new wife. Somehow I suspected that incompatible differences, or money worries, had not led to this divorce, and I was right. It is usual for Saudi rulers to retain their former wives as respected friends. Divorce is not acrimonious. It's just necessary in order to comply with Islamic law, if a king or prince is going to have dozens of children (which they like to do). Four wives is the maximum at any one time. King Abdul Aziz, the father of all seven surviving princes, had many wives in succession and 37 sons. When a wife becomes too old to have more sons it is usual that a prince, or a king, will divorce her. She remains a respected member of the royal household although she will move out of the Palace compound.

At least, that is what usually happens. When I got there all four wives' palaces were occupied and the newest wife, who was 26 and had a two-year-old child, was known as the Outside Wife. She was waiting for her new palace to be made ready inside the grounds. In the meantime she lived in a rented villa just beyond the gates, and once a week when the Crown Prince spent the night, it was surrounded by troops.

The most recently divorced wife was still living in her palace with her teenage daughters because the two girls were wild – at least by Saudi standards. Rather than risk political fallout because of their behavior the Crown Prince kept them permanently gated. They could invite their girl friends in, but there was to be no partying or clubbing within the Kingdom. They would have to wait until they went abroad for that.

In general, Saudi men are not particularly healthy; the city-dwellers don't do a lot of exercise. You see kids playing football all over the place, but I guess the *thobe* makes it awkward for grown men to run about. Also, the heat…. But Abdul Aziz brought up his sons, it is said, to "walk barefoot, rise two hours before dawn, eat but little and ride horses bareback." Aside from his weakness for tobacco, Crown Prince Abdullah is the one who appears, more than any other, to have adhered to his father's simple precepts.

The mothers of the other princes were Bedouin of the desert and the children were brought up in cities. Abdullah's mother was from a mountain tribe in the region of Taif. Taif is a city way up in the hills of the south-west. It is 20°F cooler up there, and green, and fruit hangs from every tree. Women pick petals to make rosewater and the air is scented with flowers. It feels safe. In Abdullah's youth, Taif was just a small place of mud-brick houses, and alleyways, and gardens, and the road to the desert was many miles of stony camel trails that zig-zagged down an escarpment as steep as a wall.

Later, when I would go out to camp in the desert for weeks on end with the rest of his entourage, an old man told me that when the Crown Prince was younger he would travel with a huge *caravan*, an assembly of many camels and Bedouin men, hunting as they moved and pitching camp every night as they crossed the hundreds of miles of Arabia, and the invisible frontiers between Saudi Arabia and Iraq and Syria. As the House of Saud grew rich almost beyond comprehension, Abdullah did not leave for long months of self-indulgence in Europe or America, as many of his brothers did.

He still enjoys the desert sports of falconry and hunting with salukis. He eats chicken and rice as he's always done; only now he has a western dietician to confirm that he should. He maintains the Bedouin principles of generosity, friendship, and simple living and he has a reputation for incorruptibility. You watch him and you think, there's a guy who likes a quiet life. Which is probably why he lets so many crazies let off steam.

13

Ninety Three Kids!

———

For a car buff, this was a great place to work. Every visitor had a top of the range, latest model, fancy car. Prince Faisal, a son of the Crown Prince who was well into his forties, drove a pearl-white Bentley turbo.

When I saw him I'd say in Arabic, "You still lookin' after my car?"

He'd grin and reassure me.

"Okay," I'd say. "You can keep it a bit longer."

We would sometimes get called out to attend minor injuries at the wives' palaces, and because we didn't want to summon up a soldier to drive the ambulance less than a mile, it made sense to give us a vehicle. The Crown Prince told the guys in procurement to issue us with an old runabout from the royal warehouse. They gave us the least covetable car they could find, which turned out to be a gleaming nine-year-old Mercedes 300 series with 100 kilometers on the clock. Inside it smelled brand new.

When I'd been there a while I asked for permission to look at the cars in the warehouse – a lot of them are unusual because they have been given as gifts – but the guy in charge wouldn't have it. I did ask him about one thing that mystified me though. Rich Saudis only ever have the latest model car, they hate anything remotely out of date, and the Crown Prince rides in a Mercedes 600 limousine which is discontinued.

They haven't made that model since the '80s and I wondered why he had a fleet of old cars.

"They are new cars," I was confidently told.

"But they.... "

"You do not understand. His Royal Highness likes that model. A number of these Mercedes are built for him every year."

Most days two or three of us would ride in the royal ambulance (shiny, black with a gold go-faster stripe, and made by Eagle Coachworks of Tennessee) out of the palace compound as part of the motorcade. Highways would be cleared to let us slip fast through Riyadh to the Ministry offices. We were led by black armor-plated Mercedes full of bodyguards. These were followed by the Crown Prince in his car, then four more armor-plated Mercedes and three Chevy Suburbans full of soldiers. Last of all was us in our ambulance, wearing the royal paramedic's uniform of western suits and Ray-bans, and looking like CIA.

Any ministers, friends, or hangers-on are driven behind us. No women.

We move. We go.

We'd call in at the clinic while the Crown Prince went off to sign papers, deal with correspondence, and meet and talk for three or four hours. That was three days a week. A fourth half-day was always spent at the National Guard Headquarters (the one that had been blown up).

These motorcades went out as regular as clockwork and that used to worry me sometimes. If you wanted to leave a bomb in a dumpster along the route, there was nothing to stop you – except they'd chop your head off if they caught you. There are no metal detectors at mosque on Friday either. The Crown Prince goes to mosque wherever he happens to be.

On Fridays, when he is in Riyadh, he goes to mosque at the Palace, but that is open to the public on Fridays and anyone can just walk in.

There was a direct attack once in Jeddah. It was in the early nineties and King Fahd and the Crown Prince were at a meeting in the Ministry building. A Saudi man just drove right through two huge sets of gates with armed guards idly nodding him in. He pulled up at the front steps, got out with a pistol in his hand, and at last a soldier challenged him. He made no reply, but shot the soldier and walked on. Then he shot another soldier before he was himself shot. He did not die, and neither did they, thanks to the intervention of the Crown Prince's paramedics.

When anything like that happens the culprit is said to have been deranged, and is promptly beheaded. Like Prince Musaed the nephew of King Faisal. He killed the king at a *majlis* on March 25, 1975. He had recently returned from the United States and shot King Faisal under the chin while pretending to greet him. King Faisal was a formidable and progressive figure. He cut the oil supply to America, during the oil embargo in October of 1973, in retaliation for America's support of Israel. Saudis around the Crown Prince told me that the CIA had got hold of this nephew and brainwashed him. This is generally believed.

No internal conspiracy, no anti-monarchy political stance is ever mentioned. They don't believe in giving those views an airing. It's not simply what we'd recognize as censorship, though there is a lot of that. It's underpinned by that cultural distaste for confronting unpleasant possibilities that I've often seen at the hospital.

There was better security by the mid-nineties, but the motorcade still followed a predictable route. Once we whizzed past a big garbage truck parked on an overpass and I was told it had just broken down. The next day it was still there, and it remained there day after day. Every time we passed I was seriously uncomfortable and glad we were a long way back in the motorcade. I'd go past trying not to think how much explosive it could be holding.

None of the Saudis gave it a thought. They had already decided that, *Inshallah*, we would be just fine, as we'd always been before.

Call me an old fusspot, but there were things that just kept on niggling me. The custom-built ambulances – there are two in Riyadh and two in Jeddah – are superb. The black is very classy, although perhaps a poor choice of color for a country where daytime temperatures routinely surpass 120°F. The ambulance would be parked outside wherever we were visiting, and when we came back and climbed in for the next leg, we'd gasp in a warm oven. It was just about the right temperature for turning grapes into sultanas, until finally the aircon kicked in.

We had extrication tools – Jaws of Life – which are huge snippers and pliers used to get into cars that are all twisted from a highway accident, or an explosion. But we had no helmets, face shields, or leather gloves to use with them, and shards of metal and sheets of flame do tend to fly up at you. Should there be an emergency, we'd be out there in our shirtsleeves and ties trying to prise open an armor-plated vehicle. It takes special training and tools to pry open an armor-plated car, and our tools were probably inadequate. I did make these points quite vividly to Dr Fahd Al Jabar who was in charge, but he waved a plump brown hand and smiled and reassured me in the usual Saudi style.

"*Inshallah*, it will never happen."

And then – this was in the mid-nineties before cell phones got real big in Saudi Arabia – and it is usual for ambulances to be connected to hospitals on a special radio frequency. I had another meeting with Dr Fahd Al Jabar about the fact that we didn't have radios in the royal ambulance. Oh what a nag I was becoming.

"You see Your Excellency.... " (he is Minister of Health Affairs, so you have to call him that) "If there is an accident on the highway near the National Guard Hospital a hospital ambulance picks them up, and say, there is a patient with a chest injury and an abdominal bleed that will need immediate surgery, the paramedic calls the hospital and describes it. And when he rolls the patient through those doors the thoracic team surgeon is waiting, the ER doctors are prepared, and everything is ready to expedite the best possible care. That is for anybody hurt on the street. But in the Crown Prince's ambulance, I have no way to contact the hospital."

"But the radio! The radio is a security risk we cannot permit."

"Your Excellency, should anything happen to the Crown Prince we would come into the ER unannounced. We would have to call the cardiologist or whoever once we got there. So the care that he would get is less than that of the average Bedouin picked up off the highway. We need communication."

"It is a very good point. I shall look into it. I shall see what I can do."

To this day there are no radios in the Crown Prince's ambulances. I guess they rely on cell phones now.

Every week there was one day when the Crown Prince held his *majlis* in the outer compound. Of course his paramedics, who must never be more than two minutes away from him, had to attend to. I was already learning a lot more Arabic, just from having time to watch and listen, and I liked the *majlis*. It's a consultation really, a meeting to discuss problems and issues, but in the case of those few princes that hold their own *majlis*, it's generally about bestowing favors. If you're a Saudi Arabian in need, the thing to do is find someone who can make your dream come true. And the Crown Prince never misses a *majlis*; though getting to see him is not easy.

Every week two or three thousand Saudi citizens, many obviously unwell or disabled, turn up outside the palace. Most are men, and if there are any women and children they are accompanied by men. Of this crowd two or three hundred are admitted to the *majlis* hall in the outer compound. Out of those about fifteen men will get to speak with the Crown Prince face to face.

Most of them are asking for a royal order to grant free western medical care. Normally, people without *wassta*, money, or family in the National Guard must be treated at Shimaisi, the public hospital. It's free, but it's third-world. Day after day there are hundreds of people waiting on the lawn outside desperate to be seen in the emergency room – traffic accidents by the score, bloody equipment piled up in a corner. I've taken patients over there and there are flies everywhere. Supplicants want to go to a nice hospital like the National Guard or the King Faisal.

Or they may come with other issues: a family member in a debtor's prison and unlikely to get out without help, or maybe they need land so that they can build a house. The Crown Prince might promise to consider the matter, or scale back their demands, but he never says no.

I only once saw him really doubtful and that was at a *majlis* in his palace in Jeddah. A little skinny grey-bearded man came up, leaning on a stick. He looked as old as Methuselah. I wondered what medical care he required.

"I need some money," he told the Prince. "I have 93 children and I don't have enough money to maintain my household. I need a bigger house."

The Prince blinked. He told the old fellow to come back next week and in the meantime he would give the matter due consideration.

The old man tottered back to his place in the crowd and I saw the Prince muttering to Prince Turki, his nephew.

"Impossible. Who can have 93 children?"

In Saudi Arabia, if a woman cannot have a child, her husband is entitled to a no-fault divorce, or to take a second wife. But it's not that common for a man to have even four wives in his lifetime, because they are pretty expensive to keep. Prince Turki sent someone from the palace to go and check this guy out.

He came back and said he'd been to the family house, and you bet there was a problem. The old man's children ranged from 60-something down to three-years-old. He couldn't count them, but there were people swarming everywhere. The Crown Prince gave him the money.

Late in the afternoon, after the *majlis,* the Royal party enters the dining hall and there are three or four hundred people from the crowd who started the day outside the gates, sitting at long tables waiting to be fed. A banquet follows, where the Crown Prince sits at the head table and poems celebrating his greatness and generosity are read to the grateful citizens. In the course of the day, very few have spoken to him. Most of the people in that room have simply been close to the source of power. To a Bedouin, to come from his tent in the desert, or his bare concrete house, into the Royal Palace is a thrill he will never forget.

So I'm learning more Arabic and I'm getting to talk to some of the Saudis in the entourage. I sit around near the Prince during the *majlis* and in the dull moments, I pick up the prevailing view of the House of Saud from some of the guys, who by virtue of being close to the Prince are likely to be loyal supporters.

They worry about what will happen when Crown Prince Abdullah dies. He is modest and respected, because he seems genuinely to try and treat people equally, which is the Wahhabi way. A Royal Family is by definition un-Islamic, which is part of the fundamentalists' problem. They think a council of elders should run things. Abdullah took control of the National Guard in his thirties, but was told that when he became next in line for the throne he would have to relinquish it. He defied this, said he would rather give up being Crown Prince, and when he finally did become Crown Prince all talk of giving up the National Guard was dropped. His defiance had been pretty astute. To this day there is separation of military power. Prince Sultan, who is next in line, is head of MODA, the Ministry of Defense and Aviation.

People say Crown Prince Abdullah is anti-American, but I don't believe he is. He is just a traditional Arab with no particular interest in western culture. He was always charming to me and the other paramedics, although when I remarked on this to a Saudi friend he retorted that he'd be charming too if he had that much money. This was the nearest I ever heard to cynicism. The other brothers, and half-brothers, people are not so sure about.

In 1953 when King Abdul Aziz died, he was followed by his son Saud. King Saud was never known as particularly clever. He spent much of his time driving around the country throwing gold coins out the window, living a lavish lifestyle, and doing diddlysquat for the people. Pretty soon his brother Faisal, as Prime Minister, had taken over.

Faisal had vision. He developed a system of five-year-plans that would build an infrastructure and get people educated. He was intelligent and progressive, and in due course Saud was forced out and Faisal became King. He is generally admired for having stood up to the United States in the early seventies. Up to then the western oil companies had been pretty much given free rein, and the American government had supported Israel, without being made aware that there could be consequences. Faisal showed them there were consequences, and refused to supply oil to countries that supported Israel.

In 1975 he was shot dead by the aforementioned nephew who had just returned from the States. Common belief among Saudi's today is that the CIA was behind the killing in retaliation for the oil embargo. So the power devolved to another half-brother, Khaled. But soon Khaled was so ill that Fahd had to take over as Regent. Nobody expected much of Fahd either. He was known as a playboy who liked to drink and gamble and womanize. They used to keep the Guinness Book of Records out of Saudi Arabia, because he was in it as the man who'd lost the most money in one day in Las Vegas: forty million dollars. That kind of thing can remind a Bedouin, squatting in a concrete home, with his dozen children, that the House of Saud has forty million dollars coming in before lunch.

Fahd's brothers and his advisors did some straight talking, I guess. Anyhow he shaped up, ran the country okay, and when Khaled died in 1982 he became the Custodian of the Two Holy Mosques, King Fahd Bin Abdulaziz Al-Saud. Later on he had a mild stroke, but he still functioned pretty normally.

In 1995, around the time I joined the Royal entourage King Fahd had a much more serious stroke, which was why Crown Prince Abdullah was in effect, if not immediately in name, the Regent.

Of course there was medical gossip. It is common knowledge among the medical team that His Majesty was found in his room gasping for breath, and the Syrian doctor who came in flew into a panic and shrieked for the American paramedic – who raced in and found this doctor holding the king's legs up in the air. The king was lying on his back, choking, with his mouth full of vomit and it was the paramedic who cleared his airway and intubated him. It is instilled into paramedics, from early in their training, that the airway is the first thing you clear. Anyway by that time the whole medical team had come in and they rushed him to hospital by ambulance. The paramedic (who like me was called Thomas) ventilated the patient all the way there and effectively saved his life.

When the king got well, and the pats on the back came, the Syrian doctor who had been holding his feet took the accolades and the gold Rolex along with all the others – except Thomas. He went back to the States in disgust. He didn't want all the credit, but he wanted his due. If he got credit the doctors would lose face.

Nobody said at first how sick the King was, and two young Saudi boys walked a thousand kilometers from Riyadh to

Jeddah, as a kind of plea to Allah for the health of the king. They were rewarded with about $50,000 each. This was in '96; it is a good paved road with service stations along the way and I think quite a few people wished they'd thought of it.

After his stroke the King was reported to be sick but no details were given. Three months later, when we all knew perfectly well that he was still bedridden and confused, the newspapers reported that he was one hundred percent cured of his (nameless) illness. Apparently he was taking up the reins of the country once more, and he wanted to thank the Crown Prince very much for having looked after things during his indisposition.

How we laughed. Around this time the Crown Prince and of course his immediate entourage, which included me, visited the King at his palace, which is on an island accessible by a narrow bridge close to Jeddah harbor. I was talking to his doctor who told me that King Fahd didn't even know where he was. He had been disoriented when he arrived in Jeddah.

"Where is this place?"

And he was incontinent.

The doctor said that next to the royal bed there was an 8" by 10" portrait of the King in jewels, a priceless artifact, fashioned out of diamonds and rubies and emeralds. Unfortunately it had no more curative power than the thousand-kilometer walk.

King Fahd has had to spend a long time convalescing. Every summer, during the months we spent in Jeddah, the Crown Prince would pay regular visits to the Royal Palace to see King Fahd. He would spend perhaps an hour, talking in the old man's bedroom.

The only time I have ever seen the King face to face was at a state dinner for Jacques Chirac in Jeddah in 1997. I was outside when his limo pulled up, and amazingly he could walk, but he was white as parchment and shuffled, very slowly, past the line of people; it was so sad. He is only a year older than the Crown Prince, but there was no comparison. They made him totter out of the car and across a carpet, but he was frail and obviously needed a wheelchair.

His Majesty was the host, so as the Crown Prince's paramedics, we didn't get seated at the top table this time. As usual there were many courses. Pigeon, fish, and on and on – I was quite hungry. The Crown Prince was listening and Chirac was talking, probably trying to sell a few airplanes through an interpreter, and the King was just staring into space. Gradually he was tilting forward and by the end of the first course he was leaning – and slowly more so – and everyone was aware of this and suddenly – the King almost had his face in the plate of food.

A protocol officer rapped on the table and barked a command.

"The banquet is over!"

We all had to get up and leave. That was the end of our dinner.

Nobody had wanted to help him, for His Majesty would have lost face. Once the room was cleared he was lifted into a wheelchair and steered swiftly away.

I talked to somebody on his medical team. He was full of questions.

"When the King dies, do you think the Crown Prince will keep his same medical team?"

"Now why would you ask that?" I said.

"Did you see the King today?"

"Yes."

"Why wouldn't I ask that?"

They were all worried about losing their jobs.

Years ago, before the duties of State became too onerous, and long before his illness, the King's favorite vacation spot was Spain. He owns a palace near Marbella and when he needed some kind of surgery on his knee in '98 or '99 he decided to have it done there.

Everything had to go suddenly into overdrive since the place had been unoccupied since 1984. A medical advance party was flown out to set up the facilities. It included a friend of mine from the new King Faisal Hospital in Jeddah. In a warehouse in the palace grounds they found a fleet of about fifty luxurious 1984 Mercedes with no miles on the clock at all. They had been maintained by a mechanic for fifteen years. My friend told me he tried very hard to buy these cars with the idea of shipping them to the States. But Procurement just swept them all away (I guess they had their own contacts) and brought in a new fleet of fifty '99 Mercedes for the King's convenience during his visit.

Then they stripped the whole palace – which like the cars had been kept in pristine condition by a skeleton staff all this time – and replaced everything from carpets and curtains to furniture and electronics. This is normal. In fact it happens every year, at every one of Crown Prince Abdullah's five palaces, in each of the three main cities.

The King was expected to go to a private hospital for the actual operation, and to recuperate there. Nevertheless the outdated equipment in the small palace clinic was removed and replaced by the most advanced technology. Millions of dollars were spent. Much of this stuff would never be used, for the king never returned there.

On August 1, 2005, King Fahd died. Now the Crown Prince is the reigning monarch. From time to time they show old footage of King Fahd on television after his major stroke, generally deep in discussion with a foreign dignitary at his Palace. He looks years younger than he did when I saw him. I must say I have never seen anybody recover that well. A major stroke generally leaves a weak arm and a droop to one side of the face. The person I see on television moves both hands. That is very unusual. Usually they favor one side.

I would hate to engage in idle speculation. But he in no way resembled the King I saw at the state dinner in 1997. Then again all is possible with the help of Allah.

14

Yachts and Dignitaries

I suspect that the Crown Prince's English is limited along lines of, "Hallo, how are you? Are you well? Good."

He rarely speaks English. In fact he speaks very little at all because he suffers from a slight stutter. This has served him well. People will be discussing things all round the table, and there he sits, alert, saying very little. He never takes over a conversation, but has gained a reputation as a good listener, and his comments are astute. After I had been around him for eighteen months, I heard him speak for about one minute in public and it was the longest speech I had heard him make.

I memorized an Iraqi song, in Arabic, and the Saudis at the palace thought it was really funny. One day, we were preparing to leave in the motorcade from the palace to his office and his aide said, "Tom, come here, come, come."

"Tom has learned a song," he explained. "Sing, sing," he told me.

So I did. And Crown Prince Abdullah just chuckled. Surrounded by bearded men in *thobe* and *ghutra* here was this American singing an Iraqi song about the beauty of a girl's eyes (their songs often are about the eyes because that's all they can see) – *You make me so happy* – it's well known, that song. He liked the American version.

At first I felt intimidated being around royalty, but it became routine. Two or three of us were on duty at the palace for days at a time, so we saw the Crown Prince often.

In Riyadh there is hardly any greenery except along a few grand boulevards, but the palace grounds are full of trees from all over the world. There was a jackfruit tree that had been specially brought from Asia, but we were warned not to touch it. It belonged to the Prince. One day the Crown Prince came out and walked along the marble pathways and stopped at his tree. He said somebody had been picking the jackfruit. He knew there had been more on there before.

His aides made a big fuss and in the end un-named Asian staff got the blame. It seemed odd that someone like him, with affairs of state on his mind, was also concerned about small, private, domestic things.

After a while we felt more comfortable at the palace and wanted to work out. We liked to exercise, Americans usually do. Roller-blades were getting popular, and those miles of smooth marble rolling over lawns between the sprinklers were just so tempting. So, whenever we could, we roller-bladed around the compound. The Crown Prince would purr by in the little white BMW he used for driving from one palace to another, and get a big chuckle out of what we were doing. I think he thought we were a little bit nuts. But they endlessly feed you, so you need to do something. Most people put on at least twenty pounds during their first year. It's not polite to refuse food, and from late morning onwards the sweetmeats, and little cakes, and tea just keep coming. This is true whether at his office, at his *majlis*, or in the palace, never mind the weekends.

We never knew when we would be going to a banquet. They wouldn't tell us the day before. Sometimes in Riyadh, we would think we were going to eat alone in our villa, and when dinner arrived in the middle of the evening, we would accept it. Then an hour later we would be called to dinner with the Crown Prince. As he's a Bedouin his social life doesn't start until long after dark. We would be ready to sleep, but we would have to get dressed up in suits and go sit at the top table to pick at a feast that rarely commenced before one in the morning.

He was more than courteous. We were always included at public events. The Prince's table at the Palace is like a huge horseshoe elevated on a dais, with the other long tables arranged at right-angles below. A corner of the high table was kept for us. After a few months, Saif – one of the young Saudis who'd been sent to America to train as a medic – got sent to join us on the medical team, because he'd scored well in our tests. And coming from a big National Guard family he had *wassta*. I can't say he got much opportunity to put his skills as a paramedic into practice, but he was a great fixer. And he was thrilled to get this job, because when we went to dinner there were generals and ministers at the tables below ours, and here was a 22-year-old sergeant elevated to dine with the royal party. Nobody could doubt his *wassta* after that.

He was in his element, but the Americans, there we were in our suits, sleepy-eyed, but smiling politely, and trying to appear animated, and not yawn. I'm left-handed and the greatest insult is to give or receive with the left hand, which is considered unclean. It would cause disgust were you to be seen eating with the left hand, so I would really have to concentrate to avoid causing offence, or seeming ill-mannered. And I was weary and over-fed. One week there was a succession of invitations to eat course after course in the middle of the night, and we were all feeling terrible every morning.

Finally somebody whispered in our boss's ear.

"You know your Highness – the Westerners – they like to eat at strange hours, like seven in the evening. And they go to bed long before midnight."

"Why do they come and eat with me, then?"

"Because they think that's what you want. They don't want to be rude."

"Oh, by all means feed them whenever they want," he said.

After that we tried to keep to our regular routine when we could. If there was a state dinner, with Arab or foreign dignitaries coming, we had to be present.

At Eid, the feast of fast-breaking after Ramadan, the Crown Prince would visit all the royal households and those of other important families around Riyadh. He would start at 9 pm and go on throughout the night for the next eight hours. I can't even count the number of houses, or work out the logistics. I don't know how they decided which roads to seal off, but our motorcade would glide effortlessly along to a villa, or a palace, and stop. The Crown Prince would get out and go inside. He would emerge ten minutes later, be ushered into his limousine, and we would move off through empty streets to another house, and stop. He would be welcomed in, and ten minutes later he would come out, and off we would go again. This tedious parade ended around five in the morning with the sunrise prayer (the Eid prayer, held in the square of the main mosque). Thousands of people were there already.

We were just exhausted. I was glad to be getting a lift home in an ambulance. But the old gentleman, somehow he kept going all the way through.

Wherever he is, Saturdays are his day off. No wives, no family, no work. Just the Crown Prince and about a hundred buddies. Depending on the season that may mean racing, or a vast cook-out in the desert, or sailing in the Red Sea.

At Jenadriyah, in the desert outside Riyadh, the race track extends so far towards the horizon under the deep blue sky that you can't see to the other side. There are crowds, tents, hundreds of horses, and camels, and vehicles. The annual festival out there lasts about a week around Saudi National Day. A special performance of traditional dancing and singing is put on for the Crown Prince's benefit. When I was there he was presented with a magnificent sword.

There is horse racing of course, but also camel racing, a Bedouin passion: some of the wealthier Saudis are particularly keen on it. Camels don't race straight ahead. That would be too obvious. They have a tendency to amble off into the sunset or go backwards. However, the owners generally manage to cajole a small group to assemble on the track, and head in roughly the right direction. The culmination of the Festival is Crown Prince Abdullah's Camel Race.

Traditionally camels are the Bedouin's main source of milk and meat, and only beast of burden. Racing camels are well cared for as they are valuable. Sadly, the same cannot be said for their young riders. Boys as young as four, are bought for fifty or a hundred dollars, from poor families in Pakistan and Bangladesh, and flown over to Saudi Arabia to be jockeys[7].

---

7   The use of child jockeys was banned in Gulf countries in 2004, but there remains a thriving underground trade in child trafficking. As recently as April 2009, 9 Bangladeshi children were intercepted by immigration officials in Calcutta on their way to Saudi Arabia to be used as camel jockeys. They ranged in age from 4 to 8 years old.

Many of the boys are purposely underfed to keep their weight down. During a race there is Velcro on the saddle and the wrists of the boys, but it doesn't always work. In the National Guard Hospital, I saw a little jockey with fractures on both wrists, caused by falling from a height onto hard ground. He was about eight and he sat waiting for treatment with a face of stone. He had learned stoicism. Not a wince. Many, however, never receive medical care and some die painful deaths, their bodies buried in the desert in unmarked graves.

Betting goes on. It is not permitted by the *metawah,* or in Islam for that matter, but they don't harass the rich. The Crown Prince has more than four hundred horses and likes to talk bloodstock. Almost every Saturday in Riyadh, he would travel out to his farm in the desert with his entourage and guests. It is not green but there are corrals, and fresh water, and scores of superb racehorses. All his trainers are Irish and there is one little Irish jockey working for him.

Tents would have been set up in advance, and a massive buffet lunch laid out. One of the big hotels organizes the food: shrimp, always shrimp, and traditional Arabic dishes involving lamb and rice and vegetables. I was told they were paid $400 a head, for maybe a hundred of us, every week. It was a nice lunch, but not a four hundred dollar lunch. The palace was overcharged, as usual.

Later on, after sunset, a delicious dinner would be laid out in the tents. There was an awful lot of eating. And at Taif – Taif practically finished me off. The Crown Prince has palaces in Jeddah and Taif as well as Riyadh, the same five-palace arrangement with accommodation for all the wives and families, but Taif is the most Arabic and pretty-looking. We'd travel up to the palace there from Jeddah, the whole entourage of several hundred in the air-conditioned motorcade racing up the escarpment in the dusk, round and round these hairpin bends. There are guard rails – a few – but trucks pass on the blind curves so there are quite a few deaths on that road.

In search of distraction, I'd look back down in the dusk and imagine what it must have been like eighty years ago. A long trudge by camel train, heavy rope-tied bundles creaking against the beasts' humps, climbing up and up the narrow track, endless desert darkening six thousand feet below.

In summer, it was well over 110°F on the plain, so it felt good to go up where it was cooler and not at all humid.

One time we didn't know that all the brothers (except King Fahd) were also up in Taif: Prince Sultan, Prince Turki, Prince Ahmed, Prince Bader (like a big fat spoiled baby) – each with their own dedicated staff and entourages. Nobody told us, so we ordered some food when we got there and settled down to rest.

About eleven thirty in the evening we get a message; Prince Sultan has invited us to dinner. A car is waiting. We arrive at the palace and are seated and given a lovely meal, although we can hardly eat any of it.

Afterwards we go back to the Crown Prince's palace and all the relations are there. There must be at least a thousand people, sitting on rugs on the grass beneath the stars, drinking glasses of tea. The Crown Prince is off somewhere so we pick a spot to sit down: me, and Naïf, and Dr Brewerton, who works with Dr Atiq and Dr Kaliq. Suddenly a little man picks his way through the crowds.

"Where have you been? Come, come, come!"

The Crown Prince wants us. We get to our feet, and make our way through the buzz of tea-drinking VIPs, with the little man leading the way. Now we're in a private room with only eleven people and the Crown Prince. These are just the brothers, Prince Sultan included, and a few close advisors.

And we face our third dinner. I gained 25 pounds the first year I was there.

In many ways, Jeddah was the best. Jeddah is a port on the sparkling blue sea. The Royal yacht is there, the *Al Yamamah*, it is called, after the village near Taif where Crown Prince Abdullah lived as a boy.

All four wives travel with the Crown Prince to his palace in Jeddah, where he stays for several months of the year. You would think they would all want to go to Jeddah in winter when it is beautiful and cool, but they go in July to September when it is sweltering hot. They are probably pleased with the change of scene regardless; it's a more westernized city. Relatively.

Al Yamamah is brought down from Greece, where it remains the rest of the year. The captain is Greek, and has been working for Crown Prince Abdullah since Saddam Hussein gave him the yacht in 1984[8]. Saddam did this in gratitude for Saudi support during the Iran-Iraq war. The yacht is over 300 feet long: according to a coffee-table book on board called *Super yachts*, it was at that time the seventh largest in the world. If you peer round the far side of the big brass ship's bell located right by the bridge, you read the inscription *Qadissiyat Saddam*, named after a famous Arab victory over the Persians in 637 AD. The bell is turned around, so you can't see the inscription unless you look very closely.

---

8   Re-named Ocean Breeze, the *Al Yamamah*, is now moored in Nice, France, for sale at 34.5 million dollars. It is listed as Saddam Hussein's former yacht. All references to King Abdullah have been omitted, when in fact it was his private yacht for over 20 years.

In the Captain's quarters there is a diagram of the ship with its original name taped over. You can also see by inspecting the plan that in Saddam's time there was a big bar where there is now a sitting room. The Crown Prince had it taken out. And on the upper deck, below the helipad, there used to be an enclosed swimming pool. The Crown Prince had this made into a *majlis* hall.

When the builders did this they had to take out some of the supports for the helipad, and the roof of the *majlis* hall is no longer strong enough to take the weight of a helicopter, although it still has a big H painted on it.

This was the one stressful aspect of going out on *Al Yamamah*. You've got this enormous yacht – and at times people like Yasser Arafat or the King of Jordan[9] came out on it, as well as the Crown Prince – so we're loaded to the bows with geriatrics of world significance. If these old fellows take a funny turn, Wall Street, the Nikkei and the Hang Seng start to buck and plunge, and the president gets woken in the night.

And we are responsible for their health.

So we all sail hundreds of miles out into the middle of the Red Sea and there's this flimsy helipad. God forbid emergency assistance should try to land, because we'd all be in the drink.

I don't know if they told the Crown Prince this. General Obeidh, who was in charge of the Royal Guard, was aware of it, and Dr Fahd Al Jabar, who is in ultimate charge of all the National Guard medical services, knew too. I always had an open door with him since I worked with the Prince, and by now he knew my face.

9   Considered one of the regions great peacemakers, King Hussein of Jordan died aged 63 on February 7, 1999. Palestinian leader Yasser Arafat died aged 75 on November 11, 2004.

"You know Tom, I never mind seeing you because it's always about work, you never ask for anything for yourself."

I liked that, and I would never cross Dr Al Jabar because I had seen what happened to people who did.

"But," I insisted, because I thought this was urgent, "the helipad is useless – dangerous – and it's half a day by sea to the nearest port if anything happens."

He is a plump man and he smiled like a little Buddha beneath his *ghutra,* and shrugged, utterly relaxed.

"You Americans amaze me. You plan for everything. Let me tell you about the Saudis. We are not good planners as you are. To you it makes no sense to take the support beams out. But to us, *inshallah,* it won't happen. We think ah! *Inshallah* we will never need to land a helicopter."

It's still marked with an H. But *inshallah* (god willing) nothing will happen, he can trust in Allah for protection.

Most Saturdays in the summer months in Jeddah we would glide wealthily out, four or five hours from the coast, usually to the same place between a couple of reefs where it was calm. Then we would drop anchor and the Crown Prince would entertain. There were about thirty five people in the crew, who were joined by staff and retinue and guests – say sixty or seventy people going on board every week. No women.

We would bring a lot of guests. King Hussein of Jordan came out with us one time, wearing Saudi dress including the red checkered *ghutra*. And Yasser Arafat four or five times.

There was a liquor cabinet in the Captain's sitting room behind the bridge, and although the Crown Prince does not drink, many of his retinue do. On most Saturdays the Johnny Walker Black Label would flow freely for the generals, and senior staff, and aides. The purser would be kept busy pouring whisky over ice. Then about twenty of them would sprawl on chairs and sofas, sipping their drinks, and watching porno videos. It's not my type of fun, watching porn with a bunch of drunken Arabs.

The upper level of the yacht contains the Prince's private quarters. After lunch on Saturdays he would have to leave the dining room, and walk across the sitting room – that is to say where the generals and so on were busy with the videos – to take his afternoon nap. There was always a scramble to grab the remote to shut the VCR off. Crown Prince Abdullah is relaxed about drinking on a day off, but the porno videos definitely would have offended him.

If I got bored I got one of the crew to rig up a fishing pole, so I could sit in the sun and fish off the stern. I'd have my suit trousers on, and my tie, because I was on duty and required to dress the part, but I'd have my sleeves rolled up, and a crew member with me who would bait my hook and lift the fish off so I wouldn't get dirty.

There I would sit for hours, on this vast ship, under the bluest sky, with my rod and line. It was very peaceful. And I sat there thinking, this is not bad for a boy from Marysville, California.

One day, General Obeidh and one of his friends saw that I had fish in a bucket, and was having fun, so they left the drinking and the videos, and came out on deck and decided to do the same. They're all country boys at heart. I gave the fish to the crew and they cooked and ate it.

We never remained at sea for more than seventeen hours at a stretch, except before the Arab summit in 1996. Netanyahu had just won power in Israel, and the Crown Prince invited key Arab leaders to get together, and discuss their strategy at a mini-summit, before the main Arab summit in Cario. We went out and dropped anchor, and the other VIPs came in their yachts, parked round about, and visited us. The sea and sky were deep blue and there were big white ships wherever you looked, resting complacently on the water.

Yasser Arafat was there, Prince Abdullah of Jordan, Sheikh Essa the Emir of Bahrain[10], and several of the Saudi brothers – and all the guys were hoping Mubarak would come. His enormous yacht is over a hundred years old and made of wood; at that time it was the world's largest private yacht, and it had recently been restored. We wanted to see it. However, Mubarak didn't show.

We had a smaller boat to ferry their various parties back and forth. Our Greek captain spoke terrible English, so no-one could understand him on the radio. With all this meeting and socializing was going on, I spent most of my time translating.

"OK we've got fifteen coming.... We've got thirty coming."

I spent two and a half days up there on the bridge.

"Tom, Tom, they candunnerstunn, eesneet." said the Greek captain.

"It's no wonder. I can't understand you either half the time. You need to launch the skiff to go get them."

Yasser Arafat is particularly friendly with Crown Prince Abdullah. When he became President of the Palestinians the Prince immediately gave him an airplane: a 747 I think. I don't think he has his own yacht. Little Yasser (like King Hussein of

---

10   Sheik Essa the Emir of Bahrain died of a heart attack aged 65 on March 6, 1999.

Jordan he is about five feet tall) was very friendly and laughing and jovial on the yacht.

Dr Atiq and Dr Kaliq would just raise their eyes to the heavens and say, "Tom, he is drunk off his ass. He has been drinking *all day*."

Little Yasser loved his Johnny Walker. He looks scruffy, always unshaven. If I saw him sitting beside a camel I'd throw him a riyal. But he has had a rough life. And I never saw him drunk any other time.

15

Best-paid Paramedic in the World

———

We were in Jeddah when, back in California, my father died.

For security reasons associated with being part of the royal entourage, my family had no way to contact me. They had the number of the National Guard Hospital in Riyadh, but that was all, and nobody there could give them my number at the palace. The hospital called my villa on the compound and got Kurt my room-mate, who called the palace, who got another paramedic, who came in and woke me up and told me.

I needed to go home right away.

It was during the *hajj*. The *hajj* is when millions of Muslims from all over the world visit Mecca, less than a hundred kilometers from Jeddah, and perform what is called a "spiritual journey". You have to book months in advance to get a flight in or out of Saudi Arabia at this time.

One part of King Abdul Aziz Airport at Jeddah was specially built to accommodate multitudes of pilgrims under one enormous roof tweaked into thousands of round tent-peaks like wavelets on the sea. Water comes out of misters inside and evaporates before it reaches the crowd keeping the air cool. There are hundreds of thousands of people with bags and rope-tied bundles sleeping on blankets on the floor. You have to step over them –

I call home.

"Do you want me to come home?"

"Yes."

I think of the visa. The quickest it is possible to get an exit and re-entry visa, in an emergency, is 24 hours.

I go to the chief protocol officer at the palace. To a Bedouin, family is the meaning of life.

He says, "Go back to your room. I shall see what I can do."

Half an hour later he calls me.

"There are no flights on Saudia Airlines. But the Crown Prince has given me a phone number for the director of Saudia in Jeddah and you will get a flight. Otherwise – you'll go in his own plane."

This is generous beyond belief. It's like absolutely, you are going, this will happen, it's your father.

Ten minutes later the protocol officer rings back and tells me to pack my bags.

"You are on your way."

He arrives with a Mercedes 600 and a driver and rides with me right out to the airport. He has sorted out my visa in less than an hour. We pull up in front of the Saudia terminal. There are six people waiting and one of them is the head of the airline. They take me by the hand and put me onto a flight which has been booked first class from Riyadh to New York and through to California and back.

I am in Marysville within 24 hours.

I guess they know how to find things out. And wow, can they move things along when they want to. Nevertheless I was surprised by what happened next. At the funeral, among all Dad's flowers appeared a vast floral display on a tripod stand six feet tall, with a card engraved with the familiar royal crest, the crossed swords under a palm tree. It read, "From the Royal Palace, Jeddah."

We sat in the pews and I muttered to Mum that it looked like Dad had won the Kentucky Derby.

When I got back to Jeddah the Crown Prince wanted to see me.

He held my hand and murmured, "How is your mother?"

I was really touched by his kindness and respect. They are such loyal people.

We went to the '96 Arab summit in Cairo so that the leaders could discuss their stance towards Israel in the light of recent changes. This meant flying to Egypt in the Crown Prince's private 747. It was an overseas trip which all the staff liked, because overseas trips mean presents. When you leave Saudi Arabia even for one day, you get thousands of dollars in an envelope as you board the plane.

There is one man whose job is to carry the two black suitcases. I was told that those cases were filled with a million dollars – no less, ever – in American hundred-dollar bills – so that should there be a revolution and, like, no ATM within reach, it was the emergency fund. This guy's everyday duty was to flip open the suitcase and hand out chunky envelopes with wads of sequential dollar bills inside.

The paramedics and servants received $3,000 and the doctors, $10,000. General Obeidh, the big stocky fellow in charge of the Royal Guard, who spoke English with us, and another resident General would get $25,000 each.

So we get into the plane with a spring in our step, and immediately ahead is what looks like a brass phone booth.

It is an elevator up to the Crown Prince's private bedroom and living quarters.

On the regular level there are sofas and chandeliers and low tables. The sofas have seat belts, and the buckles are gold-plated and engraved with the royal palm-tree and crossed-sword motif. The generals and the entourage would spend the flight in this lounge area being attended to by the crew of beautiful Moroccan girls whose hair was not covered. As we embarked each girl would be given a rose (and presumably an envelope as well).

At the very back there are thirty first-class regular seats for the staff, snugly buckled in by the same gold-plated engraved seat belts. There is also a fully equipped surgical suite, with a ventilator and all the key surgical kit, even burls to perform brain operations at 35,000 feet in case of head injury. The suite is checked and stocked by medical staff before the Crown Prince embarks on any flight, and it is where we store our paramedical equipment for the journey.

This summit was the largest meeting of Arab leaders in over twenty years, and they had booked the entire Heliopolis Meridian hotel, not far from the airport.

We land to find that each entourage has been assigned a general (there are lots of generals in Egypt apparently) who issues every individual with a special security pass. Mine tells whoever looks at my name and Californian image that I am a particularly fresh-faced, dependable Saudi diplomat.

And we get a number, and this is our car number in the motorcade that is to whisk us to the hotel. I have never seen so many glossy black twelve-cylinder Mercedes 600 sedans in my life. I think they must have rounded up every limo in North Africa for this. Three of us – Dave, Saif and I, have our own car and driver. For the three days of the summit he will sit in the parking lot and that car is for us, and no-one else.

The hotel is surrounded at each corner by sandbags with a machine-gun nest. It is packed. All three of us have to share the same room. We step out onto our balcony and every rooftop as far as the eye can see has soldiers with machine guns on it.

The Crown Prince, of course, has a suite. The late Emir of Bahrain, Sheikh Essa, has a suite at the end of the hall. When we walk past his door is always open. He is another tiny man, hardly more than five feet tall with a big grin all the time, and he beckons gaily to us.

"Come come, sit! Have tea!"

Saif and I thank him and take tea with the others in his room. The Emir wears a dagger in his belt and an enormous Rolex on his skinny little wrist, with diamonds and rubies set into solid gold. I am over-awed. When we leave I mention it to Saif.

"If you had told him you liked it he would have taken it off his wrist and given it to you. He is traditional, and it is an old Arab custom."

Next morning, all the Mercedes are lined up to take everybody to the convention center where they are having the meetings, about fifteen minutes away, and I notice – everybody notices – the only car that doesn't fit in.

This is a long stretch Cadillac limo in white, with running boards along each side and the back and grab-handles on the roof. Muammar Gaddafi of Libya refuses to use a Mercedes and has flown his own car over. When we drive into town he has his bodyguards ride outside it. Two of them are black women with huge breasts, dressed in skin-tight camouflage jump-suits, wearing row upon row of gold bracelets down each arm and pistols tucked into black webbing belts. They are perched on the running boards in high heels. The Cadillac skims past all the men in *thobes* and one of these girls looks just like Donna Summer.

What a showman. Michael Jackson couldn't do it better.

For several days our job was to sit outside summit meetings. The bodyguards were doing the same thing. All the Arab leaders were there. I had seen Hussein, Little Yasser, Mubarak – he is close to six feet tall and stocky, with that Arab moustache, but I had seen him before at the Gulf Co-operation Council in Qatar. I saw President Assad of Syria[11] for the first time. When he walked by us he would always smile and say, "hallo, how are you?"

"Seems like a nice fellah," I murmur in Arabic to the Saudi standing next to me.

"In Syria, there was a town that demonstrated against him. He had it surrounded by soldiers, and they came in and killed every man woman and child and bulldozed the town to the ground[12]."

"Oh."

"They have a hotel there now. But nobody will stay because they think it is haunted."

From time to time people would leave with a few bodyguards and then go back in. I wanted to be able to say I'd spoken to Gaddafi, and I told Dr Kaliq I would take the chance if I got it. He looked real worried.

"Whatever you do, don't tell him you are American. He hates Americans."

---

11   President Hafez Al Assad of Syria died aged 69 on June 10, 2000.

12   The Hama massacre occurred on February 2, 1982. The Syrian army bombarded the town of Hama in order to quell and uprising by fundamentalist Muslims. It is estimated 7,000 to 40,000 people were killed.

So Gaddafi comes out, flanked by two guys, and I just kind of step up and say, "Hallo, Mr Gaddafi, how are you?"

"Fine, how are you?" he says, and shakes my hand.

So, it was less than a meaningful exchange of views. I'm still proud that I've stood toe to toe with Muammar Gaddafi.

What a prima donna. There is a double curving staircase that rises from the lobby of the Meridian – and this lobby is packed with TV crews, littered with cables and cameras. The world leaders would stride in wearing preoccupied expressions, turn sharp left to the bank of elevators and be whisked upwards. Gaddafi saunters in, effeminate, slinky, minces up the stairs two or three steps, poses for the photo-opportunity, and sashays on up like he's in a Busby Berkeley musical.

He has another side. One day, when the rest of us were slumped on gilt chairs outside the meeting room, two or three of his bodyguards took the opportunity to go shopping. This happened to be a day when the meeting broke up early and their boss got back before they did. Too late, a taxi pulls up in front of the hotel and these men step out laden with glossy carrier bags. Right out there in front of the Meridian Gaddafi has been waiting and he strides up and beats the living shit out of his own bodyguards. In front of everybody he beats a guy and kicks him to the ground. It's the scandal of the Arab summit.

We were probably the best-paid paramedics in the world. Very often the Crown Prince gives presents. Everything is organized in advance. And because you are in this environment, full of demanding people, it rubs off. You can easily get spoiled.

The Crown Prince went to Syria to see King Assad, and it was rush rush! A last minute meeting – We're going!

Get ready! Get ready! So we packed up our medical gear and flew to Syria on the Crown Prince's plane at short notice.

When we landed they didn't have enough cars for us. Six of us with our medical equipment had to pile into a little Toyota. We drove to the hotel, a Sheraton. At first they told us there was no room at all. Finally they arranged one single room and we all had to share it. I can't remember how we organized who got the bed, but five of us had to sleep on the floor. We were up most of the night attending a state dinner anyway, so we only had two or three hours of sleep in 24.

At this time the Crown Prince's team included a rather camp doctor from Florida. On the flight back he did not stop complaining.

"Oh! That was *So Awful*. They had no food for us, no car for us, no room!"

I said, "You know your envelope? How much did you get?"

"Ten thousand dollars. But it wasn't worth it."

I scanned him for signs of injury. He looked perfectly well to me. A little tired, perhaps, but –

"How long you bin in Saudi Arabia?"

"Ten years."

"I would stand in the corner on my head for ten thousand tax-free American dollars. You have been here *way* too long."

It's very difficult to earn that kind of money back home. Plus we were getting paid a good salary, as well.

Not long after I started working for the Crown Prince we flew to the meeting of the GCC, the Gulf Co-operation Council, in Qatar on the Gulf. We stayed at the Sheraton, which is shaped like a Pyramid, and everyday we would assemble down either side of a long hallway as an audience for the distinguished visitors going into the conference room. Right after the conference every member of an official party was given a Gucci watch in gold and silver, the numbers on the face sparkling with diamonds. With it came a card in Arabic which said, *"With the compliments of the H.H. Sheikh Hamad bin Khalifa Al Thani of Qatar"*.

More senior people got one with diamonds encrusted all the way around.

A little man came to our hotel rooms and handed them out. He must have had over a thousand of these watches, in little wooden boxes. I was told that they were custom-made for the conference and that no-one else in the world had one.

In downtown Riyadh there is a used-watch store. Well, I happened to be wearing mine when I walked in and saw two on the shelf. I showed the guy who ran the shop.

"Ah yes," he said "every year, after the GCC, it's is the tradition that whoever hosts it gives out watches and afterwards all the household staff of the Crown Prince come in and sell theirs. They are indeed specially made. But" – and he pulled open a drawer – "this is from the year before, these are from the year before that."

Some were superb. They were all different models, mostly undated, although the older ones said where they were from – Syria.

"Those are not the popular ones," he told me.

No-one wants one that says *"Syria GCC 1990"*, because that's old.

Whoever hosts the GCC used to give away only Rolexes, but now they're not so fussy. It's Omegas, all sorts. But it's still watches, because according to Islam everyone is the same before God.

Everyone wears the same *thobe* and *ghutra*, no jewelry, so the only permissible displays of status are useful things like pens and watches. Just occasionally, I have seen cufflinks on the *thobes*.

Most of the servants sell their gifts. For a long time, sitting unused in the palace grounds at Riyadh, there was a scaled down version of an MG roadster (a three-quarter version of the car in *Love Story* that the Crown Prince had bought for his son when the boy was about eleven). It was all handmade, hand-sewn leather seats, little Kaboda diesel tractor engine in it, real neat. I got into it and drove it around the compound once. The Crown Prince gave it to his servant in the end and the next day it was up for sale at twenty thousand riyals.

Shortly before the GCC meeting, while the Emir of Qatar was holidaying, or otherwise spending time in Switzerland, his son the Crown Prince assumed power[13]. I think he just told his father not to come back.

But we could go. We were the first official government entourage to visit the new Emir, about six months after the coup. In that time they had (I couldn't believe how fast) built him a palace: huge rooms, acres of Persian carpet and marble floors, gold taps, crystal chandeliers.

I felt I was living one long episode of *Lifestyles of the Rich and Famous,* but that was because I hadn't yet been with the Crown Prince long enough to get spoiled.

Lofty from Tennessee, was 42 years old, about five feet two, chubby, and looked like a troll. He'd been a paramedic on the team for seven years already when I came, longer than

---

13   On June 27, 1995, Sheikh Hamad Al Thani deposed his sixty three year old father Sheikh Khalifa Al Thani in a bloodless coup. Allegedly Sheikh Khalifa was squandering the countries oil revenues.

anyone else. He spoke fairly good Arabic. He had hardly any paramedical skills left. He had been there too long. It's like playing a musical instrument; you need to keep in practice.

But he was a good politicker among the Palace hierarchy and they treated him like a pet. After a few years there he had converted to Islam. He still drank and smoked, but on duty or around the Saudis, he was devout enough. This gained him respect among Saudis. Most of the Westerners thought he was a cynical opportunist.

I was told that in the first five years he was there, he'd been to Bangkok every single holiday. He was no oil painting, but in Thailand with a pocket full of money, he had all these beautiful Oriental women clambering all over him and he loved it. One of them was particularly special to him, and he sent her money, rented an apartment in Bangkok for her, and sent her to school to learn English. They were to be married.

The Crown Prince's favorite holiday destination is Morocco, and he has a palace right next to the King of Morocco's not far out of Casablanca. So, the year before I arrive, Lofty goes to Morocco with the entourage, visits Casablanca as usual, and meets Fatima.

He is smitten. Fatima is a prostitute, but absolutely gorgeous. She is twenty five years old and five feet seven, she has wavy ringlets down to her knees, and olive skin and green eyes, and a hard edge. She's tough. Fatima also has a four-year-old daughter, out of wedlock, which in a Muslim country makes her the lowest form of life.

Lofty's trips to Thailand dwindle and he starts going back to Morocco for holidays. He sets up Fatima in an apartment in Casablanca. Tells her not to be a prostitute.

I don't know if she carried on turning tricks until they got married, but married they did get, and he brings her back, with her daughter to Saudi Arabia.

The Saudis around the palace knew the woman's history, although I think he told everyone that Fatima had got a divorce because her husband was abusive.

So I come to work at the palace, and Lofty is top dog among the medics. He has pretty much free rein. The Prince likes him, all the Saudis like him. If he wants something from the hospital administration he generally gets it. More to the point, if the Crown Prince is visiting Morocco it's Lofty who can put in a word about which paramedics should go.

Everybody kisses up to him. He can make a difference to your pay worth thirty or forty thousand dollars a year, because you can be boarding the royal 747 and collecting an envelope stuffed with cash, while the rest of them are sitting on their butts back in Riyadh.

However, at this point Dr Fahd Al Jabar comes onto the scene. Dr Al Jabar is new. Lofty has no clout with him. And Lofty finishes his career over $80.

It's 1996, and the paramedics get a *per diem* allowance whenever they are called upon to work outside Riyadh city limits. This stands at 300 riyals, about $80. Every Saturday we go to Jenadriyah, which is only fifty miles away, to the Prince's farm, and we get our allowance. We are clearing 1200 riyals which is about $300 on top of our salary. Not to mention *per diem*s for visits to Jeddah, Taif, and other places.

Lofty has been there long enough to remember when the daily allowance was 500 riyals, and he has watched it go down once. Now the administration proposes to reduce it to 150 riyals. The guy is already making six or seven thousand dollars a month, but he's got greedy. He wants this extra 1200 riyals and he doesn't want it reduced. And then one day he notices we didn't get a *per diem*.

"That's outta town, we should be getting our *per diem*s for that," he says. Bustles in all indignant to see Dr Fahd Al Jabar.

"We have an agreement."

"I will look into this and see what I can do." Dr Al Jabar dismisses Lofty and calls down to his staff.

"Bring me that man's payslip. I want to see his salary."

He looks at it. Lofty's taking home $128,000 *per annum* in pay, overtime, and *per diem*s, and that figure does not take into account the cash in the envelopes or the watches. This is more than the American emergency room doctors make at the National Guard Hospital.

"I didn't like the way he demanded the 300 riyals," he informed his staff.

"I don't want him working out at the palace any more. He can work at the emergency room at the hospital if he wants."

He probably didn't like Lofty's influence at the palace either.

General Obeidh, Dr Atiq and Dr Kaliq all were astonished. They had liked him and wanted him to stay. But he had not treated Dr Fahd Al Jabar with respect.

Lofty was demoted to the ER, but was an awful paramedic. He'd had no practice in seven years and now his private life was not so much fun as he had to get by on $40,000. His wife was not happy. Shortly afterwards they moved back to Tennessee where he put a down payment on a house.

Fatima's little daughter, a cute kid who had spoken only French and Arabic when she arrived, was now five and a half and no longer liked to speak Arabic. She generally spoke French, but had a smattering of English. She and her Mom would be all right.

As for Lofty I am not sure. When he left (it's amazing how much we all knew about each other's lives) he had less than $100,000 in the bank. He owned an apartment in Casablanca that all of Fatima's family now lived in, and part of a grocery store in Tennessee that his mother lived above and ran as a business. I heard he bought a new car when he got home.

16

Malcolm

———

Prince Bader bought a yacht. He had it built in New Zealand for seven million dollars. It was 110 feet long, three decks high, nicely laid out with accommodation for 25 people, and could be run with a crew of five. The back deck was stepped down to the water line and had two air compressors to fill scuba tanks. Prince Bader has a lot of young sons, so they could now park their jet-skis and fill their tanks and dive in the Red Sea.

This brand new gleaming boat slid into the private dock behind the Crown Prince's palace in Jeddah. It was moored alongside the majestic bulk of *Al Yamamah* and looked real elegant.

Prince Bader was anxious to impress his brother and invited him for an afternoon's sailing. Two of us, the paramedics, went aboard first. The decks were smooth wood of the palest gold. The Captain, who was from Seattle, told us that this wood is unique to New Zealand and they are not allowed to export it. The only way to take it away is to buy something made there. Say, a yacht.

We waited in the ship's lounge where fresh fruit, and pistachios, and so on, were set out for refreshment, should His Royal Highness desire a snack. Prince Bader hurried in to check on the effect. He started picking out pieces of fruit and tossing them into space, screaming, "This is Not Right!"

A white-robed minion scuttled in and replaced mangoes and re-adjusted the grapes.

The Crown Prince came on board and we sailed proudly into the Red Sea.

We were just fifteen minutes out of Jeddah when the boat swung about and returned to its moorings.

We tied up, and luncheon was served. The dining room seated only fifteen, so we shared the table with Prince Bader, Prince Sultan, our employer and a few of the advisors. Conversation was none too animated. We got off the boat.

This was something of an anti-climax. As soon as I could, I asked Dr Kaliq what had happened.

He whispered, "The Crown Prince didn't like the little boat. It rocked too much."

Prince Bader was quite upset. I think he was mortified and hurt. The Crown Prince was not interested in anything smaller than a ship, smooth as glass, and feelings were not mollified by the way he condescendingly called it, "The Little Boat."

It was a beautiful vessel and personally would have been my choice.

Days later, I was sitting on the dock in the sunshine thinking I could do with some time off. I had been in Jeddah, working in an all-male environment, for weeks, and it was at least a month since I had seen a woman's face. I stared up at Bader's yacht. On the bridge I glimpsed a beautiful blonde. This was the Captain's wife. She was kept out of sight of the guests, sequestered, unseen.

One reason I hadn't had any time off was that we were a paramedic short. Chuck had had to go; he'd been drinking on duty while in Morocco. Security found booze in his room. He'd sent a servant into town to buy it.

If you are an American who is a hopeless alcoholic, I guess it seems obvious that if you spend a couple of years in Saudi Arabia, which everyone tells you is drier than the desert, you'll shape up.

Then you get there and discover *sidiqi* at about 200 proof.

Chuck had got married when he got to Saudi; he'd found a female alcoholic called Suzanne. If Chuck and Suzanne were not at work they were stumbling drunk. They had both been married before and had children back home in the States.

Sid is not well tolerated. I have felt terrible after drinking it. You can kill yourself with it. It will ignite with a match. You keep it in your freezer, but it doesn't freeze and a bottle lasts for months. Chuck and Suzanne would get through two bottles a week. I know this because my friend Kurt used to sell it to them. His price was 150 riyals a bottle, but Chuck had to pay 200 because Kurt didn't like him. Few people did; he and Suzanne were pretty worthless.

They saved not a penny and after Chuck was booted from the palace he went back to the emergency room. But it's hard work there and he and Suzanne quit and returned to California certain that the hospital could not function without them. I believe everyone was glad to see them go.

I go away on a long holiday, return to Riyadh feeling terrific and we're off on one of the Crown Prince's long hunting trips to the desert.

There are beautiful parts of Saudi Arabia, with mountains and trees and even water, but where the Prince most likes to go is way out in the desert, hundreds of miles from anywhere, just flat sand and bleached camel-bones and patches of scrub stretching to the horizon in all directions.

I spent many weeks in the desert with the Crown Prince. He stopped doing camel caravans a long time back. It's the usual motorcade out (he rarely flies within Saudi Arabia), and the highways are blocked off. We assemble; we're ready, four hundred National Guard soldiers and huge trucks full of communications equipment, hangers-on, servants, dogs, the falconer and his birds. Altogether an entourage of about a thousand people in limousines and jeeps and army vehicles, and suddenly we're off and running at 100 mph down that empty highway that runs straight as an arrow way out into the desert. Our ambulances have a hard time keeping up.

One time, I flew into camp 48 hours late in the daily supply plane, a Hercules C-130. They have web seats, like a sling, and I'm sitting there with my knees pressed against bags of rice and hundreds of terrified sheep bleating in pens in the back. They kill 90 sheep a day to feed everybody at a desert camp; it has to be done *halal*, so there are butchers on site.

Coming in to land, I see dirt roads – we're always way after the end of the highway – and trailers grouped in a circle around a big *majlis* tent. There's the satellite dish getting signals from space, water trucks, peripheral tents, animal pens, and jeeps. Everything for life and work except women.

We always camp a hell of a long way from Riyadh. We have a medical tent and caravans to sleep in. There are usually two American paramedics, two Saudis, and two of the Crown Prince's doctors. When we Americans are on duty, under the desert sky, striding across eddying sand, we wear our suits, shirts and ties, and Ray-bans as usual.

This time I climbed into the back of the ambulance and there was a new paramedic. There he was, arranging things. I introduced myself. He was a quiet fellow, ex-Marine. Just kept on taking stuff out of cupboards, lining it up, sorting it into groups. I was getting curious.

In the end I said, "What are you doing?"

"You know, I really like to organize ambulances. I'm not a very good paramedic, but I'm really good at tidying up," he said, without meeting my eye.

He didn't want to socialize or learn Arabic, but preferred to spend every evening in his tent. He must have been bored out of his mind.

Everyday they would set up a tent in a different part of the desert and we would motorcade out there and have lunch with the Crown Prince. Afterwards the Saudis would gather and talk, drink tea, or shoot guns. By early evening we would be back at camp and then our responsibilities would be finished, although we must never be more than a few minutes away from His Royal Highness.

In the evening they bring in two semi-trailers filled with firewood and have a huge camp fire. The Bedouin, the National Guard, the medical team, and everybody who was servicing the camp, I liked hanging out with them, and we'd sit around and drink tea and smoke and talk. Mostly, life in camp consists of Saudi men sitting around talking and smoking waterpipes filled with *sisha*, tobacco in different flavors. It's not a loner society. At home, they'll go out to a coffee shop at night and sit together with their water pipes just the same.

The evening was when I made my social calls. I had a little circuit, going from one tent to another, in warm air that smelled of petrol and grilled meat and tobacco. Mostly we would sit outside in the dusk with pipes and tea kept warm over a brazier, although the tents were nice inside, hung with pretty cottons and littered with Sony Walkmans and bundles of spare *thobes*.

It gets chilly when the sun goes down. It just slides very fast below the horizon like a great red ball, and that's when you go inside your tent, and appreciate the carpets on the floor. They put the flap down and since it's the middle of the night and time to eat, the food's nearly ready. They have a big metal box with coals inside, and little pillars each side and you set the pots of tea on it. They wrap lamb and vegetables in foil and bury it in the coals and it cooks.

Anyone of the tent sides can be folded back to let in the breeze or, if you are cooking, to let the smoke out. They are adept at camping. They have been doing it for thousands of years.

What the guys talked about a lot with me was cars. But sometimes falconry, or occasionally gossip (although there isn't a lot of that unless you count tales of the Crown Prince's two errant teenage daughters).

One story was about Majid, the Crown Prince's son. He had a Porsche Carrera and got stopped by the traffic police for driving fast and recklessly.

Now the police don't usually stop expensive cars, in fact if they were to stop every car of any description that drove fast and recklessly they'd never go home, so Majid's driving technique must have been truly woeful.

"You are driving badly. Get out of the car."

"Do you know who I am?" demands Majid. "I am the son of the Regent. Why did you pull me over?"

"Because it's my job," says the policeman.

Majid slaps him across the face.

Every nearby policeman comes running and that includes a Captain.

"Right, add 'assaulting a policeman' to the charge. Take him away."

Back at the police station, somebody calls the palace.

"There is a big problem here. Somebody in the police wants to put the prince in jail."

Crown Prince Abdullah personally rings the Captain.

"What happened?"

"Well, Your Royal Highness, your son was driving fast and recklessly and slapped a policeman."

"Normally what kind of punishment would a person get for that?"

"Two days in jail at least."

"Fine. Put him in jail for two days to show him he is no better than anyone else."

So it was a story that reflected well on the Prince (our host, employer and ruler).

More often than not, they wanted to talk about western women. They talk about sex a lot, as a substitute for doing it. Frankly, they are fixated. And I can't count the number of times I've been asked —is there like a shot, or something, you can give me to make me a little stronger in bed? This is before Viagra, which they now buy over the counter.

One night I met an elderly gentleman who was quite closely related to the Crown Prince. He carried a stick, like a shepherd's crook, to help him walk, and puffed his chest up to look good. The first thing they always ask you is whether you are married. At the time, I wasn't.

"Do you have a wife?"

"No, but I'm looking around."

"Oh," he said, with a gleam in his eye "you know what? You need to get one of those American women. I hear they do *everything*."

I said *"Really?* I'm looking for a nice young Saudi girl."

"Ach," he said, "you don't want one of those. They just lie there and do nothing. Now one of those Americans...."

"You know" I said, "I know some of those American girls. Maybe I'll get one for you."

"Ach," he says, "What am I going to do with her? Put my leg in her? I'm eighty-four."

As night fell some of the Saudis would drive further into the desert with their packs of salukis to hunt rabbits. These dogs are built for speed, with sleek coats and long legs that skim across the sand, and they can weave and dive and chase down a rabbit in the desert and hold it. Like the falcons they are trained not to kill their prey because whatever they catch must be killed *halal*, its throat cut by a knife, and allowed to bleed to death.

In the old days the Bedouin would follow the hunt on horseback. Now they follow their salukis — or the falcons — in Jeeps. The hunting animals and birds wear radio tracking devices and the Jeeps have GPS. You see up to twenty vehicles criss-crossing madly in every direction across the desert, chasing the signal from their own radio tracking device as all their birds follow the one rabbit.

Here I was, watching some of the most prized, best-trained birds in the world and the only falcon I ever owned was Malcolm, and that was a sad story.

Not long after I first came, when I was working at the National Guard Hospital, I bought him one day down at the *ouq* in Riyadh, in Bahtaa. Saudis pay tens of thousands of riyals for a really good falcon, but Malcolm was small, so he wasn't going to be very good. He was sitting in a cage looking forlorn, as they all did. I was going to buy a bigger better bird, but when I raised him up and let him down I saw he had a broken wing, so he was worthless. And Malcolm was a bright little chap.

I went to the book store and bought a book on falconry.

You don't have to get a baby bird; you can train them at any age. Down in the *souq* you buy the stand, which you just drive into the dirt for the bird to sit on, and the hood, and all the accessories, the leather strap for his foot, and the glove. Pretty soon I could call him over and he would fly from his stand and land on my arm. The Saudis loved to see me with him on my gauntlet.

They have to be hungry all the time when they are being trained. I had him for nearly nine months in my apartment. He lived on a stand on top of my wardrobe and there was newspaper down, and I would have to get up if he swooped down at my head when I was asleep. They must eat fresh, raw meat.

Then my private life intervenes. I need a holiday, I haven't been away since I came nearly a year ago and I don't know who will care for my bird. I have a cage for him, but he is used to being on top of my wardrobe where he can fly whenever he wants.

I have this little French-Canadian girlfriend Noelle. So I leave the bird with her, with very specific instructions – he is to have this fresh steak everyday and you have to let him out to fly around everyday as well.

Well, it's winter. I am away for three weeks. The first thing I face when I come back is two phone calls. One to say Noelle has been having sex with the Bangladeshi man that trims the hedges around the apartments, and another to say she's been doing exactly the same with the Saudi ward clerk in the hospital.

I call her up. How's she been, how've I been, how's my pet?

"Your bird's fine."

"I'm going to come and collect him."

So we get together and have a major row. Who told you about this? Who's been talking to you?

And poor little Malcolm is sitting in his cage sort of sideways with snot running down his beak. A bird can get cold and sick especially if it isn't able to exercise.

"And," I say "what the hell did you do to my bird?"

"Oh he's always rattling around in the cage making noise so when you were gone I just left him out on the terrace."

"I *told* you, you *can't* leave him in the cage, and you *can't* let him get cold. I told you specifically outside was too cold."

"Oh just take your bird and get out. Here's his food."

She gave me this Tupperware box. The meat was rotten.

"This is what you bin feeding my bird?"

The morning after I took him home, he was dead.

The Bangladeshi thought he had got a one way ticket to Canada. The charge nurse, who was a good friend of mine, though Noelle didn't know that, told me Noelle had been trying to get a flight to London for an abortion because she was pregnant by him. The whole hospital knew this within hours.

Noelle left her room mates without saying why and one day we heard she had gone back to Canada. The Bangladeshi used to ask people if they'd heard from her, but no-one had.

In the end somebody told us she'd had the baby. She didn't look after Malcolm though.

17

Fugga Hunting

———

I talked to a man from LA, a friend of Prince Bader's kids, who'd gone up to Canada and paid $5,000 for a peregrine falcon. They're a highly endangered species, but Prince Bader wanted one. This guy was a black Muslim who'd met the prince's kids when they came to California to go to college. He would take them clubbing. Now he's become a kind of companion and fixer and gets them the latest of anything. It's become his job: procuring stuff – cars, or computers, or whatever.

Problem: he can't ship a peregrine falcon out of the States, so he and the bird go back up to Canada. Prince Bader sends a private jet to collect it and gives him $25,000.

When it gets to Saudi the prince sells it to one of the other princes for $100,000. This other prince won't be able to breed it. He has only got the one.

The Crown Prince had a home built specially for his falcons in the palace grounds at Riyadh. It had glass walls like a greenhouse so they could respond to light, but it was air-conditioned, and had a solid roof. There were about thirty birds in there and I liked to go visit Mohamed, the keeper. He told me Khamis, up in the mountains, is where they were bred. I used to watch him exercise them. He would put meat or a dead pigeon on a rope, and swing it around and the birds would swoop down and right before they got it, he'd yank the rope away, his long fingers whirling it just out of reach. And they'd make another circle. All the birds had to be exercised.

Mohamed the falconer was on my circuit when I went visiting out at camp. I handled one falcon, a beautiful pale grey bird, almost silver, that the Crown Prince had recently bought for $25,000. The lighter the color the more prized the bird; animals can't see them coming so they are better hunters.

The Bedouin had this little boy in camp, and he'd go out at night with the flashlight and catch *jaraboua*. They jump. They are like kangaroo mice. *Jar*, it means rat, so I called him *jar walid*, rat boy.

The Saudis kept saying, "But he's not a rat!"

Here's what they would do.

They have a bed of coals out in front of the tent and they halal slaughter the mice. They slit their little throats and let them bleed to death and then throw them whole onto the coals, turn them over a few times – and when you are sitting there, drinking tea, they come into the tent with foil and this whole plate of steaming mice. Mmmm! The hair cooks off of 'em, but the skin's still there. And the guts and intestines. You are supposed to pick off the bits.

They would say, "This is really good, it will make you very strong in bed, you'll be able to go all night!"

"How come," I would say, "'whenever you try to feed me anything that is gross and disgusting, you tell me it is going to give me this"

– I'd make a rigid arm –

"and I'll go all night long?"

We have lizard to eat too. Thubs look prehistoric. They are flat and light brown with a long tail with spines sticking up and can grow to be several feet long. If they bite you I have been told you have to break their back before they will let go. They are kept for food. At the hospital I had one as a pet, and it never bit me. I eventually gave it to a nurse who let it go in the wild.

But in camp we'd have barbecued thub, the whole thing, guts and all. As usual you pick the meat out and leave the bones and intestines. This is the Bedouin way. Catch it, kill it halal, and chuck it on the fire. Nomads have to eat anything that moves. Of course it tasted like chicken.

One dark night the wind was howling across the desert. A shower tent had been set up for the soldiers and they were all bending into the wind and struggling across to take showers. I'd brought one of those dual-line stunt kites, from America. The type you can make duck and dive and swoop in the sky. So, me and another paramedic, we want to fly my kite. The soldiers have those luminous glo-sticks that you break to see by and be seen. We tie glo-sticks onto each end of the kite, and up it soars, it's like six feet wide, and this thing can dive and go sideways, and we're dive-bombing the soldiers as they scamper into the shower. Of course some of the other soldiers are watching and laughing.

There's fifteen minutes of this and then we see headlamps bouncing across at speed. Two Suburbans roar up full of soldiers armed with machine guns under the command of Prince Majid. He's been over at the *majlis* tent with the Crown Prince and all they can see are red and green lights darting up and down, and this way and that, and they think it's a UFO or something.

So now Prince Majid is fascinated, he thinks my kite is really neat, and I'm thinking, am I supposed to give it to him?

;w the answer to that. But I'd drug this 6-foot kite all
/ from the States and there was no way I was giving it
up. I thought to myself, next time I go, I'll buy him one.

Before they set camp, they send up a little Egyptian guy to
make sure that the whole area is clear of snakes. And when the
Crown Prince and his party are about to go fugga-hunting, the
snake catcher goes out in advance to check the ground. A couple
of times I went with him to watch. He had a long aluminum
pole with a pincher that would grab them behind the head and
pop 'em in a big canvas bag. He left the snakes in the bag for a
week or two, they were all OK, and he took them back to the
snake house at the National Guard Hospital.

I walked right by a pit viper, just a baby, which he saw.
He was good. By the end of the time we were there he'd have a
whole bag full.

We were at a big camp up near the Iraqi border. They'd set
up the Crown Prince's tent about fifteen miles from the main
camp, in a place where there are fugga roots under the sand.
These are something like a truffle. In the market fugga costs
about $100 a kilo. It's rare and expensive and only to be found
in certain spots.

So we'd follow the Crown Prince and his party, strolling in
their *thobes* and scanning the ground. They have special little
narrow-bladed trowels on long handles and they'd see a little
sprout and poke about in the dirt, pop it up, and cry out happily
if they'd found a fugga root.

The Crown Prince was intent on the desert sand. The
Royal fugga shovel is spray-painted gold. Everybody was quite
enthusiastic when he found a root. He always had someone
standing next to him to take it.

He would fugga-hunt most day[...]
border. Then he would get bored [...]
we'd all walk slowly back to the tent [...]

They cooked some for us.

"It is the Arab truffle! it will mak[...]

It was a bit gritty and sandy, but [...]
it tasted okay.

You get huge sandstorms (called *Shamal*) out in the desert, even in Riyadh. You can see hardly anything. Much worse than a California fog. It is like being blinded, and if you're driving you have to pull over, and stop, and the sand gets driven in everywhere. After one of these storms out at camp, I was with the snake catcher when he caught a big non-poisonous snake.

I was raised in the country, and I played with snakes as a kid, and owned a boa constrictor. So, I borrow this feller from him, and swing it over my arms, and carry it across the dust which is still settling, over to the trailer occupied by Dr Atiq and Dr Kaliq.

"Look what I found in my bed."

They jump up onto their couch like they're on springs.

"Oh Mr Tom! Take it out Mr Tom! Please, please take it out!"

So I drop it on the floor, looking alarmed.

"Do you think it's *poisonous*?" I ask.

They're whimpering up there like two little girls.

I played dumb for a while, then hauled it back off the floor and took it out. I kept a straight face. But it was a payback for those guys for putting us in a crap trailer. They kept the huge luxurious one for themselves, and there were only two of them, and there were four of us.

a place with a shower and bathroom of course, but
. The camp's satellite dish was as big as a house, so
were proper telephones and most of the trailers had them.
eirs did. But if I wanted to call Riyadh I had to use their
phone.

Wherever the Crown Prince is he must be in communication.
He is forever on the telephone. He's not, so far as I know, a
person who has to keep a lot of notes; I never saw him writing
anything down. And wherever he is, even if he's on the phone,
a television is on in the background. He had a widescreen TV
in the palace sitting room at Taif and surrounding it were
29 smaller televisions with other channels playing. This, I was
told, was for His Royal Highness's convenience, so that he did
not have to channel-surf.

Even out in the desert he would get Al Jazeera, BBC World,
ESBN, Saudi 2, all the Arab news channels. He made topical
jokes about mad cows – You guys eating a lot of beef lately?
MTV he does not care for at all, he is fastidious about avoiding
sexual vulgarity, but the sports channels he loves, especially
horse racing. And he can play his Nintendo on the big screen
television as well. As far as I could see television was burbling
constantly; at informal dinners, like on his yacht or Prince
Bader's yacht, or when he was with his coterie at the palace in
Taif, there was always a set playing in the room. There are no
newspapers around. It's just constant TV. So it's a selective view
of the world.

They liked to shoot too. Guns are not a problem to own. It's
buying the bullets. If you buy a .38 pistol they don't care, but
bullets have to be recorded by the police. They will have you
account for those if anyone gets shot with a .38. I asked a Saudi
·v about this, because down at Bahtaa I was offered an AK47

for $1,500. But rifles are cheap by comparison with hand guns, which will cost more than half as much again.

The Crown Prince would have with him in the desert, in its velvet case, his gold-plate Kalashnikov, besides .22 pistols and shotguns and hand-guns. His best friend is a Moroccan billionaire called Mr Iraqi, who apparently made a lot of money out of his dealings with the Prince. I don't know how.

But I don't think he is an arms dealer.

They were all shooting guns one day near the big luncheon tent and Mr Iraqi is like a court jester, shooting a shotgun and the rest of them are throwing things up in the air for him to shoot. Crown Prince Abdullah and Prince Turki and General Obeidh and the rest of them are showing him how the gun works. So he's enjoying it no end, BANG! BANG! he shoots and he swings round.

"HEY! Did I do OK? Am I doing all right?" And he's waving the gun and he's got it pointed at half the House of Saud and to a man they hit the deck. They're all screaming into the dirt –

"Folk, Folk, FOLK!" – Which means, "Up! Up!"

"Oh.... OK," he said.

Prince Turki was a favorite nephew of the Crown Prince and well liked by us as well. He had been educated in America and was I think the person who explained most to Prince Abdullah about how Westerners think. Prince Turki wanted to surprise the Crown Prince by getting him a Humvee. These are like outsized jeeps with a wide wheelbase and great for the desert. They hadn't been out long.

However, this wasn't going to be just any Humvee. The Crown Prince is a very tall man, so Prince Turki when he ordered it from the States specified that the roof and doors must be raised four inches so that there would be more headroom. Also it would be stretched, with an extra door in the middle, so that it would fit the Crown Prince and all his brothers. Nowadays you can rent them in Las Vegas a block long, but this was the first stretch Humvee ever made. The Humvee company took lots of pictures before it left the States for publicity purposes. They had never had one modified to this extent, with no expense spared, the front was customized, and there were new rims on the wheels, and genuine fine Morocco leather seats, and interior trim, and GPS, and so on. It was a big rush to get it done in time for the Prince's camping trip, not at the off the shelf price of $56,000, but for a quarter of a million.

Prince Turki told us the big secret when it was ready to fly over from the States. He hired a private cargo plane to bring it. Here it comes and it's all dusty. Two of the seats haven't been put in. Last-minute worries.

Anyhow it gets polished and fitted up and brought to the camp site. The Crown Prince knows nothing about it at all.

Surprise.

"Here is your car, your Royal Highness. Prince Turki had it made for you."

The Crown Prince looks delighted and gets in. Saudi Royals sit in the front seat, on the right – but the Humvee transmission cowling comes right down on the passenger side and leaves only inches for your feet. There is not much foot-room.

There are tracks across the desert. The Chevy Suburbans and Toyota Landcruisers have a standard width of wheelbase, so the ruts are already made. But the Humvee has a low, very wide wheelbase. So one set of wheels are on bare desert and the other in a rut, and it's a rough ride anyway, the Humvee.

The caravan of forty cars sets off out into the desert to the luncheon tent. We follow. We watch the Humvee rocking along. We drive a quarter of a mile and the whole caravan stops. The Crown Prince gets out. I see the familiar tall figure in his flapping *thobe*. He strides back down the line, gets into a Chevy Suburban, and we move on.

The Humvee we never saw again.

I asked what would happen to it. It'll be banished to the warehouse, they told me.

He likes what he likes, is deeply conservative and dislikes unfamiliar things. Sometimes I suspect there might be a little bit of psychological one-up-manship going on there too.

18

Under Arrest

———

The only time I was ever on Saudi TV was up at an airbase near the Iraqi border. There are runways for miles across the desert and a small ground staff stationed out there. We were camping not far away, so the Crown Prince and his party paid it a visit. He was greeting all the officers, so they set up chairs and cameras. The officers came up and shook his hand. I was sitting two rows back, next to Majid the Prince's son, and we were filmed for the news on Saudi Channel 2.

I noticed how when people greet the Prince they'll kiss him on the left shoulder, as a sign of respect. He will let people do that, but he will not let anyone kiss his hand. He thinks it is demeaning to the other person. He is a stickler for that. You can even see in the TV footage that he pulls his hand away when an officer tries to kiss it.

The other princes, they'll put their hand right up in your face.

Hereditary monarchy, with families the size they have, is a poisoned chalice. For a start they don't get into positions of power until they're old, and it's a lot of responsibility for a person who may not be in their prime. More importantly, it's got built-in conflict potential. By the time they get power, they're looking right ahead to the succession.

Every action of the Crown Prince carries a political interpretation for the future. Whatever he does, somebody interprets it as a sign of favor and somebody else gets offended.

Khaled is a son of King Fahd who is now a man in his 30s. He is fabulously wealthy since he received two billion dollars at the age of twelve; he gives millions to good causes (which are often a cover for malevolent political groups, but in the early 1990s he would not necessarily know that). He had great power and influence in his life as the favorite son of the king, but when King Fahd became sick, and no longer wielded as much power as he used to, Khaled did not cut quite so much ice.

According to palace gossip, when he asked for the hand of one of Crown Prince Abdullah's daughters, Abdullah refused. Now if this really happened, it was a huge insult. Cousin marriages are routine in rich Saudi families, so there wouldn't have been a problem about that. There may have been a suspicion that he was trying to consolidate a power base which would in due course cut out Abdullah's own sons.

The Crown Prince would have known that inferences would be drawn from his refusal, whatever his real intentions. These inferences could inspire repercussions.

This sort of thing was going on way above my head. Mostly what I saw was politics at my own lowly level, which meant at all costs avoiding confrontation with Dr Al Jabar the Ruthless.

At the palace in Riyadh, I got to know Thad. He was an American sports physiologist who had worked for some athletic teams in the States. The Crown Prince is among the few senior Saudis who look after their health, he swims and exercises, so they hired Thad to keep him motivated and figure out different exercise routines. The Crown Prince liked Thad and worked with him three or four times a week.

Thad lived on the hospital compound with his wife and two children. There was no set time for his duties. He always had to be on call, because there'd be a phone call – "The Prince wants to exercise now" – and he would have to order a car from the palace, and go over there, and he'd be driven back later.

But six months out of the year we're not even in Riyadh, we're in Jeddah for three months, in Taif for a month, or we might go to Morocco for a month, and Thad had to travel with the Crown Prince. He got fretful.

He said, "You know, this really isn't what I thought it was gonna be. First off, I have to call the driver from the palace to come and get me, he has to drive 10 minutes to collect me and 10 minutes back, so I need my own car."

There is something people who work at the palace get, which is self-importance. It starts with this feeling "The Crown Prince likes me" and it's got a lot to do with the lifestyle and having money.

Anyhow Thad had got self-important, big-time.

He said, "When I go travelling for a month I want a villa for my wife and kids in Taif, and one supplied in Jeddah, because I don't want to leave them. Plus I want more money. I'm not making as much as I thought."

He was on call 24 hours a day, but only working three or four hours a week.

"I'm gonna ask Dr Fahd Al Jabar for all this and if he doesn't give it to me, I'm just going to go to the Prince."

I said, "Let me tell you – please don't do that. Don't mess with that man. You can request politely, but don't demand. Don't threaten him."

Thad didn't take my advice.

He went to Dr Al Jabar and said I want a car, a villa here and a villa there, I want my family flown all over, and moreover I want more money.

Yup, that would be nice.

"Well," says Dr Al Jabar, "let me think about it. Thank you for coming. I appreciate your coming by."

No sooner was the door closed behind him than the telephone was picked up and Security was called.

"Do not let that man back into the Palace."

Thad now had no access to talk to the Crown Prince.

Dr Al Jabar told Security, "I want you to go to his house and pack him up."

He called Public Relations.

"I want you to get an exit visa for that man, his wife and the children. Send them all back to America. I want them out within 24 hours."

A new trainer arrived.

The Crown Prince said, "Where's Thad?"

Dr Al Jabar said – "He didn't like it here so he went home."

Dr Al Jabar didn't become a Minister of Health Affairs for the National Guard because he's stupid. He is a pediatrician by training. He used to be in charge of the King Faisal Hospital in Riyadh, the most famous hospital in Saudi Arabia, but got fired by King Fahd. Some Royal came in demanding this and that and he told the man to get lost. This got back to King Fahd and he lost his job. Then the Crown Prince hired him, originally just as an administrator running the one hospital, but later he got Ministerial status. I guess his appointment was another subtle political statement.

Saif and his friends were gleeful about working in Jeddah, because there is a well-known bordello there. It's mostly Moroccan women who look Spanish. A lot of the palace staff would go over there even though it was very expensive. One night with a girl would cost about $800 – which is more than most Saudis make in a month. And with that they would get a bottle of Johnny Walker which is illegal too.

Like the Empire Club, this place must be protected by a royal. Anyway I was invited to go to this brothel, but I claimed a previous engagement. Then they invited me to a party, so I thought I'd go. It was at King Fahd's farm about an hour outside Riyadh, and actually hosted by Prince Khaled.

"Yeah, I'll come. Will they have beer there?"

"Oh yeah, there'll be beer."

I go to Europe or the States, and I'm there for weeks before I think of wanting a drink, but in Saudi if someone offers me a real beer – being it's illegal – I'm gonna drink it just because I shouldn't.

We drive out there with the sun setting over the desert, and they have the little Filipino guys in their tuxes and bow ties serving drinks, and a full bar, and all kinds of food. In a separate room there is coke, hash, and little pills nicely set out. Little cross-top tabs, look like bennies, which I didn't know were still made, pharmaceutically. I don't know of any medical use for them.

"What are those?"

They were bennies all right, so Naif took two and I took two, and we chattered and chattered, and chewed gum, and sipped cold beer, and stayed awake all night. It was mostly guys, and then there was an influx of western women.

Some seemed to be nurses that worked nearby and then there were.... other girls.

"You want one, you can just take one," whispered my Saudi friend.

"I'm happy with my beer," I said.

Later, I ended up talking to one of these girls.

"Where are you from?"

"I'm from England."

"So you live here?"

"Oh no, we just came here for the weekend."

"You often come for the weekend?"

"Every once in a while they'll call, and send a plane and we'll come over."

There must have been thirty or forty girls from escort agencies in London. And there was probably the same proportion of western women who worked around. We had a good time. Saif didn't take one of the girls either. We were there for the beer.

There is a major social scene with the young Saudis. There are lots of parties in the great private houses in Jeddah. In Riyadh you see streets of severe, un-ornamented villas, it's all quite uniform, but Jeddah is more cosmopolitan and laid back and used to trade and foreign influences. People are not so afraid of being seen to be different, so you see every kind of style and beautiful homes. It's the closest Saudi gets to Beverley Hills.

You only get to party if you've got money, or *wassta,* or both, and it can kill you if there's not a lot else in your life. I had a friend, his father worked in public relations for the King, so he was very well connected. Mohamed was raised for several years in California, and like any teenager he liked to go out and party and drink, and when he came home he carried on doing the same thing. He had several drunk-driving accidents. In Saudi Arabia that's going to put you in jail even if you don't hurt anybody. It's an automatic one hundred lashes and jail. But as soon as he got arrested his father would be down to the police station and he would be released. This was like three or four incidents: he'd be drunk, or drunk driving, or drunk in an accident and released without charge. Then he went to work for the state oil company, and I lost touch. Until one day somebody said, "You heard about Mohamed? He was killed, drunk driving."

And I thought about it and I knew Mohamed thought he was untouchable. If his father had let him suffer the punishment, he would probably be with us now.

In the mid-90s, where in Riyadh it's either black Mercedes or white Toyotas, in Jeddah all the young blades would have their Dodge Vipers and their Lamborghini Countaches and their Ferrari Testarossas, their Lamborghini Diabolos, their Ferrari Mondero 360s, and then of course the Porsche, which was cheap for them. Hundreds of thousands of dollars, they cost, these cars.

Osama Bin Laden could have had this lifestyle and there are a lot of younger members of his family who do. Although I am sure these days they would not be so anxious to tell Westerners their surname.

We'd been working at the Jeddah palace and had a night off. I was with Saif, and he was driving down town, crawling through the old city there, that's Balad. There were lights over the stalls in the market, lights in the rooms above, people were starting to cook and you could smell spices.

"Where are we going?"

We were turning down a back alley. Saif liked to smoke hash, so I guess I knew the answer. Anyhow we were approached; a Somali guy had come up to the window. What did we want?

Saif scored and we were out of there, but then he took me down another street and said, "See all those Somalis on the corner?"

Somalis wear little round hats, and when it gets chilly at night, they put old western jackets over their *thobes*.

"They all got *sid* under their jackets."

"Really?"

I've been in Jeddah a couple of months and I fancy a drink, and now I know where to go.

A week or two later, I get a Pakistani taxi driver to take me. Being blond and blue-eyed, I get thirty Somalis descending on this taxi like flies.

"Buy this, buy mine! Mistah!"

"Buy here!"

"Best *sid*!"

"Here, here mister!"

"Mine is better!"

I seize two bottles and shove the money out the window. I can feel six hands grabbing it.

"Let's get out of here. Go, go, go!"

We move, the Somalis scatter, there's a little police jeep leaving the curb right across the street. As the bodies melt away I see the cops have been enjoying this whole spectacle.

"Shit."

We go up the street and around the corner. A conversation I had only the day before flashes through my mind. I'd been talking to a Saudi at the palace about how Saudi policemen are small and skinny and polite, and how they ask nicely if a person will please get into their police car. I'd seen it many times at the hospital, with people like drunk drivers. Whereas in the States the cops are burly and they clamp handcuffs on, the guy gets hit with billy clubs, gets thrown into the car – and my Saudi friend says, "Yeah, in public our cops are like that. It's when you're behind closed doors you'll get your beating. Don't you fool yourself."

So this thought takes a nanosecond, and at the top of the street the police jeep blocks us.

"I'll take care of this."

I'll try bluff.

I get out.

"Could you please move your car? Because we're trying to get by."

You know what? It doesn't work. They look at my ID and the driver's ID and look in the car and there are the two bottles of *sid*. So, one policeman drives the taxi back to the police station. Without comment they put us in back of the little police jeep and the poor little Pakistani man, he is whimpering.

"I'm a good Muslim. They're going to send me home. I haven't done anything wrong. I shall be in disgrace with my family."

He is very upset.

"Don't worry. I shall tell them you had nothing to do with it."

Like my word is really going to make a difference. I'm feeling terrible. So we get to the police station and the two cops that have brought us in are with this senior officer and he sees a Westerner in the lobby. I can hear some of what he's saying – voices are raised – it's like *Why? American! Trouble! You're just gonna cause trouble here.*

So I mutter to the taxi driver, "I think it'll be OK, don't worry."

He doesn't say anything. Maybe he can hear more than I can.

They tell us to come. They unlock doors. Ahead of us are barred cages as big as a room, about twelve by twelve, packed with men in *thobes* who are standing like people on a subway train.

We are marched right past all this and left to wait in a nice office with a couch.

We sit there.

I'm thinking about calling the American embassy which could give me options like: get thrown out on the first plane, or get thrown out later after some Saudi lawyer has found a loophole and I've spent a few days standing in the cage.

I can hear doors crashing shut.

"Just relax," I whisper.

The taxi driver stays crouched over with his head in his hands.

Then in comes a guy in smart uniform, about thirty, speaks perfect English.

He says, "In Saudi Arabia we don't drink on the street, you know."

"Oh no, I wasn't – I was getting it on the street to take it back to my hotel to drink it there."

I can hear my own voice, it has risen a couple of octaves – I finish up, "I swear to God. There was to be no drinking on the street."

"You had two bottles."

"Yes."

"How much did you pay for that?"

"A hundred and fifty riyals a bottle."

He smiles.... this could be the guy who beats the soles of my feet.

"They sell it for fifty. They ripped you off because you're an American. Where you from?"

"California."

"Oh. I got my Bachelor's in Police Science at UC Davis in California."

"Really? UC Davis Medical Center was my base hospital when I was a new Paramedic."

"Where do you work?"

"I work for the Crown Prince." His face didn't flicker. "And you know, this would really embarrass him, if one of his medical team got arrested with a couple of bottles of *sid*."

"I imagine it would," he said. "Just remember, if you're going to drink don't do it on the street."

I protested again.

"OK," he says at last, "We're gonna forget it."

A great weight is lifted. I try to maintain my contrite and ashamed expression, but inside I'm just bursting into song.

"If you ever want to come over, like for a drink or anything, here is my number." He gave me a card; he was a Captain.

As he took me to the door he said, "You want your *sid* back?"

"No," I said, "just keep it."

I had totally lost the desire to drink.

The Pakistani gave me a ride.

"In my whole life," he said "I never see anything like that. I cannot believe they let us go."

"You know," I agreed "they do treat Americans differently."

"Now I've seen it with my own eyes I know it's true," he said. "Americans are treated different."

We were both very relieved.

Back in Riyadh, the endless round of state banquets continued. I used to keep the menus, these beautiful menus in Arabic – the food is always the same: fish, pigeon – and they have just one big stack of menus they give out. I would write who was there on the back of mine. When the Chinese delegation came, we were all standing around waiting for them, and General Obeidh, who is in day to day control of the Royal Guard, and speaks English, and is proud of everyone of his 33 children, was with us. I asked him what the Chinese were doing here.

"Ah, we're buying some stuff from them," he said.

"What kind of stuff?"

"Just some military stuff."

"Like tanks, or planes, or what?" I said.

"No, ballistic missiles."

"Really?" I said. "How far will they go?"

Well you don't want to ask too many questions or they think you're CIA. But I was always curious and they liked to keep us in the dark.

"Well I can't tell you that."

He is a big stocky fellow in military uniform with the Saudi royal emblem they all wear on the *ghutra*. Now he looked sly.

"But I tell you one thing – they'll reach Israel."

I'm wasted as a paramedic.

The reason we were dressed up to look like spooks was that the Crown Prince didn't want people to think he was ill. William Perry, who was at the time Secretary of Defense, came to Riyadh twice when I was there. The first time was soon after the Al-Khobar tower bombing, he pulled up in his big motorcade with Secret Service, American soldiers, and people from the Embassy. They were assembling a big satellite dish in the front yard. I turned to, Doug Simmons, a slim guy 6 foot four, who I worked with, and said, "Dyawanna see something? It's gonna kill them that they don't know who we are. We'll go stand out there and watch them. Somebody will come up and ask who we are."

So we stood with our arms folded, legs spread, Raybans on. Didn't say a word. Just watched as these guys got the satellite dish set up outside the Crown Prince's palace.

Finally a man came up.

"I'm the Vice Consul."

"Pleased to meet you."

Pause.

"Who are you guys?"

"Sorry, we can't tell you that."

"Seriously," he says.

"Well, we work for the Crown Prince."

"Yeah, but in what capacity?"

"Well we're really not allowed to say. Sorry."

He left. We sniggered. That's gonna kill him for the rest of the day not knowing who we were....

Just to mess with their heads. We had to find some ways to keep ourselves amused.

They were an interesting bunch of guys working with me. They didn't all spend their time drinking. Dave from Florida, who worked at the National Guard Hospital, like a lot of Westerners, was in transition to something else.

Dave was saving money to go home, so he could bump up his flight hours, and get his jet engine rating. He did it too. He landed a job with Delta as a co-pilot. Sadly, he got laid off after September 11th. Just another case of acute irony.

At the Palace we had Steve, an ex-Navy Seal in Vietnam. He was a massive guy, looked like Santa Claus, big belly and grey beard; he was in his late forties. He had a degree in theatre management, and he and his wife, who was a nurse, were in Saudi Arabia in order to save up the money to start a theatre in their hometown. They spent five years in Saudi and he's done it. He acts in the plays too.

Generally three of us worked together, me and Chuck and Steve. The Crown Prince wasn't real good with names. There was the Fat One –

"Where is the Fat One?"

"He is on holiday Your Royal Highness."

Chuck was younger than Steve, but didn't look it.

"Where is the Old One?"

The Old One was off duty and probably out buying *sid*. I was the Young One. I liked my nickname. If you went on holiday and were gone for a week or two the Prince would notice, and there were at least a hundred people in his entourage. Maybe we stood out because we were the only Westerners except Dr Brewerton.

We usually had a Saudi paramedic with us. Some of the other shifts were dismissive about their skills, but I was glad to have them because they knew the system, were native speakers and could be facilitators. Salim, who had come bottom of the Atlanta/Chicago EMT class, spent most of his days schmoozing with the bigwigs, trying to increase his status, but Saif – aside from drawing my attention to Somali alcohol dealers – contributed a lot. He'd find out way beforehand when and where we were going, and if we were flying he'd make sure they didn't forget to factor in the medical team, but got us a car, or a limo, and a room.

I think the Crown Prince valued our image. The suits, the Raybans, the black bags made us look like the Men in Black; we were status symbols.

At the GCC in Qatar, all the rulers were strolling down the hall, and President Mubarak of Egypt and the Crown Prince were walking together in intense conversation. When he got up to us, he excused himself for a moment.

He came over.

"Is everything all right? Your room is OK? Do you need anything?"

We all say everything is fine. He interrupted the President of Egypt to talk to us, but also to show him that he was attended by an American medical team (and maybe there was a subtext: these are not, Mr Mubarak, a bunch of American spooks, and I hope the suspicion never crossed your mind).

The Crown Prince always called us Doctor, because there is no Arabic word for paramedic. I got used to being called Dr Tom. I did try to explain what a paramedic is, as a lot of other medical disciplines don't have our emergency training.

If you're some place and somebody yells, "Is there a doctor in the house?"

A doctor will normally stand aside for a paramedic. In an emergency you want to see a paramedic, not a dermatologist.

19

California Culture Shock

———

I quit the Palace in 1997, packed up in Riyadh, and flew back to California.

I was having a terrific time and saving money, but your skills suffer if you work at the Palace for too long. It had now been nearly two years since I did what a paramedic is for – saving lives in an emergency. If I stayed another two years, I would start to lose the confidence and assertiveness you need to be effective.

And it's a young man's game. There are paramedics in their forties and fifties. I'd known plenty. They get very good, but our work doesn't make us like the human race any better. Year after year the overdoses and drunk drivers come in, the same self-destruct button pressed, the same problems to patch up.

Of the paramedics that worked in Saudi too many were running away from their own mistakes. The ones I admired were often the ones with another career in mind. I liked the work, but I couldn't see that it was going to take me in any direction I wanted to go. Like a lot of us, I hankered after a completely different career.

In my case, it was law. When I first started as a paramedic in the States it wasn't well paid, and I wished I'd stayed on at college and gone to law school. But now I didn't want to do law to make money, but because sometimes people frustrate me.

I'd taken a cheat to court before I left the States, did all the work, read the books, spoke up and defeated some smug lawyer. I had prevented an injustice and it felt good. Lawyers – they always think they are smarter than anyone else – but I was well prepared for this and my opponent wasn't. I destroyed her in court. I enjoyed it immensely.

I don't want people to be bullied. That's my motivation. Being a paramedic makes you assertive, and sometimes aggressive; when a patient is in my ambulance I will fight for them. I found it much the same in court.

So I figured I already had a lot of college credits, and if I went home and got a few more, I could get my degree, which would get me into law school.

I needed to pick up credits fast, so the career counselor advised me to do sociology. I would go to school full time, do sixteen units, and work part-time in an emergency room to pay my way.

Just one thing I hadn't factored in. I hadn't lived in my home town since I was eighteen, and very few of the people I used to know still lived there. I had come from a huge college-dorm type social life on a compound with three thousand people and Brendan's (an illegal bar) right across the street to go to after work.

In Marysville I met reverse culture shock, big-time. I got set up in an apartment, I got a phone – and there was nobody to call.

I never thought it would happen to me. In Saudi, I'd seen one or two friends who'd been there a long time and I'd thought – he's gone native; he could never settle back in the States now. Like Mark. Mark was from Massachusetts and had been a paramedic in Saudi Arabia since he was 22 and that was seventeen years ago. His Arabic was really good. He was gay, and as a gay man he had an easy life. He didn't run any risk of getting caught with a woman. He could walk down the street in Riyadh with a boyfriend, arms around each other, and that would be socially acceptable. So of course he would get invited to loads of Saudi parties and have local friends.

He'd quit briefly during the Gulf War and then gone back. He had been in Saudi through his formative years and readily admitted he could never re-adjust to life back home.

But not me. I told myself I could have a good life anywhere, make new friends easily. But I'd been used to the compound, everybody popping in and out of each other's houses, and now I was isolated in an apartment in Marysville.

I'd spent my time in Saudi doing a more interesting and challenging job than I would ever find here. I'd been functioning much like an emergency physician. I had been responsible for the survival of a world leader. I had worked in the busiest emergency room I had ever seen in my life. On my quick decisions people's lives depended.

But back in California it was like Oh yeah? You worked in Saudi? They'd feign interest for a while, but it was hard for people to relate to it. You imagine your friends are just going to be fascinated with your stories. And you quickly learn that after ten minutes they want to get on with what is going on here, and they are just being polite.

They will sit there and listen, but then they lose patience.

After four or five months, I stopped telling people. They had no idea.

There is a scene from Rambo near the end, where he's come back from Vietnam, and he's falling apart crying, and he's got his old commander talking to him and he says, "I was in Vietnam. I flew a gunship, I drove tanks, I was in charge of million-dollar pieces of equipment, I come back to America, and I can't even get a job in a fuckin' carwash."

It was almost that way with me.

It's like how the Vietnam vets hang with each other because they know what it was like. Other people don't want you to elaborate.

At one point I went to work in Gridley hospital. It's located in a suburb of Chico, which is a college town, fifty miles from Marysville. Chuck was from Chico – Chuck that had married Suzanne and got sacked from the Palace for being drunk – I knew where he worked, so I talked to somebody that worked there, and said, "You know Chuck?"

Yeah, he said, he died of cirrhosis of the liver. He was 44 and had been back in the States two years. Chuck it seemed was one unhappy man, wherever he was.

Most Americans have very little interest in anything outside America. I have an older brother back in my home town. He was a huge outdoorsman in his time – a certified PADI dive instructor, he went to LA to qualify. He was about twenty three then, and he came home and spent his days driving a forklift for Sunsweet at ten dollars an hour. But then he got offered a job as a diving instructor in Jamaica. I was fourteen or so and thrilled.

"MAN! You got asked to go to *Jamaica*?"

He was like, "Oh those jobs, they don't pay anything."

He never left. I remember how frustrated I was for him. Very often it's fear that makes people stay with what they know. He's a skilled stonemason now, lives within five miles of where

he was born, does superb work, but isn't the most reliable ....
he likes a drink.

I go back and some of the guys I worked with are still in the
same hospitals, doing the same jobs. It's safe I guess; nothing
out there, across the sea or over the border, seems relevant to
their lives. I guess they think this is as good as it gets.

I take my nephew over to visit a nurse from Calgary, Canada.
He's just started college, he's a bright kid, and he's sitting on
the couch –

"You're from Canada," he says.

"Yes."

"Where is Canada anyway?"

She gasps. "You are not serious."

I look at her. "He is dead serious."

She says, "It's like one of the biggest countries in the world.
There are nine provinces." He's looking blank. "Right across
the top of America. From the east to the west coast."

He goes, "Really? I just thought it was some little small
country like Alaska, somewhere."

So I sat L-SAT and did okay, and in a year and a half I had
completed my degree. I had not had one minute during which
I wasn't either working or studying. I was interviewed and
accepted at the Lincoln School of Law in Sacramento.

I took the pre-law course which is six units and cost me
about $1,000; it's two classes.

Then it came time for the semester to start.

I needed to come up with $11,000 for the next two
semesters, plus the books I had to buy. I could get a bank loan.
My mother volunteered a loan as well. I could see this getting
stressful, down the line. There was one other option. I decided

to come back to Saudi for a year, and save enough to pay for one full year of law school plus living expenses. So when I went back I would have nothing to do but study.

Well, that was the idea.

I came back to my recruiter.

"This time," I said, "find me a job in Jeddah – I'd rather not work in Riyadh."

Generally, there are not a lot of jobs in Jeddah.

She called me back and said, "Would you be interested in going back to work with the Crown Prince?"

I wasn't. There was a lot of sitting around doing nothing, and your social life suffered, because you couldn't maintain the ties. And if you live in a place like Saudi Arabia your social life is more important than it is at home – it's your support network.

Then I got offered a job in the new King Faisal Hospital at Jeddah that had just opened. When I left, the only King Faisal Hospital had been the one in Riyadh, a very good hospital patronized by members of the House of Saud and other wealthy people; this was an offshoot. And I knew the city was a lot less conservative than Riyadh, so I was delighted.

Besides – diving every week on my day off? I'm there, I'll take it.

I get to Jeddah and I know why I'm back. I'm deep in a love-hate relationship with this country.

Two Canadian girls come with me on the flight from the States. Neither one of them has been out of Canada before. We are in the same orientation group.

I try to give them some advice.

"You are both tall blonde women, you will get a lot of attention from Saudi guys and it will be in your best interests not to date them. To them, all western women are whores.

So be careful – If you drink don't do it outside the compound. You only have to have alcohol on your breath, and you're in jail. Never, ever get into a car with a man other than a taxi driver. In Saudi Arabia bad things do happen."

Yeah, yeah.

We go through orientation in Jeddah and I'm the only one in the group who's been in Saudi before. I'm getting déjà vu.

When I first came to Riyadh in '93, a Saudi doctor named Khaled put us through orientation. He put on a good talk because he had spent time in America, been to university there. And the girls were whispering *Wow! He is so-oo handsome.* He was six feet three and wearing western clothes, a married man apparently with two children. The girls were very disappointed (though some of them looked like they might try their luck anyhow).

"I want to dispel some myths about control," he announced. "The way women in Islam are expected to behave. You might think the *abayah* is restrictive, but our women themselves prefer the modesty of this garment. They wear it because Saudi men treasure women like precious jewels; we enclose and protect them. We don't expect women to appear in public alone. They are always with their menfolk or at home, and we keep them covered because we don't want to share their beauty with other men, or have them incite lust."

And another bunch of crap. There is no crime, no AIDs, no homosexuality. You can just leave your wallet full of money out in the open anywhere; Muslims don't steal.

Shortly after this orientation, a fully covered woman came into the hospital with her child about five or six years old. I thought she was Saudi, but from behind the black *abayah* came this American accent.

"You're American" I said, stupidly.

"I'm Khaled's wife."

"Oh, right," I said "How long you been here?"

"Eight years."

"Really? How do you like it?"

There was a pause.

"I absolutely hate it."

Some of the girls got to be friends with her. Khaled wanted a second wife. She didn't want this to happen.

"Fine," he said, "leave. Go back to America. The children are staying here."

She was staying solely for them. He treated her like a whipped dog. She couldn't leave without an exit visa, signed by him. She tried to commit suicide twice.

In college, at University in the States, he treated her wonderfully. He was very westernized, people said.

So, I'm at orientation in Jeddah now and here comes the speech. In Saudi Arabia crime does not exist. There is no rape; if you rape you are executed. Robbery does not happen; if you steal you lose a hand. There is no crime. You may think we are restrictive of the women. In fact we feel our women are like precious jewels that must be protected. Nothing must happen to them as we care for them so much. Homosexuality does not exist. (I sit deadpan. I've never been hit on by so many men in my *life*). Somebody asks about dangerous insects and snakes. Nothing to worry about, there are no snakes in Saudi Arabia.

We had a snake breeding house back at the National Guard Hospital because they often needed rare anti-venom and they were running a program to develop it. I went to have a look at the snake-house, in the hospital grounds; they had scorpions there as well.

There are seven different poisonous snakes in Saudi. Five of them are pit vipers. There is the Egyptian cobra, big and black, but not hooded, then there's a little black snake that is hardly thicker than wire, and if that bites you you're dead in thirty minutes because there is no anti-venom for it. They don't bother to develop the anti-venom because by the time you get to hospital you'll be dead anyway.

The doctor in charge explained all about the snakes and the kind of path they make through the sand, and showed me this is a poisonous one and that isn't. The little Egyptian guy, the snake-catcher to the Crown Prince, took me through where they kept the snakes in tanks, and took one of the Egyptian cobras out and put it on the floor.

They told me the anti-venom development program had been going on ten years. In that time they had never produced one drop of the stuff. If we got snakebites in the hospital, we used anti-venom bought from France. So I don't know why they'd been milking the snakes. They produced a scorpion anti-venom that we never would use because it made you way sicker than a scorpion sting would. We got lots of those stings, in Riyadh, because the Bedouin sleep outside, but even the Saudi doctors would not use the scorpion anti-venom from the snake house.

They have a lot of programs like that in Saudi that just look good on paper.

Anyhow we're through orientation with me suppressing my derision; we're not in Jeddah a week and one of the Canadian girls is going out with a Saudi.

The guy has a brand new 750 BMW, and the girl is from an island off the east coast of Canada, some rock stuck out in the Atlantic, she's never been off the island before – and she comes in all flushed and exultant.

"We went to a Palace!" (It was just a big villa.) "We drove in a 750 BMW! And there were drugs and real booze...."

"Carole" I said, "If you go out with those Saudi guys, they can do anything they want to you – rape, sodomy, group sex, anything, you have no recourse whatever. There is no way you could have got them in trouble. And they know it."

"Oh they wouldn't do that! That's *so* ridiculous. Abdul was very nice."

"I am sure he was. That is not the point. Legally, because you are a single woman, if you are in a house with a single man, anything that happens to you is your own fault. Saudi men and women are brought up to believe that a man does not have control over his sexual urges. All men are insatiable and that is why women are covered up."

"Well they wouldn't know we were going out together just by being in the same house! There were other people. We're not like *doing* anything, we're just friends, that's all."

"There is no concept of friendship between a man and a woman here."

"Of *course* there is."

I'm beginning to feel like her grandfather. She's 22.

"Listen, Carole. I have lived here before. I can tell Saudi men that within the compound girls come over to my villa and watch DVDs, and make popcorn, and go home. I would not lay a hand on any of you. Saudis do not believe that. That is just stupid, they say. What would you be doing with a woman except sex?"

"They've got sisters, for heaven's sake."

"They are brought up apart from their sisters. And believe me they would *kill* their sisters if they thought they'd been in a house with a guy. They think women are stupid. It never crosses their mind that you might make your own choices."

I've never once heard a young, unmarried Saudi repeat anything a woman has said. Women are not well respected by men of that age. I can't count the times I've tried explaining to them in their own terms.

"This is why God gave us a mind, to decide what is right and wrong, which is why a woman can be in a room with a man and they do not have to have sex. Men are not like dogs with bitches in heat."

None of them agree with that. They tell me I am totally wrong.

"Well these guys I know are not the same," Carole says.

"Look, if you are caught with them you are the one who will get punished."

I dug out the newspaper story about the Canadian girls I knew who'd been caught by *metawah* in the Lebanese guys' house.

"Oh!" she said "but this was a long time ago. That was 1994! Things aren't the same now."

"Yes they are. It's no different now."

"You're just jealous because you didn't get to ride in the BMW," she said.

Carole has been in Saudi Arabia for a few years now and has had a long line of Saudi boyfriends. She is being passed around a bit. But she feels like Britney Spears. And you can't tell people; they've got to find out for themselves.

Socially, western women are damned if they do and damned if they don't. Saudi men flatter them wonderfully, and are often extremely dashing, but if these girls go with them they're called Saudi-shaggers and western guys don't want to know them anymore. This is hypocritical. There is an undertone of racism about it. But most guys would be fastidious about a girl who's had unprotected sex with partners whose previous encounters have necessarily taken place in some hotel room in Bahrain.

On the other hand if western girls never associate with Saudis at all, they're accused of being narrow-minded.

Jeddah is to Riyadh as Paris, France is to Greenville, SC. In the malls you'll see Saudi women in black *abayahs* with sparkly beads on, or a little lace trim. Some of them are even buttoned, and what is more, now this is really *risqué*, they'll wear them unbuttoned up to the waist so you can see the designer jeans underneath. That would never go in Riyadh – the *metawah* would be all over 'em. They insist that the *abayah* should be shapeless and uniform. Recently they confiscated a hundred thousand *abayahs* at a factory and destroyed them because they had too much shape. They had a tuck at the waist, and maybe even some glitter.

20

Royal Patients

In December 2000, I took one look at the new King Faisal Hospital, Jeddah, and knew it wasn't going to be a re-run of any experience I'd yet had.

It had been open for less than a year when I came and was built to supplement the King Faisal in Riyadh which opened in '73. This way, the royals wouldn't have to go all the way to the capital for their treatment.

From the outside it's five storeys high, elegant, plenty of glass, surrounded by shrubs and palms, big pillars fronting an imposing lobby – pretty much what you'd expect of a five-star hotel. Inside I'd give it seven stars.

Patients are driven up to the main entrance along a curving marble lane between well-watered shrubs. They are helped out of their cars into the lobby, where they see a magnificent chandelier suspended over marble floors with gold inlay. Off to the right is an elevator with gold-plated doors, big enough to put a hospital bed in plus a sizeable medical team.

There are no shared rooms. The hospital has 250 beds and every room is private. They all have ante-rooms, and private bathrooms, and in the bedrooms the medical equipment is concealed inside cherry wood cabinets beside the bed. When you first come in to see a patient you have to walk through the generously sized ante-room complete with big wooden doors at both ends, and past the couches and chairs and so on. When the two sets of big wooden doors are closed, and a patient has a seizure or stops breathing, you can yell for help, but no-one will hear you. The new King Faisal has been conceived as a hotel with a series of audience chambers, not a hospital.

There is a separate entrance for VIPs, and they have suites. Besides their ante-room, bedroom, and en-suite bathroom fitted with the usual crystal chandeliers and gold taps, they have a sitting room and a dining room. In every sitting room there is a couch, coffee table, and chairs, and the hospital management have installed hundreds of the biggest ten-thousand-dollar flat screen televisions on the market. Every dining room has a table to seat twenty. The patient's room has a plush bed which rises at a tilt like a hospital bed, although the headboard and footboard are carved wood. And there is another low seating area in the bedroom with a television.

You would think it was a suite in the Waldorf.

Patients are generally courteous and friendly. They don't have financial problems. They are mostly from the 30,000 strong Saudi royal family and entitled to free treatment here. Every adult male has an allowance, and most of them have government jobs as well, thanks to their connections.

The other patients are rich businessmen with *wassta*, and their families. They pay. The House of Saud is coming to terms with a treasury that is no longer limitless and has begun to take fee-paying patients. Indeed the King Faisal Specialist Hospital, Jeddah, has redefined itself as a private establishment, albeit heavily subsidized by the government.

Marble floors, crystal chandeliers, glossy pot plants and leather couches line the corridors. There were cloth couches when the government first took over, but they stripped them out and bought new. The director, Sultan Bahavri, ordered a vast hand-carved desk for himself at a mere 80,000 riyals (about $30,000). Anywhere else he'd be doing a 12-step program for shopaholics.

Every painting and photograph was taken down and replaced at around the same time. I was walking down the hall one day, when I saw four rather ugly Islamic scenes propped against the wall. There is usually something from the Quran in sinuous calligraphy, but instead there were these monstrosities, with men getting ready to hang them, and I saw the price tag for the four: another 80,000 riyals. Like it's turning out to be a magic number. I asked, to confirm, that this was indeed the price of just those four, because they were hanging dozens of them. It was all on credit, because the management didn't actually have the money yet. The House of Saud used to spend without regard, but now they have to budget.

If you walk down the hall at the King Faisal you can tell how long ago an important member of the Royal Family came in, because of the perfume. If it's overpowering you've just missed them, and if it's faint they've been gone a while. Everywhere they go, they are preceded by two men swinging heavy incense burners, so that the place will smell good. The burners look like foot-high, square chimney stacks intricately carved out of dark wood, with gold twiddly bits on each corner. Sometimes they are inlaid with semi-precious stones. They stand about on shelves or mantels with smoldering charcoal inside to make the incense linger, and then they are borne in advance of the royal party: apple, cherry which is very popular, even bubblegum smells waft everywhere.

I hadn't been working at the hospital long, when one night I was asked to come up to the VIP suites (the ones with the dining room, sitting room and flat screen TV) and start an IV. They call the paramedics a lot for that, because most non-western staff are too intimidated to stick a needle into princes, princesses and government ministers. Even western nurses have told me there is pressure – don't mess up! You only have one chance! You can't stab them more than once!

And Saudis have very tough skin. Anyway – they call it canulation. I followed the smell of roses and the patient turned out to be a young Saudi princess. She was really quite pretty. About fifteen of her girl-friends were hanging out in the suite, with their *abayahs* off, looking like expensively casual American college students. I was certainly intimidated, but I started the IV and it was fine.

As I left one of them snuck over and said, "Where can I smoke around here?"

For her to be seen smoking in public would be scandalous. But above the emergency room there is a balcony where you cannot be seen. So she followed me, without even bothering to put her *abayah* on, and we walked out the emergency exit onto this balcony, and sat, and smoked a cigarette. She'd got a cellphone in her hand and we got talking and I said, "Can I use that to call my mom?"

They are very generous like that. It was eleven or twelve at night, so daytime in California, and I gave her the number and she dialed it, and handed over her phone.

"Hallo Mom, what are you doing?"

She told me, and asked me the same, and I said, "I'm sitting out on a balcony smoking a cigarette with this *princess*."

"Oh! No! You're gonna get your head cut off! Over there!"

"It's all right – Fatima, say hello."

She took the phone, grinning.

"Hello Fatima. Thank you for letting my son call."

Afterwards the princess said, "Oh, your mother's so sweet".

In the following days I saw them all out there smoking.

So, most of the patients were pretty nice.

One day, however, there was a little boy about nine or ten in the hospital, and I was in the emergency room when they asked for somebody to take the child up to the VIP suites. I knew he was somebody important because the Executive on Duty and all the administrative staff were fussing around this little kid. And the VIP floor has some rooms bigger than others, and he got the biggest of all. He turned out to be the son of Prince Naif (who happens to be head of the secret police as well as the *metawah*).

"Where are you from?"

"America" I said.

"Oh," he said, "you are the brother of Sharon."

It was intended as an insult. His anti-American views were instilled even at that age.

Royal patients are not treated like regular folks. Their doctors are deferential and conflicted. On the one hand they are scared of hurting them, and on the other they don't want to ignore any symptoms, or see them get any worse. One time a young prince, in his late thirties this time, came in because he'd got a pain in his side. His doctor had told him to come to the King Faisal for ultrasound, blood tests, every precautionary investigation you can think of, and they called me to do an IV. Frankly anyone could have done it; he had huge veins and was very fit and easy to canulate. I was mystified.

"What's the problem with you?"

"Nothing much," he said. "I told my doctor about this little pain, and all of a sudden I've got to have all these tests."

"I'm so-oo glad I'm not a prince," I said.

"Why?"

"The more important you are, the more needles they stick in you."

He laughed.

I said, "It's true. If I had tummy ache they'd tell me to take two Tylenol and go home, and if it doesn't get better come back tomorrow. They will do every conceivable test on you to make sure they don't miss anything. They've even done studies in the States on this – government officials, movie stars – the more important you are, the more tests you get, and the more needles."

He still stayed for the full check-up. But he was unusual; he was health-conscious and willing to go through a bit of discomfort to be on the safe side. Royals can dictate their own care and many of them are not willing to put up with any discomfort at all in order to get well. If they don't want to take their medication, ain't nobody gonna make 'em. If they have a rip-roaring infection they need an intravenous antibiotic, but if Her Royal Highness doesn't fancy having a drip in her arm then her doctor will give up and prescribe tablets, which will do little good. No patient gets the best treatment if their doctor's scared to get firm.

Princess Leila dictated her own care. She had ovarian cancer and had flown to the States to be treated at Johns Hopkins. She knew her case was terminal. Having been prescribed Demerol there for pain relief, she was now home in Jeddah and addicted.

The conventional treatment in the States is to start cancer patients on a painkiller, proceed through chemotherapy and other treatments, and finally show them how to administer patient-supplied analgesia. This is usually a patient controlled pump pre-filled with morphine; the patient just has to press a button and it keeps the pain at bay.

At Johns Hopkins the Princess was told that she would need to have her pain relief changed on her return to Jeddah. But she decided otherwise. She turned up at the King Faisal, swathed majestically in her *abayah*, demanding intramuscular Demerol every four hours. She would not accept an analgesic patch, or a patient controlled pump, she didn't want a drip. She liked the needle. She would come into the hospital three or four times a day for her fix.

You could see her coming. She didn't like her driver to go over 40 mph an hour, and Saudis drive like maniacs, so from the upper corridors I'd see this Jaguar crawling up the freeway with all the cars kshoo, kshoo ripping past. The nurses would scatter. (Oh NO, don't let her see me). And she would walk in –

"I shall have my injection and sleep after it. I will be woken at 5 o'clock when I shall have a meal. After my meal I shall have another injection." She would sometimes stay all day.

At this point I have to explain (and I know it's a shock) that patient confidentiality occasionally breaks down. In this case I knew a nurse. We shall call her Emma. She was a pale, delicate English blonde. Emma told me what happened when Princess Leila got up to the women's ward.

She told her doctors how much Demerol she wanted, and what anti-nausea treatment she would have, and which nurses would treat her. She did not want anybody from the Philippines, or South Africa, or anybody black, or a Saudi. Only white or western nurses. That left just three girls: Bridget, Tracey and my friend Emma.

Now this princess was in her early fifties, but during her early years she had undergone a whole lot of plastic surgery on her backside.

"She's had surgery from her knees all the way up," Emma confided, adding (you know how the English are masters of the elegant understatement) "She must'a been a real fat whacker before she had it done."

Bridget, the Charge Nurse, was a big Irish girl and she administered the injection perfectly. On the next shift Tracey, who was Canadian, came out of the suite looking stunned.

"Hell, her ass is hard as a rock, I had to run up with it and stab her. You do it next time," she said to Emma.

There is a perception that English nurses are prim and deferential, and my friend played it for all it was worth. In she went.

"Good morning Your Royal Highness. My name is Emma and I am from Surrey, in England...." And how had the Princess arrived?

"My car is outside. A Jaguar."

"Oh really...." and so on.

Then it came to the injection.

"Bend over! just a little prick!"

Normally, you just mark the place and do it. But Emma prodded gingerly and this behind was hard as a table-top. Normally when you do an injection you hold the syringe like a dart, and it slips neatly into the skin.

Emma decides to hold it like a hammer.

"There we are! it'll be over in a minute...."

She stabs the royal buttock and the syringe just bounces back. And again. She cannot get the needle to penetrate. She's getting desperate.

"Have you done it yet?" The woman is already drugged up to the eyeballs, and what with this hard shell of skin – she could sit on a bed of nails, she can't feel a thing.

"Sorreee," sings Emma sweetly, "I forgot to put the needle on."

The needle hasn't broken but it's now bent at the tip. It hasn't penetrated at all. She just puts a bigger needle on, the biggest possible, and draws back like she's about to compete in some discus event.

"OK, here we go!" And BOOM. "You might feel a little stinging."

The Princess turns her head. "I don't feel anything."

"Oh, that's good then."

Emma pulls out the needle and gives the place a rub with alcohol, sticks a plaster on, but blood just keeps oozing through the plaster. It won't stick at all.

"What are you doing?"

"I'm just holding the plaster to make sure all the medicine goes in."

"Stop." She pushes Emma's hand away.

Four hours later the Princess comes back to the hospital and Bridget goes in to see her.

"I do not want that blonde girl again! She made me bleed."

A day later she had crossed Tracey off the list, because she made her bleed as well, and Bridget had to say, "Look, I am the only nurse you will accept and I am not here all the time so what are we going to do?"

"Let me see the other nurses."

Princess Leila knew all about the scar tissue, but it wasn't her problem. It was like Deal With It.

Here comes Irene, a white South African. She is introduced and the way she sees it is this, "I have been chosen! I'm a better nurse than everyone else!"

Irene had visions of being the private nurse, if she kissed up enough. This sort of thing does happen and private nursing offers better money.

The Princess decided that Irene was the only person who could inject her, but of course Irene was not there everyday. She would come in then, and sleep – it was her choice – on a trolley in the emergency room until Irene came in the following day.

Irene went home on holiday and returned with so-called anti-cancer drugs for Princess Leila. In South Africa you can buy these things over the counter if you know the right people. This was not only unethical, but illegal, and could have got her struck off immediately. There was no way that any drug was going to change this patient's future. She had terminal cancer.

Just before Princess Leila died she came in and gave Bridget an *abayah* and some perfume and a gold necklace. Now if you receive gifts or cash you have to go to the Executive on Duty and declare it. Bridget went down quietly and did this, but he waved her away.

"Wear it, wear it. The necklaces are two a penny here – keep it, fine."

Bridget was getting ready to go home and Irene saw this stuff and suspected that Bridget had got it from the Princess and was quite upset. And when Princess Leila died, the driver came into the hospital with a donation for the Emergency Department, and Irene approached him and said, "Where is mine?"

"Sorry," he said. She was a greedy girl. But sick people are so vulnerable.

There is no way anyone who isn't Royal could get narcotics on demand like that. Most doctors in Saudi Arabia are exaggeratedly paranoid about drugs. A woman with trigeminal neuralgia used to come in. She had had surgery in Europe for toothache and was left with agonizing pain in three parts of her face. She would walk into the Emergency Room with her son, always with a bandage or scarf covering her face, and a raised pulse rate. Strong prescription drugs were the only thing that worked. She started on 100 mg Demerol, 75 mg Voltren, and 25 mg Phenergan the anti-nausea drug, and she would have 60 mg morphine sulphate tablets at home. She only came to us when the pain was so bad that the morphine did not work. Sometimes that was twice a week, sometimes once a fortnight, sometimes not for months.

The Saudi doctors decided she was a drug abuser and needed to go through detox. One day she came in and they told her, "Forget it, you're an addict. Take two Tylenol. We will get you into rehab."

But then, she wasn't a princess.

Their paranoia about drugs is based on ignorance. They will give a quarter of the recommended dose of any opiate-based medicine. I had a discussion with a Saudi doctor over giving painkiller to a child, which he wouldn't do.

"But you can get addicted!"

I pointed out that there would be no reason in this instance to repeat the dose. Occasional use is what opiates are for.

"Oh no," he told me, "one time you give these drugs and people get addicted!"

Doctors routinely under-prescribe painkillers in the States too, in my view. There they do know better, but a liability paranoia pervades.

Saudis get addicted mostly through social contact with drugs, the same as people in the west, not through long-term pain relief. There is a big party scene with rich Arabs and minor princes, where there is coke and hash, and some of them smoke crack. One time the ambulance team was put on standby to take a young prince to rehab. They all claim to be Prince Somebody and it means very little until you know who their father is. But being a prince helps a lot in trying to date western girls. Anyhow this guy was spending 5,000 riyals a day ($1300) on crack, which is a habit and a half.

His doctor told us he would go for a week or two partying, and then sleep two or three days. He and his family wanted us to lurk outside their palace, snatch the guy as soon as he went to sleep, and whisk him away. There are two drug and alcohol rehab hospitals for wealthy Saudis and one of them is up in Taif, about an hour and a half away. I said Okay, but why don't we forget the lurking, and just go in and do what we do in the States? I wanted us to go in with leather restraints, which in America can only be used with a police order.

I didn't want to keep watch like some spook. But they made us wait in the ambulance outside the garden walls until he went to sleep, which of course he didn't do. He was there by himself; there was no party going on, just this guy, flying – We were not allowed inside. So after six hours – and there is nowhere to go to the bathroom, in an ambulance – they let us go. The doctor kept telephoning anxiously, emphasizing that this was highly confidential. Like there was some Saudi version of the National Enquirer we were going to tell.

Two or three days afterwards we were told, "He is willing to go now."

We trundle out to the palace again: me, another paramedic, and the ER physician from the hospital. We are joined by the palace physician, and shown into the room where he is sprawled alone, incoherent and drugged.

I had to sedate him with Haldol. He slept most of the way up to Taif. Thank god.

Seven years after I first came to Saudi, I'm back and meeting with the same old predicament about what Allah really intends. A young Saudi has overdosed on heroin in our parking garage at the King Faisal in Jeddah. He is dead, nobody knows how long he's been there, and they call the ambulance.

He is stiff; he has rigor mortis and a needle in his arm. We put him on the heart monitor, it flatlines. Pupils fixed, dilated. Game over.

Then the Executive on Duty – the EOD is responsible for everything in the hospital on his shift, and in this hospital that can mean members of the royal family, VIPs and visiting statesmen – says, "Why did you not try to save that patient?"

I tell him about the rigor mortis, and the flatline, and how long this person had been without oxygen. And that we had no idea how long he had been dead.

"You should have tried."

I remember the correct approach.

"When someone dies, and God takes them away, there is no grabbing them and bringing them back," I say.

He doesn't argue with that.

One of the English nurses told me she met such a very nice man in the Protocol Clinic. She'd only been working there a day, and she was told, "Take this Madeira cake to the chap in that suite," and say "Here is your English cake brought by an English nurse."

The Charge Nurse assures her this guy will be impressed. So in she goes and the man, who is a tall fat African in magnificent robes, is charm personified – asks her where she's from, how's she settling in.

She walks out, and gets talking to her friend. He's a lovely man, they agree; he's got a cuddly quality. He's called Edith, the other nurse says, and my friend frowns and says that's a funny name for a man.

The Charge Nurse hurries in for a minute and they ask, "Who is he? The nice fat man – Edith?"

"Not Edith," she mutters, "Idi. Idi Amin."

She disappears. Well, these two girls have never heard of him. When I explain later about the thousands of murders and the heads in the fridge they are quite taken aback. The Butcher of Uganda – he lives in exile in Jeddah. As I write, well-trained professionals are fighting to save his life, as he is in our ICU following a stroke[14]. Princes keep dropping in to pay their respects.

His two sons are high-profile on the party scene. Both are dark, good looking and well toned, and one of them has a Harley. Like Paris Hilton they are famous for being famous and make the best of it.

The American consulate holds functions, and they have a regular bar with real beer and liquor, all legal because you're

14   Idi Amin died in the King Faisal Hospital Jeddah on August 16, 2003.

on American soil; it's not easy to get on the guest list. Anyhow, I walk in to one of these functions, and the two Amin sons are there, in my own Consulate, hitting on all the western chicks. It's an outrage, I think. Drinking our beer and hitting on our girls. And they're Muslims. One is in his early thirties and the other is about ten years younger. One is known as Smokey, or Stoney or something like that; can't imagine why. I guess they got the number of the Swiss bank account before the old man keeled over. Frankly, I do find it hard to relate to the will of Allah in this case.

Adnan Khashoggi, the billionaire arms dealer, owns a villa next to the hospital. He came in to the hospital one time and saw a very pretty, very new, Canadian nurse, in her early twenties. He introduced himself, but she had absolutely no idea who he was, and you could see his ego deflating.

"Surely you must have heard of me?"

"Never, I'm sorry."

"I'm Adnan Khashoggi, the arms dealer, you must have heard of me. I own the palace next to the hospital. It's right over...."

"Oh? I didn't realize that was a palace."

By Saudi standards the villa he owns is modest, but there is a sign saying *Khashoggi* on his gate.

Anyway, he has this pain, and purports to be very important, so she books him into a private room on the VIP floor.

The Executive On Duty comes along and says, "Who'd ya put in there?"

She explains. Adnan Khoshoggi, arms dealer, VIP, and so on —

"Oh that Khashoggi," he says. "Put him in a regular patient room, he's no VIP."

Kasshoggi was born in Mecca in 1935, and his father was the personal physician to Saudi's founder King Abdul Aziz. Add to this mix the billions in his bank account and I'm not quite sure what it takes to be considered a VIP around here.

21

Rolls Royce for Sale

In a strange way, I really love it here.

I was glad to be back in the Kingdom of Saudi Arabia. You might think, because this account is mostly a catalogue of a crazy screwed-up society that I wasn't. But, I'd come from a crazy screwed-up society of a different kind, and it's not just the social life here, or the opportunity to dive in the Red Sea when the mood takes me, or any of those things. More than anything, it's the place. Saudi Arabia isn't the dustbowl you see from 35,000 feet. It's beautiful and mysterious. It's got a history.

Jeddah has an old quarter that's more picturesque than anything in Riyadh. I got to know the city when I was working for Crown Prince Abdullah. One time, his western medical team stayed in King Faisal's old palace on the corniche, while the Prince and his entourage went to Mecca. As infidels, we were not allowed in the holy city, so we had to stay behind. King Faisal's Palace is rare because it was never demolished, while most buildings are torn down when the principal inhabitants die, or otherwise desert them.

There's not a big market for used homes in Saudi, because of the *djinn*.

God created man and *djinn* to live on earth. *Djinn* are all around us, but they whirl about at such a high molecular speed that we cannot see them, though they can see us, just not very clearly. They live and die, are born and go to hell or heaven, in a kind of parallel universe, sharing our space. But when a house is left empty, the *djinn* remain; they don't move out when we do, so it would be inappropriate to move in. They might be offended.

There is no sign of this belief abating. Near the King Faisal Hospital in Jeddah there is an apartment block which used to be military housing. It has been kept empty for well over twenty years. But money is a little tighter than it once was making re-cycling an attractive option, so the hospital bought just over a thousand units there and refurbished them. They are starting to move hospital staff in: Westerners and Filipinos mostly – Saudis absolutely would not live there. It must be haunted by *djinn*.

Exceptionally, King Faisal's old palace in Jeddah was also refurbished, but only for the use of visiting dignitaries. It is called the Guest Palace. In Jeddah palaces can be of any design, some are traditional Arabic with sinuous shapes carved along the tops of the walls, some are classical, like the White House with pillars and a portico or a dome, or like a mansion in the Deep South with verandas and a double winding staircase leading out of a huge foyer. The Guest Palace is vaguely Arabic, with ornate ironwork (painted gold) and a hint of the southern Mediterranean. There are trees all round and the garden walls are topped with clay tiles like you see in Italy or in pictures of Ancient Rome.

Inside it is superb. Every detail is exquisite and carefully thought out as befits the Bedouin tradition of hospitality (*djinn* aside, Royalty do everything possible to make visitors comfortable). I stayed there again when I was with the ambulance service at the King Faisal because Vice-President Dick Cheney came. We were seconded to his entourage and accommodated in the Guest Palace.

Cheney has a pacemaker and has had two or three heart attacks. When we get there the physician assistant briefs us on what medicines he's on.

"But" he adds "– if anything happens you're it. I'm just here to keep the crowds back."

So that was reassuring. They sent sniffer dogs to check out our ambulances. I was talking to the protocol officer, and I told him how I remembered when King Hussein of Jordan stayed here, and how the paramedics had the run of that whole place for the three days while the Crown Prince was in Mecca. We didn't have a lot to do, so we just looked around.

And here I come again and it's all been re-done. There are genuine old masters on the walls, soft intricate carpets, and Limoges china with the royal emblem. A lot of the people that get to stay are just staff, really, like us.

I said, "Do you get people stealing things, ever?"

"All the time. When the Libyans came, they stole everything that was not nailed down. Paintings, silverware, dishes, rugs, they just cleaned the place out."

"What do you do?"

"We can't say anything; there would be a diplomatic incident. Things go missing all the time."

There is a Persian rug in the main greeting room, the *majlis* room in Faisal's day, which was made for that room. Even the Libyans couldn't take that. It has got to be 75 yards by 75 yards and it is all handmade. It's wool and silk, lots of blues and greens and dainty designs. It must have kept scores of people employed for months. I know that one like it, only about three yards by two, took three people nine months to make.

I think the Crown Prince does suffer from a lot of theft. I think of this as a personal insult to a host, though I suppose for most non-Saudis, used to a government where the money is tax money, the victim is just an anonymous bureaucracy.

When there was money, and it's not like they're broke now, but it's not the kind of gold-rush of the seventies, companies from the west persuaded the Saudi government into a lot of wasteful expense in a push to make Saudi Arabia look more like Miami. It was all done with the best of intentions. In Dammam, Riyadh and Jeddah they paid for high-rise apartment complexes with five thousand units in each one. They were built for nomadic Bedouin who were not consulted and didn't want to live there.

These buildings are still there: small identical self-contained cities, virtually empty. They filled them up with Iraqi refugees during the Gulf War, but essentially they're ghost towns. The Bedouin prefer the desert.

And while nearly all the water in Saudi Arabia comes from desalination plants on the Persian Gulf and the Red Sea, in Jeddah the streets are falling apart because of sub-surface flooding. A friend of mine in the Geological Society says the desalination plant piping is so poorly constructed that 25% of it is seeping up under the tarmac. Partly because of wastage like this, water is becoming such an expensive public resource that there has been talk about metering and charging for it. Saudis don't understand that; it would be like a tax, and what do they know of tax? As good Muslims they pay a proportion of their income, the *zakat*, to charitable causes, but it's the job of their rulers to provide things like water and freeways.

In the meantime, seepage is destroying the streets. You drive along and a kind of sink-hole has developed. My Z3, before I sold it, was getting beaten to death by pot-holes. One night I was walking home and I saw a piece of the road had vanished, and it was three feet wide and ten feet deep. There was no sign to warn you. Anyhow they're fixing the leaks now.

Contractors come in, build and leave, often getting away with shoddy workmanship. Sometimes the root cause may be *bakshish*, back-handers. In any case there is not enough expertise among Saudi nationals to spot faults. Nor is there any maintenance to prevent decay after these projects have been completed; nobody really understands that maintenance matters. Native expertise is lacking, not because the House of Saud hasn't poured money into training (they have) but because there has been no social or cultural change to obliterate *wassta* and *bakshish*, and the lack of motivation that follow from them. Ten years after I first came, bright people with good brains are still going to waste in this country.

In Riyadh there are freeways with overpasses built by Americans, and Saudi drivers can deal with those, but in Jeddah we have British streets with roundabouts and 65% of all traffic accidents in this city happen at a roundabout. If you're a foreigner with no foreign license you need to take a test, but if you're a Saudi male tall enough to see over the steering wheel you don't.

There is no such thing as driver etiquette. Roundabouts are approached in the spirit of a stock car race – nobody has right of way. People come in at you. I've been in three accidents there and one was quite major. The guy that hit me was in the hospital for a couple of weeks, and one of the girls riding with me broke three ribs and fractured her lower spine and had concussion. It was one in the morning, I was in the roundabout, and he just came and broadsided me at 60 mph. Like, Yo, anyone who's there just better get out of the way. I was driving a 1982 Olds Cutlass, he hit the front – They have posted a speed limit, but it's not enforced very stringently.

But it does give you a sense of freedom to drive.

There is an old airplane parked on a roundabout near the old airfield in Jeddah. It's right up on a stand. The old airport got built way back, in the forties maybe, and then outgrew the location, so that side of town is run down now. All the old airport buildings are there, the old tower with the windows busted out, and the airplane. That was America's gift to King Abdul Aziz in the early forties when the old warrior was frail and nearly blind[15].

In 1945 King Abdul Aziz and President Franklin Delano Roosevelt met on an American warship, USS Quincy, in the Suez Canal. The aging king lumbered towards FDR, who was sitting in his wheelchair and said, "Aren't you lucky you have something like that to move you around." FDR had an extra wheelchair and gave it to the king. It became one of King Abdul Aziz's most prized possessions and a symbol of their friendship. They respected each other. The aging American president had bothered to find out what the customs of the country were, although FDR

---

15   In 1953, as King Abdul Aziz lay dying in his palace, President Eisenhower sent his personal physician to examine the king. While examining his body – covered in scars from the many battles he fought to unify Saudi Arabia – the doctor commented, "The history of Saudi Arabia is written on the scarred body of this dying king."

was a smoker and a drinker he abstained in the King's presence. They exchanged gifts. He gave the King an airplane; it was a Dakota complete with an American flight crew.

Churchill was less well advised about Saudi customs. I guess the Brits were arrogant about the Middle East. The British used the Arabs to fight the Turks, but only Lawrence of Arabia, a soldier, seems to have respected the culture of the Bedouin. At the end of the Second World War, at the same time America was courting Saudi oil, Churchill came along. He smoked his cigars and drank in the presence of King Abdul Aziz, who was too polite to say he found the smell offensive. He was not taken with Churchill.

One time, down in the car souk in Riyadh, I saw an ancient right-hand drive Rolls Royce limo on display, not for sale. It was covered in dust, but when you peered in you could see its wonderfully plush back seat. The story goes that Winston Churchill, having decided to present King Abdul Aziz with a car, did not realize that Saudi royalty ride in front, next to the driver, on the right, or that the left hand is considered dirty. It was a bit of an insult therefore to give him this limousine. He never once travelled in it and it remains in Riyadh, pale grey with dust, as a curiosity.

There are lots of Rolls Royce in Saudi Arabia. They are not a highly regarded car, though some rich Saudis may have a new one. The old Rolls Royce you can pick up for nothing. In the seventies they were not well engineered, their technology didn't change and those old cars break down a lot. So what the Saudis do, or rather what the Bangladeshis do for the Saudi market, is take out the Rolls engine and put a Chevy Caprice engine and transmission in. I looked at a '75 Rolls Royce and lifted the hood and found a fine Chevy transmission and engine in there; they'd moved things round and sorted it out very well. An improvement, very well done. A Chevy master cylinder and brake system, Chevrolet aircon – so it would be cheap to maintain; any competent mechanic – like me – could work on it. I drove it, it ran fine, it just needed a paint job and would have been good fun to drive.

It was 10,000 riyals, about $2,500. In the States you couldn't even buy the grille and the little lady for that. I didn't buy it and I guess I'm going to tell you why, later. I still think about it though.

Every tree in Jeddah is less than fifty years old, except one. A rich old family has this big tree in their garden, and for years it was the only tree in the whole city. The family was so big, that there were always sons and grandsons living in the family house, so the *djinn* were never forsaken, the building never pulled down and the garden never built over. And the tree thrived. People used to come from miles around to look at it.

The old houses are in Balad, the old town. Jeddah one hundred years ago was about one square mile of crooked cobbled alleys and stucco-faced houses within ancient walls surrounding a port. A small group of Saudis has banded together to preserve the old buildings, but they are considered pretty eccentric.

Some of the houses down in Balad are the size of apartment blocks, up to six stories high, usually with lockup shop premises at ground level, because the people who lived there were traders. The houses are made of block coral faced with stucco; you can see the white coral where the dull pinkish stucco has fallen off. They have a kind of wind tunnel that captures the air and funnels it down; it's like a central well that runs from the top of the building, and has adjustable vents to catch whatever air there is, and direct it around the house. It's an ancient form of air conditioning. And there are wooden projecting bays that have shutters and screens pierced and carved in a delicate filigree pattern. They block out the sun, but let in air. Sometimes you see mysterious paneled wooden doors at street level, strengthened with ornate wrought iron.

That's where the wood went – for carving, for doors and windows, for ship-building, and as fuel. It's been so long since anyone saw an old tree in Jeddah that much of the wood must have been brought by ship around the coast, or down by camel train from Taif, a three-day journey. It's all called rosewood, and maybe it is. The buildings are around 300 years old, and if they do knock one down, they know now that there is a market for the carved window bays. They sell them, the whole thing, either genuinely old or artificially antiqued, in the *souq* in Balad. The traffic down there is chaotic; the sun is glaring, there is just enough room in the lanes for vehicles. Walking is a struggle, you're pushing your way through crowds all the time – "See this, See this, Buy this, Good Discount Mister" – and you pass the dusty carved window bays leaning on top of heaps of junk. It's an artful pastiche of neglect. The shopkeepers know exactly how much they're worth.

Trees are being planted. The city is quite lush with palm trees and greenery on the central reservations and roundabouts, partly because of the water tankers constantly crawling around, but mostly because of the faulty desalination pipework. Tall palms rustle softly in front of hundreds of garish signs advertising pharmaceuticals, electronics, watches, jewelry, tires, baby milk and internet access. Signs in Jeddah are generally in Arabic and English, although the English spelling is not always correct. A shop opened with a sign that read *Al-Fucker Chicken*. It stayed for a couple of months before finally being removed due to the large number of complaints.

In Balad they sell gold. The gold *souq* goes on for blocks, and you find breastplates of gold – necklaces, belts, a gold rose the size of a real rose. All these are dowry presents. Gold is how Arabs all over the Middle East keep their money; about 50% of a family's wealth may be in this form, which is why the market is so huge. Governments come and go and are sometimes unstable. The Iraqi dinar used to be on a par with the riyal. But gold jewelry you can always sell. Gold is sold by weight, usually regardless of workmanship. I have never figured out how the intricate jewelry gets paid for. I can pay 43 riyals for a gram of necklace, or a gram of solid ingot. Saudi gold is high quality; it is mined in the western province, and the lowest level of purity you will be offered in the *souq* is 18-carat.

I once saw a 24-carat gold cuff made entirely of miniscule beads. It was beautiful. It was expensive because of the workmanship and the solidity of the beads arranged in geometric designs. It looked like something from a tomb. You couldn't buy that by weight. It was very heavy too.

You can haggle in the gold *souq*. You can beat them down to a certain extent on their gram price. But you always pay a premium as a Westerner and some people send Asians to buy on their behalf.

Jeddah is a port, so that means trading and fishing. Commercial fishing boats chug out beyond the pollution of Jeddah and you get big fish at the fish *souq*: sharks, squid, lobster, shrimp, all on ice – they get sold straight off the quay, some alive in tanks, some flapping helplessly on the slab. Occasionally you get vast creatures from the deep that nobody can identify. The restaurants buy their fish on Friday mornings, which is the best time for Westerners to shop; it's their Sabbath when most people stay home.

There is daring new architecture now, not so much in Jeddah, but certainly in Riyadh because it is the capital and the official seat of power where resources are concentrated. The Faisaliah Center in Riyadh is spectacular. It's just one mighty tower like the nose-cone of a rocket (they're big on phallic symbols in Riyadh) with a multi-faceted globe like a giant disco ball balanced in space near the top. Inside the tower there are offices, a shopping mall, convention center and an exhibition hall. There is another tower about a mile across town, roughly the same height, that looks like someone took a bite out of it – they are so tall, and you're driving into Riyadh and you're still in the desert and you see these huge buildings from dozens of miles away.

Prestige projects like these get put up by European contractors and Indian laborers. There's been no change in the Saudi attitude to manual labor. But there's one new thing in the Faisaliah which is a women-only floor in the mall. All the shops are owned by Saudi women and only women are allowed to shop there.

I know a Saudi girl who was raised in the States and she opened a shop in the Faisaliah. Her sister is a training to be a doctor – treating women only, of course. Their father is quite wealthy. They like to work. They come and go from their home at all hours; one goes to medical school by taxi, the other takes a taxi to the shop, and so on, at regular working hours just like girls in the west.

This has been noticed. Religious people from the community visited the house and sat down and discussed the daughters with the father. They expressed serious reservations about his capacity to be a parent. They told him he was not a good Muslim. His daughters should not be out at all hours doing as they pleased; they should be at home and controlled.

This man had enough backbone to assert his own opinion, which is highly unusual. He told them he was satisfied that his daughters could run their own lives. There are stable Muslim families all over the world where the women earn an income, but necessity has not yet driven Saudis to see the point of it.

22

Bad Hair Dye Day

———

Early in 2001, things were about to change for me. I got an unexpected opportunity, because somebody I respected got fed up with arguing with the hospital management and quit.

At that time, managing the hospital's clinical services was the responsibility of the short man, with dyed black hair, from Little Rock, whose office I sat in to watch the Twin Towers fall. Clinical Services at the King Faisal is nine departments: Radiology, Emergency, Ambulances, Respiratory therapy, Laboratory, Procurement, Staff Management – other than nursing, running it is the biggest responsibility in the hospital.

He used to be Manager of Laundry Services at the King Faisal Hospital in Riyadh. He was transferred. There had to be *wassta* involved with that large of a promotion.

He knows nothing about equipment, people, anything. He's paralyzed with fear of making any decision, in case it is the wrong one. He has some good heads of department, and he blames them when things go wrong and takes credit if they go right. The Saudis pat themselves on the back and think he makes the right decisions. He is a yes-man. Most Westerners get frustrated trying to deal with him and resign.

The manager of the ambulance service was an American called Pete. He had been a paramedic for twenty years, and had a Bachelor's degree in Business Administration. Born in Saudi Arabia he spoke fluent Arabic; he'd been an Aramco brat, raised there until he was nineteen.

That is the kind of guy you want to run your ambulance service. But, Pete was getting paid like a rookie paramedic.

The Director says, "I'll give you a year to show me what you can do, and then we'll adjust your salary."

After a year Pete says, "Right, I need my salary adjustment now."

"Well, just wait a while longer."

All the time this Little Rock guy was telling the Saudis how much money he was saving them. Frustrated, Pete said he didn't need this and left to go to Florida.

The next best qualified is me: paramedic over twelve years, Bachelor's degree, and Arabic not quite as good as Pete's. So I get the job.

My boss is five feet two, a hundred and forty pounds, in his fifties, balding and what remains of his hair is dyed jet black. One night we had to pick him up in the ambulance, because the hair dye that he'd bought in Saudi was not the same as the stuff they sell in Little Rock, and he'd had an allergic reaction. He was treated in the emergency room with anti-histamines because he had bronchial constriction, shortness of breath, and his whole face had puffed up like a big red wrinkled apple. He got his breath back, deflated, went home and got in the shower where the hot water opened up his pores and he reacted all over again. We had to go and fetch him a second time and bring him back for more Benadryl.

I managed the Ambulance service for a while, but the stupidity of this guy and the way he took credit, was very frustrating. I have a problem with people demanding respect.

I think it should be earned. So, I transferred and started developing a training program which was outside his jurisdiction.

I'm in management now, so I get to see how the finances work. The Royal cabinet pays, because the service is dedicated to the royal family, and it provides the hospital with three years funding. However, this time there was a caveat: if you're going to carry on, you've got to become 50% self-supporting.

This is the first time a hospital dedicated to Royalty has ever been expected to make a profit, and I don't think the management quite grasps the situation yet.

Profligate spending quickly racked up billions of riyals in unpaid debt. Our boss pays himself 260,000 riyals a month, which is about $80,000 a month. He has a new car that cost around $80,000. So salary, plus car and villa – Oh, and there is the $30,000 desk in his office, which makes him feel good.

Within a year and a half of opening, the King Faisal was broke. If they run out of money and can't meet payroll, there are no apologies. They just keep the staff hanging around until the Financial Director has trotted back to Daddy and begged for more money.

It is routine in Saudi Arabia for employers to run out of money and not pay their staff for months. A paramedic I know at the airport, where there is a dedicated medical staff, went four months without pay, and I had to lend him money for food. The Pakistani and Bangladeshi gardeners out there were almost starving. The management was like "Too bad – you'll get it when we can give it to you."

We had a staff meeting when they last ran out of money. One of the senior administrators stood there listening and said he didn't see what we were making a fuss about.

"In North America you people very often go without pay."

He really believed that. A resentful hubbub arose.

"Never does that happen, never."

"Oh I'm sure it does," he said. "And you are all lucky to have a job, and to be here at the King Faisal, which is one of the finest hospitals in the world."

One of the nurses stood up – a woman.

"Do you realize," she said "that there is a worldwide nursing shortage and we can go anywhere? You're lucky to have us here."

"There is no worldwide nursing shortage. You are here because there are no jobs where you came from," he said.

People just got up and walked out. About twenty staff resigned that day. He is no longer allowed to speak at those meetings; they send a more diplomatic director of the hospital to address us now.

The hospital needs to recruit more board-certified North American anesthesiologists. This guy, the undiplomatic one, announced that they would pay them $110,000 a year. A clued-up Saudi anesthesiologist told him that would not be enough. Out of school, just starting, people who can do that job are getting a quarter of a million dollars.

He said it was not true. He could not be convinced.

The way a lot of hospitals recruit is by mailshot. They send them indiscriminately worldwide to every board-certified North American doctor in the specialty they want. The clued-up Saudi happened to have been sent one that day and he said, "Why would I accept a job here when I have offers from an American hospital: $325,000 US per annum, to start."

He typed out a memo and sent it that afternoon, but has never had a response.

So now they get third-world doctors who may not be so well trained. I am organizing a training program, and I get paid three times more than a Syrian doctor. There is one really good Egyptian medical school, and a lot of bad ones without American or British exams, and they tend to hire whoever comes along. Frankly you get what you pay for.

The King Faisal traditionally employed the best doctors, but now our top American neurologist and Canadian neurosurgeon have been let go, so they will get someone cheaper and inferior. Saudis have not realized that twenty or thirty years ago, when they first started hiring from the west, things were very different, especially in Canada. The money then was double or triple what you could get in North America, and they got the best and brightest beating a path to their door. Wages are now on a par.

The advantages to working in Saudi now are the facilities, generous vacation time (exotic locations are just a short flight away), and the fact that it is tax-free. That's all. There is a world-wide shortage of the skills they need, but their mindset has not changed. They know that their money is no longer limitless, but still think they can choose the best and are doing us a favor. People find them arrogant and dismissive of the dedication we bring to the job.

After 9/11 many Westerners left. The hostility on the streets, and the small matter of not getting paid, meant that about seven out of every ten western doctors and nurses have now been replaced by people from India, or Lebanon, or Syria, and a few of them have been trained to the standard that should prevail.

I've got angry about this, but only in a controlled way.

I just say, "You know I'm very angry right now." Just in case there's any doubt.

The Head of Personnel was trying to get me to hire some British paramedics. But back then they were not trained the same way we were, and our hospital was supposed to meet North American standards to stay within our accreditation. Canadians and South Africans copy it. British EMT, emergency medical training, with its one probationary year, was equivalent to our EMT, but their paramedic training was different. It was four weeks in a classroom and six weeks of clinical hospital work, and then you qualified for a paramedic license. They didn't upgrade to our system because there was a powerful lobby claiming paramedical expertise for doctors and nurses. Now the British Paramedic system has expanded to include a degree program and the training is a lot more extensive and in-depth.

But back then I was determined not to hire Brits. I said to my boss "I carry a drug box with 37 drugs in it and I have protocols, North American protocols, that are three hundred pages thick – and if I hand this drug box to a British paramedic who is licensed and trained to administer only seven different types of drug, what's he gonna do? He is not licensed to administer them and if he does, and he kills somebody, whose fault is that gonna be? How can he be expected to work to a level he's not qualified to?"

"But they're paramedics."

"Yes their license says that, but it is not the same. I will not hire them."

"But they are cheaper and available. The American overtime is expensive."

They think they've found a solution to a financial problem, but it's ad hoc, and as usual the implications of cutting corners haven't been thought out.

I have learned to explain my objections in the gentlest, simplest, most salesman-like (that is, emotionally manipulative) way.

"We can do things this way. That's fine. But X number of people a month will die. That's perfectly OK if you're willing to have that happen. If not, we'll have to do it a different way. I'll do whatever you want."

This way I get results.

When we first started I was given free rein and plenty of money to set up the ambulance service as I wanted. I got the best equipped outfit I could and it is a good system.

And then the financial crisis hits; they've run out of credit.

Now they decide to cut back the ambulance service. This is when I point out that if they cut back from two ambulances to one, then one ambulance will be out on an emergency and there will be another emergency elsewhere. This happens on average twenty times a month. Probably four to six patients per month would therefore die. Would they accept that every month? Because if so that would be fine.

When I put it like that, they back off. Our customers are princes, and they can't risk a prince having a heart attack with no ambulance to pick him up.

We routinely run out of supplies, because when the budget was first allocated suppliers extended large amounts of credit. Then they did not get paid. There are a lot of western structures, like contract law, that have not have time to settle in to the culture here. They can break contracts with impunity, and they will. Friendship, brotherhood – they'll go to the wall for a friend. But a contract with a western employee, or a western company – well, there is no disgrace in failing to honor that.

This isn't the only hospital in the world where inefficient management wastes money. It isn't even the only service in Saudi Arabia where it happens.

In my new capacity as trainer, I go to help with training the Red Crescent. I am told they've bought Automatic External Defibrillators (AEDs) to equip all their ambulances. These are the best thing in pre-hospital care, because anybody with a little training can put one of these things onto somebody in cardiac arrest, and it automatically analyses whether to defibrillate or not. Passenger aircraft have them installed, so that the stewards can use them. You even find them in shopping malls in the States. The machine speaks to you: Shock Patient Now. Check Pulse. No Pulse. Start CPR.

Cardio-pulmonary resuscitation was invented forty years ago. Pre-hospital it was estimated that 9% of cardiac victims survived thanks to conventional CPR, and this figure remains the same today. The big change comes when AEDs are put into use; the survival rate can be as high as 60% if applied quickly (within 4 minutes).

So I hear they've bought automatic defibrillators for the hundreds of Red Crescent ambulances which provide pre-hospital care throughout the land. They have these machines, which speak in Arabic. I'm shown closets full of them. They're returns: they're not in the ambulances any more.

"They're broken," the manager of the Red Crescent explains when he shows me.

"All these? But these are great, they save lives."

I take a look, they're regular machines.

"Let's take one back to the guy at the hospital who fixes the medical equipment. Maybe he can tell you what's wrong."

I put one in the trunk and drive back to the King Faisal. The technician calls me. "Where's the charger for this thing?"

I ring the Red Crescent. "Mr Dawisha, where's the charger?"

"Oh we didn't get the chargers," he says. "They were extra."

I call the technician who says, "How they gonna get them to work if they don't have chargers? Batteries run out in about two weeks."

I call the manager and tell him, and he puts all the machines back in the closet.

You can see what happened. Handover of hundreds of machines.

"Here is the warranty, and here are the battery chargers, and here is the bill."

Now the Procurement guy wakes up.

"We thought it cost so much?"

" – Yeah, but of course you need the battery chargers and the service – you gotta rotate the batteries and charge new ones like any other defibrillator."

The procurement guy won't have them. He'll do without. He wasn't expecting extras.

So now nothing works. Hundreds of thousands of riyals have been wasted and there are cupboards full of useless defibrillators. As usual there have been two steps forward, a load of money spent, and ten steps back. They would have been perfect, those machines, and would have saved lots of lives.

This is the way it is.

On the outside the King Faisal still makes the Ritz look like a dump. It is sparkling clean; there is a huge staff to do that. I have been in several Saudi hospitals and it outshines all of them for good first impressions. But for medical care it would only get two stars now.

If there was any good reason for this, if Saudi Arabia really did have a third-world income, fine. Admittedly I probably wouldn't be here, but – I'd have some sympathy with low standards of care. As it is I just get frustrated. It's not like the House of Saud is salting away the entire wealth of the country in some bank in Geneva, like Bokassa or any other dictator you could name. The problem is more that your average middle-management Saudi with *wassta* cheerfully accepts kickbacks to buy unnecessary foreign products, so the government's money leaves this country anyway (and for government money, read "the royal family's income from oil" – because there is no income tax).

Bakshish is normal. It is not talked about, but is an accepted part of business. For instance we were going to buy new infusion pumps for the King Faisal Hospital. We trialed three different types in the emergency room and the intensive care unit, and reported on which ones were best. Nurses and doctors were exhaustively questioned. Unanimously, they rated the infusion pumps one, two, three in order of preference. The one the hospital eventually bought five hundred of was the worst one, because the manufacturer offered the largest kickback.

After the Gulf War was the first time the Saudi government had ever been in debt, or talked of saving money. At that time I was at the National Guard Hospital, and we were asked to cut back our expenses by 15–20%. By and large we did. Then one day some flunkeys show up on our housing compound, where there are three thousand people, and they've bought 1,500 Sony Trinitron 27" televisions and we all get one in our villa. Why? Because the commission, *bakshish*, for the purchasing office was huge.

The apartment I live in now is a simple one-bedroom apartment, nothing like as well fitted as apartments I have stayed in before, and they pay around $10,000 a year for it which is a lot for this country. There is another western compound which has luxurious apartments in lovely grounds, and instead of 58,000 riyals, which is what the hospital pays for us, those apartments cost 50,000 riyals. Why can't we live there? I ask. Because of *bakshish*, I am told. The apartment I have is worth about 25,000, not 58,000 riyals. But the procurer gets his kickback and the hospital pays.

There is a disincentive to being conscientious when you do a business deal as conscientiousness is not what brings benefits. We were buying new cardiac monitors for our ambulance and wanted the Lifepac Ten, which is pretty standard in the States, and costs about $8,000. The guy comes and shows us a list –

"These cost $16,000."

"That's wrong," I say.

"No," he says, "from this supplier, Lifepac Ten are $16,000."

"Well, I have a friend who runs a medical supply company in Sacramento, he'll ship 'em right over to us for eight thousand bucks plus shipping."

"No," he says – he's so patient with my dumb American ways – "you don't understand, it has to go through this system. You can't just buy them."

"These people are gouging you."

"It's OK," he says.

Everybody understands the way things are. All down the line prices are inflated, and at the end of the line the Crown Prince pays.

Years ago I learned to say "the Crown Prince would like this" and "we are required to have this" when buying equipment. So the Crown Prince wants us to have a backup monitor, or whatever, and Procurement would give it to us because no-one would ever ask him. Nobody would ever have the balls to ask him direct whether he really wanted a piece of kit he'd never heard of. His name was just bandied about.

The system is well accepted and never openly discussed; the Crown Prince must know about it and maybe he thinks of it as the perks his employees get and the way they keep quiet and loyal. His fifteen palaces are remodeled every year and the stuff sold out the back door. This would not be approved procedure, but the warehousemen have a highly desirable job. They strip the palace of all the furnishings and televisions annually, but they haven't built any new warehouses in twenty years. It must go somewhere. The warehouses are not even full. If the royal DVDs and VCRs were stamped with crossed palm trees and a sword, you could probably trace one or two of them to the *souq* in Balad.

23

By GPS.... to Mecca

During the day Jeddah is quiet. At eleven at night it's still warm, the Red Sea is sparkling black in the port, the city's all illuminated, and there are traffic jams and plaintive music. Parked cars line the sidewalks along the corniche, and any little square of grass is just perfect for a picnic. Out of the trunk comes the Hibachi grill and the blanket to spread on the ground, and the Arab families start cooking and talking.

One of my first dates with Nicola, we went to the corniche. They have a kiddy amusement park open at midnight, and I won her some stuffed animals. It was pretty easy, and they wouldn't let me play any longer, so we walked along the corniche by the sea. I bought some fireworks, and was showing all these little kids around us how to use them safely. The Saudi boys would hold fireworks in their hands and set light to them, but I told them there's a better way. I got a coke can and secured it with stones and put the firework in, lit it and moved well back. It worked. Nobody lost a hand.

Anyway some of their parents came over and asked us to come and have tea. It is rude to refuse if you are invited, and it was Nicola's first real social encounter with Arabs, who turned out to be Syrians. They were very nice and made us special coffee. We sat on the pavement with the cars whizzing by behind us. The girls were fascinated by Nicola. She told them her name was Harriet. I didn't bat an eyelid. I knew she'd just found out her name means Nic(Fuck)-ola(Allah). It's not the best name to introduce yourself by in Arabic-speaking countries.

Their kids are funny. There's one little boy in our compound who speaks only Arabic.

He jokes, "I'm gonna scratch your car with a knife!"

I whisper back – "You do that, and the police will come! And put handcuffs on! And we'll never see you again."

He helped me work on my car.

Nicola hadn't been here long when we started going out. She's English. Now we're married and exploring Saudi Arabia together. She works with Saudi girls at the hospital and tells me a whole lot I didn't know about them. I show her what I know of the countryside, but not by Rolls Royce. It was Nicola that drew the line.

We like driving up to Taif. Straight across flat desert and then you see the mountains rising sheer ahead of you, the long climb up 6,000 feet. You'll be going up and a truck will come right at you, in your lane, and you'll have to get all the way over to the shoulder onto the grit, next to the drop. My wife goes very quiet at moments like this.

Near the top you are greeted by a tribe of baboons. Saudis throw rocks at them, so the baboons recognize the *thobe* and *ghutra* and scatter. If Westerners come they know there is a fruit stand a little further up, so you come back down and they'll be waiting for bananas. They will take them and peel them – if there are no Saudis nearby.

The baboons make no noise unless they're upset or angry, when they shriek. Each male has a group of his own, and gets jealous. They're territorial and move fast. They have long canines and will turn on the packs of wild desert dogs and rip 'em up. Some of them will turn on humans. I know because it's happened to me, there was a baby away from the mother that I wanted to feed, and the male charged me. You are not supposed to look the males in the eye. I shot back into the car that time with Nicola scolding me for taking the risk. It's nice to have somebody looking after you.

I took her to Al Heet. This is a beautiful cave about twenty miles outside Riyadh. The opening is an immense gaping hole in an escarpment; it looks about a mile wide and a mile high. You could put the Faisaliah center in it for sure, and you walk in feeling the size of an ant. You find yourself going downhill, first gently, then a steep climb down over rocks in damp-smelling darkness, for nearly a mile, until you find you are on the shores of an underground lake. When I lived in Riyadh some of us explored it. I have never dived in that lake, but I have been told that it is about ninety feet deep, and branches off into dangerous underground tunnels. We were down there four or five hours, it was huge.

In the days of Abdul Aziz, it is said, the water lapped right up to the mouth of the cave. He camped there with his army and watered his horses and men, before he entered Riyadh to kick out the Al Rashids, when he was a young warlord in 1902.

Nearly all the water has been pumped out. The water table right across the eastern province has become much lower than it was. This is because in the sixties the Saudi government decided they could develop a different economy and tapped into the deep underground aquifers that lie beneath the whole central plateau, in order to irrigate the land. A bushel of wheat cost $6 then, and they got hold of the notion that Saudi Arabia could become self-sufficient in it. They said they would subsidize people who'd volunteer to farm wheat by paying $30 a bushel and giving them tractors and pumps, so they could flood the desert and grow the wheat.

As a result the water that would have supported existing levels of farming for about five hundred years disappeared in fifteen. That's when geologists told them there would soon be no water. So they stopped.

The eastern province is honeycombed with caves. Once, in Riyadh, we had a huge storm and the ground about a mile from the hospital just opened up, and I saw hundreds of Saudis looking down into a hole. Down as far as you could see was hollow; this entire time people had been driving and walking on a layer of dust and rock that was maybe only thirty feet deep over a huge cave. Government guys came and just buried it all up again.

What you notice in a country which hasn't got pressure groups (and it's illegal to join together and question the government here) is that things, like the ground suddenly giving way, are never explained. You just learn to accept the decisions of a paternal, private state, the way you just accept being given a 27" TV, or not having a defibrillator when you need one.

Even history is sensitive; you might think because there is one small Saudi group dedicated to preserving old buildings that they have a voice. They only have a voice because as individuals they have *wassta*, and even then they can go only so far. This country is as much the cradle of civilization as anywhere else in the Middle East and parts of it have been settled since pre-history, but Saudis are not encouraged to think about that because Wahhabis don't like to acknowledge any influence before Mohamed.

One of the oldest trading cities in the world was found when photographs taken by satellite showed old roads under the desert leading to a trading center somewhere in the Empty Quarter near the Yemeni border. Archaeologists came from America and excavation began. When they got to a certain point they realized that this must have been a Jewish settlement – the oldest ever found in the world. Oh dear. Everything stopped and the scientists went home. Nobody else will be allowed to excavate there for as long as the Wahhabi have any influence.

You see steep escarpments, flat on top, and on these high plateaus you find circles of stones, thirty yards across, stacked by somebody, with another pile of stones in the middle. And at the bottom of the cliff face there will be piles of fallen stones anywhere from two to eight feet high. I tried to find out what these stone circles are for. For worship maybe? When were they put there? I asked a guy at the museum about one that's close to the compound in Riyadh and he could only tell me it was pre-Islamic. Scholars like him are curious, but enquiry is generally discouraged.

Near to Taif, on the side close to the coast is the *wadi*. A *wadi* is a depression in the desert that usually fills with water in winter, and this one gets the run-off from the hills down a steep, rocky cliff. The beds of the streams are spidered with petroglyphs, incised nobody knows how long ago. You can climb the cliff and find symbols for the sun, a horse, a man, and other strange marks like a line with a half circle under – nobody, not even the Saudis, has been able to tell me what they mean.

There are petroglyphs on cliffs all over the desert, and far inland near *wadis* that now have only salt in the bottom of them. Many of the animals they depict are extinct in Saudi Arabia now, like the gazelles. Other petroglyphs are quite new, and incised in the rock perhaps within living memory, because they show guys with guns, but nobody seems to know quite why they were made. You have to climb right up the dry beds of streams to find some of them. You disturb chameleons among the rocks, and see strange plants and insects.

You're never alone in the desert. You'll be coming down the *wadi* and suddenly find hills covered with sheep, and goats, and at the roadside an old Bedouin, or a young boy hawking the milk out of leather bottles.

One time Nicola and I were hanging around in the desert with this Australian guy and his wife. We looked at the map, and the Aussie said, "Well, in Saudi Arabia, the sun sets in the East."

"No," I said. "Are you sure?"

Not long afterwards we bought a GPS.

Mecca, you are strictly forbidden to enter unless you are a Muslim. You are not even allowed to approach it; there is an exclusion zone for miles around, like a *cordon sanitaire*. But Mecca is less than an hour, sixty miles, away from Jeddah, and there is interesting countryside all around. In fact there is an unusually lush-looking strip of land coming out of Mecca, between the Taif Road and the Christian Road, but when you drive alongside you can see it is a river. And it stinks. All those millions of people coming for the *hajj*, and no proper sewage system – so it all oozes off into the desert, and once a year a big trail of greenery springs up along the riverbed, and the holy poo, as Nicola calls it, has made the desert bloom.

Anyway the GPS is on, and Nicola's just got her telephoto zoom to play with. I'm driving along the Christian Road, and we've just passed this malodorous green trail, turned left, and kept on going. We come across a village where people have been firing bricks in low mud houses, beehive shape. There are grates inside and they put the bricks in, keep feeding the fire, and then seal it up. They break out the clay later to get the bricks. Thousands of years they've been doing this, and here's a whole village still devoted to it, like in a Bible story.

Nicola, in the passenger seat wearing tee-shirt and shorts, and no *abayah*, spotted some Saudi men having a shower outside and throwing water at one another. We stopped some distance away, because she insisted on photographing these guys. Then I drove on, following the GPS.

"If we go right, we will hit the Christian Road again," she says, happy with her pictures.

"No," I say. I like a change. "Let's go left and see what there is."

You see mirages on the road, like water, which are just tricks of light and heat. But suddenly there is a city two hundred yards ahead. Tower blocks round the outside, lots of minarets. Uh?

"Tom, we really should turn back."

"What?"

"The GPS says that's Mecca."

I braked and did a fast U-turn. We would have been in a lot of trouble.

Mecca is much, much more than a place of pilgrimage in the sense of Canterbury, or Santiago de Composte'⁀ or even Jerusalem. It is a hotbed of fundamentalism, and afte   ⁀⁀ revolution, in 1980, some *metawah* began an ur The House of Saud appeared to have been challer it was kind of odd that the National Guard's guns were used, and the King and some of the princes, who were expected to be present, happened to be away. A lot of fuss and sixty-three public decapitations later, the rebels went quiet, but the city still has a fanatic aspect.

All the same I have been into Mecca, three times.

I went through in the motorcade coming back from Taif once, with the Crown Prince, so they didn't check our cars. And in my early days at the King Faisal I was in the ambulance with a patient, and the driver wanted to go round Mecca, which would have taken half an hour longer, so I told him to go straight through. They waved us through that time, because we were an ambulance.

Then once, in the ambulance when there was no rush with Mustafa as the driver. He is a very nice gentle man who studies Islam, and he gave me a tour around Mecca. It is an ordinary enough city, except for the massive Kaaba inside the mosque, and I got out and went in a shop and had a shwarma. Nobody stopped me. They gave me some funny looks, but they thought I must be a Muslim, otherwise I'd never have dared. I speak Arabic anyway.

Mustafa showed me the ancient Christian graveyard, which he said was fifteen hundred years old, from before Mohamed's time, and he said that they know who was buried there, because the names have been copied from the tombstones. He showed me the Great Mosque, which has ornate arcades all the way round and extremely tall minarets, and told me it is a thousand years old. When I pointed out that it didn't look as old as that he agreed, and said that anyway there had been a mosque there for a thousand years, which I am sure is true.

The black stone-built cube, the Kaaba, in the middle of the Great Mosque's courtyard, is what Muslims are really praying towards when they face east. It is said to have been made by Abraham and his son Ishmael. It is about forty feet high and covered with a vast cloth known as the *Kiswah*, which is replaced every year (it is cut into pieces and gifted to various dignitaries or organizations). The cloth is produced at a special factory in Mecca at a cost of about 17 million riyals ($4.5 million). It is made of 670 kgs of pure silk which is dyed black. About 15 kgs of gold thread is used in the gold-embroidered calligraphy which runs in a band about two-thirds of the way up. Always included in the embroidery is the Islamic profession of faith the *Shahadah* (There is no god but Allah, and Mohamed is his prophet), which also appears in white on the green background of the Saudi flag.

Mustafa told me that in Mohamed's day the locals used to go inside and pray to their idols, and they would have nothing at all to do with Mohamed. So he and his followers left for Medina, but eight years later they returned, and this time Mohamed conquered the city and smashed the idols. He announced that the Kaaba would be a Muslim shrine from now on. The Kaaba stone is set into one corner in a silver ring. This is a smooth black stone, which is supposed to have been sent by Allah (although it could be a meteorite) and as they walk around the Kaaba seven times, praying, most pilgrims try to kiss the stone. In 1941, when the Kaaba flooded, old photographs show dedicated pilgrims attempting to swim around seven times

No-one at all is allowed inside the Kaaba: it is kept empty. The keys are held by the Bani Shaybat tribe. However, as a reminder of Mohamed's clearing of the Kaaba, once a year they open it up and somebody extremely important is picked ɔ sweep it out. Members of the tribe greet visitors to the inside of the Kaaba on the occasion of the cleaning ceremony.

It is a huge honor to be asked. The time I got left behind at the Guest Palace in Jeddah for three days, was the time when Crown Prince Abdullah was the chosen one. So Saif, who never prayed, but smoked, and drank and was a womanizer, went as one of the official paramedics. The most holy, awesome thing for a Muslim is to be permitted inside the Kaaba. He told me that as soon as the Crown Prince had swept it out, with a broom spray-painted gold, then the whole group went in, Saif included, for their prayer.

I teased him – God's up there saying, "I can't *believe* they let Saif inside my Kaaba. Is that *Saif* in there?"

He said it's just bare inside. There is nothing in there, except a few lanterns against the gloom. The floor is made of marble and limestone, and the walls are lined with marble inlayed with Quranic inscriptions reaching about half way to the roof.

The yard within the Great Mosque is over 200 meters in every direction, and has to accommodate hundreds and hundreds of thousands of pilgrims all day, everyday, for about ten days, as they arrive to take their turn in running counter-clockwise around the Kaaba. It is just one of many rites of the *hajj*, which includes trekking outside Mecca to Arafat for a sermon, and throwing stones at three pillars where Ishmael drove away the temptations of Satan.

One of the British Muslim nurses at the hospital told Nicola it's a lot like being on *Survivor*. It takes six days, drinking out of dirty wells, not being able to go to the bathroom properly – Millions of people sleep out, divided by language and country of origin. Trucks come driving by and helpers fling *nan* bread at the happy campers.

It's every person for themselves, and you have to sprint to get round the Kaaba seven times; everyone wants to get as close as possible.

"If you don't get there early, forget it, because it's about a kilometer if you're on the outside ring. *Seven times!* The trick with lobbing the stones," this nurse confided "is to stand at the back or you'll get hit."

So many tasks to perform, so little time – and that's just the pilgrims. Behind the scenes, the Red Crescent and the airlines and the hotels, organize food and shelter and medical care, hundreds of ambulances and doctors, for two million people who come here, and go home, pretty much simultaneously in the space of two weeks; it's a formidable feat.

Every year someone falls over and the hordes move so fast and so very close together that there will be a trampling. There is a pedestrian tunnel where one year the lights went out, and people panicked, and hundreds of people were crushed and suffocated to death[16]. The Stoning of the Devil is exceptionally crowded and dangerous, since 1990 over nine hundred people have died while performing the ritual. After the 2004 *hajj*, out of concern for safety Saudi authorities replaced the three pillars with 85 ft long walls; many people were accidentally throwing the stones at people on the other side. The Ministry of Hajj's website reads, "Be peaceful, orderly and kind. No crushing."

But if you are a Muslim the best time and place in the world to die is at the *hajj*. The medical team told me that many old sick people come wishing to die there. It is Saudi Arabia's reminder to over a billion Muslims worldwide that the

16   On July 2, 1990, a stampede inside a pedestrian tunnel (Al-Ma'aisim tunnel) which leads out of Mecca towards Mina and the Plains of Arafat led to the deaths of 1,426 pilgrims.

Holy Mosque is the most important place on earth and that they, and only they, are welcome guests. Every good Muslim who can afford to, and is well enough, should perform *hajj* at least once. Rich people do it more than once, and now I hear that *hajj* visas are limited to five in one lifetime.

It takes place in the twelfth month of the Muslim year. If you fly out of the country at that time, you see thousands of shaven-headed men and boys wearing the special white towels intended to make everyone appear the same (in the eyes of Allah there is no difference between a prince and a pauper). They and their white-clad womenfolk will be carrying zam-zam water. This is a sign that they have completed their *hajj* and have visited the Well of Zam-Zam, in the grounds of the Great Mosque, which is where Ishmael's mother Hagar found water after a difficult search and a prayer. God made a well for her and nowadays it has a pump and goes through a purification system. The pilgrims believe it has curative properties.

They also claim to believe you can live on it without food.

There was a regular British Muslim, Dr Bashir, who came to work at the King Faisal. He and his wife turned up fresh from Leeds, where she had been brought up as a Muslim too. Socially, they behave like an ordinary Yorkshire couple in most respects.

Here he discovers the buddy culture of Saudi men, and likes it, and all of a sudden he clamps down.

"Get out of bed, it's dawn. Get on your knees, woman; we have to pray."

Five times a day. She is miserable; her husband has become a fanatic. He is smacking her around for the first time. YouTube, a popular video sharing web-site, contains a number of videos showing a Muslim cleric giving specific instructions on the correct way to beat your wife.

She is not entitled to leave unless he gives permission, she's on his passport and she has a child now, and is totally alone in Saudi because he has found God. He runs with the boys all the time – sits around drinking tea and talking – and she is isolated at home with the baby. She has no family here, she has no language in which to speak to other Muslim women and nothing much in common with them, but she can't behave like a Westerner. If she leaves the country her daughter stays, because she belongs to her father, not her mother.

And Dr Bashir – I asked him, "You know the story of the Well of ZamZam?"

"Of course."

This is right after he had been to *hajj*, and when you've done your pilgrimage it is like a purification from that day forward; you are inspired to become an even better Muslim.

"You know they say you can live on zam-zam water. You believe that?"

"Certainly."

"But you're a British general practitioner, a family doctor with a scientific education...."

"You can't understand. You need to be a Muslim to understand the Holy City and all the wonderful things in it."

"Did you know there is a Christian graveyard in Mecca over 1,500 years old?"

"Nonsense. Who told you that?"

"I've been there, I saw it."

"*You* were in *Mecca*?" he said.

He looked at me as if he wanted to kill me. I had soiled the holy of holies just by visiting.

I just wanted everybody to lighten up.

Prophet Mohamed was a great military leader, as well as a religious one. He engaged in a long list of holy wars. Those conquered in battle were generally given three choices, accept Islam, pay tribute, or die – whereas Christianity began by glorifying meek obstinacy and didn't get violent until later.

Mohamed was born in Mecca and the Arabs of the Hejaz (the western highlands) were his original followers, which is why this part of the world still contains the Two Holy Mosques, the other one being at Medina.

I read a good story one time where Mohamed went to a village where they worshipped two small gods and he told them, "You must worship Allah as well, or we go to war."

"OK," they said.

And then after a while he said, "Sorry, Allah's got to be the only one."

So he converted the whole village to Islam without having to fight them. He tricked them.

Mustafa told me Mohamed never did say it was wrong to drink alcohol. He just got tired of everyone showing up to the mosque drunk and he said that to be under the effects of drink and come to the mosque is a sin. So to pray five times a day – you needed to sober up. He disliked prohibitions and he got his own way kind of sideways, without direct confrontation, if it was at all possible.

There were Jews here in his day, and even more in Medina; there are still Yemeni Jews, but none have survived in Saudi Arabia. In Mohamed's lifetime Islam spread, and his descendants the Caliphs took it even further afield. Today, estimates of the Muslim population range from 1 billion to 1.8 billion, making it the world's second largest religion after Christianity.

24

Unsung Heroes

———

One other ambulance driver I know pretty well, besides Mustafa, is Abdullah Al Daboush. In some ways he represents the man in the street to me, because he is traditional and unquestioning and he has his problems, but in general Allah has been good to him.

Abdullah – it's like a cut-out picture of the average Saudi, this, but it's all true – has two wives (he's thinking he needs another) and thirteen children and makes 2,500 riyals a month which is about $800. He's close to fifty. His older sons contribute to the household expenses, and Abdullah, his children, the older sons, and their wives and children, all live together.

He runs a car, which is wired together and has no aircon. He's a fat fellow, and amiable. He wants a new wife because he wants more children, and he wants more children because it's more hands to keep the camels and milk them. The fact that there is a wheezing Chevy Caprice, rather than a herd of camels, and jobs are available only if you get good schooling, and he can't afford private education for his kids – that hasn't hit him yet. As soon as he gets his monthly salary he's down at the pharmacist, buying over-the-counter Viagra at thirty dollars a pop.

Education is free but religious, and it isn't enough; you need influence as well. The advantages of producing a small number of highly educated children, rather than maintaining your reputation for virility, are not at all obvious.

Immigrant workers are different. They don't get free education. One of the other drivers I have is Sudanese and on the same salary as Mustafa. His four children are all in a private school at the Sudanese Consulate. This does not offer the social and intellectual advantages of Jeddah Prep, or the Continental School, or the American International School, which might cost tens of thousands of dollars per child per year, but at least it shows an awareness of what the future holds.

Some of the skilled immigrants are heroic. They spend their lives working entirely for the benefit of their family back home. There's a Filipino nurse at our hospital, like a lot of them she's supporting an extended family in her village. She's been here ten years and she's just got her third sibling through university in Manila. She said to me, "Now I can finally work for myself."

She'll never marry. She's typical. And every holiday, she goes home. It's a family loyalty thing. The Saudis have the same thing. They take care of the old people, they nurse them until they die, and I admire that.

At the other end of the scale, I know a Canadian doctor who is delighted that his son is going to school here. At the American school in Riyadh and at Jeddah Prep there are the best teachers, no crime, no drugs. All the rich Saudis want their children to go to secular, demanding schools like this, and this doctor's son has made a young Saudi buddy. This thirteen-year-old Saudi boy gets driven to school everyday watching TV in the back of his own Humvee. His family owns the largest yacht on the Mediterranean.

Come vacation time, they invite the Canadian kid for a month. And when the family goes into town, like Cannes or Bandol or somewhere, the entire restaurant is taken over and surrounded by bodyguards. The kids are getting bored on the boat, so they ask for jet-skis. Oh, OK then, says the father, and sends them into town with $25,000 and two bodyguards to buy them.

They were dining out somewhere nice in Juan les Pins one night, and the doctor's son didn't have a suit, so they fitted him out at Armani for $3,500.

He came back with incredible tales and the doctor said, "Wow. Never lose contact with him."

Just don't fall in love with his sister.

Even Prince Naif, who heads up most of the quasi-religious state bodies and is presumably pretty close to the Grand Mufti, admits that there is a conflict in this country between traditional values and prosperity.

On the one hand, you have many top jobs going to the least competent because of *wassta* and corruption, so you need to put competent foreigners in key positions to get anything done.

On the other, you need to get rid of all these foreign workers and replace them by Saudis, because otherwise, money is leaking and evaporating like the water under the Jeddah streets, and you're creating a perfect growth medium for discontent.

A year after the Twin Towers blew up Prince Naif gave an interview in which he said that there were over seven million foreign workers and the hard currency leaving the country was approaching fifty billion riyals a year: the Saudi government was, "working with companies to set up centers for training Saudis."

There is nothing in the Bedouin lifestyle or history that makes them time-keep. Even the shops — many are owned by Saudis, but run by Indians, or Pakistanis, or Filipinos.

In the gold souk, most of the work these days is done by Indian goldsmiths. It's a huge trade and they are expert; you just draw them a picture of a piece of jewelry, they tell you to come back in a couple of days and they've made it for you. The government is trying to Saudi-ize that, too. They sent a bunch of Saudis to Bahrain to learn goldsmithing. They're gonna come back and train other Saudis. In theory. But they have a hard time finding people to fill the places.

There are Saudi security guards at the hospital. They will sit in a chair with no book for eight hours just staring at what is going on. They are perfectly happy. It would drive me crazy.

Ten years on from when I came, there are still no Saudi paramedics to speak of. In every walk of life messages about the need for proper training fail to penetrate the thick heads of middle managers, who are in their jobs because of, guess what, *wassta* and corruption.

A lot of these people will have done Business Studies at university, because they imagine that they will go straight into a managerial job. They have no concept of starting at the bottom and working their way up, and no work ethic. In their lives, the third world immigrants do the actual work, and people like them sit in the office drinking tea and "managing" the whole thing.

That's the way they think it will go on being, but it won't. Fifty per cent of the population is under 21, and they can't all do car theft.

We're developing a new Emergency Medical Technician program at the King Faisal. It's an intermediate program of one year's duration. I intend that it will train Saudis to a level of competence and dedication never before seen, and also make money for the hospital. Most of the entrants to the course will be young university graduates who have discovered there are no jobs in management, and whose families will sponsor them.

It can be difficult to train Saudis because their previous education has taught them to learn by rote. Before any examination they are told, "This is what you are going to have to memorize." So they memorize it, pass the test and forget it.

I figure if I set up a good training program for the King Faisal, I will screen applicants myself and pick the interested, motivated ones. This way I should be able to raise the current, roughly 20%, real pass rate on courses like mine, to a 75%–80% real pass rate.

My superiors are not happy with that. They want the usual 100% pass rate. I tell them that at paramedic school in the States, we have to pay for our own training, and have one year's experience as an emergency medical technician, before we can apply for paramedic school – and still our failure rate is close to 30%.

If you have a pass rate of 100%, I tell them, I guarantee you that these are not good students. They are not gonna be who you want to work on your own mother or father.

They still look baffled. I just grit my teeth and keep selling. I remind them about all the other programs that have started in the Kingdom. Entire schools have been started before to train Saudis in ambulance service work. They have all fallen short because of this, "We enter, we pay, we're gonna pass" idea on both sides.

Democratic ideas that seem obvious to us are not to them, because as yet these ideas have not taken hold through necessity. Necessity seems to be the mother of social change. And as yet, life still looks really sweet from behind Sultan Bahavri's desk.

There are a few Saudis working at the King Faisal as ward clerks. It's a menial job. They speak English because they've been there a few years, and this is unusual, they are keen to learn. They want to better their position.

So I talk to these ward clerks about getting onto the EMT course. Everything would be worked out for them.

They're keen, but they all say, "How can I afford to quit work for a year? Never mind pay for the course?"

I approach my boss.

"We've got these guys who are intelligent and keen to learn. They have been with us for over two years, so we know they speak English. They have a strong work ethic and have had excellent evaluations in their time here. Would it not be in our best interests to give these guys a scholarship? Just a few of them? Because when they are finished it will benefit them, and the hospital. Westerners come and go and get trained and leave. You invest in Saudis, they'll be here for years."

"But you're running that program to make money for the hospital!" he says.

"But this is for the hospital. It's in our long-term interests. It's just three or four places."

He still didn't get it. I am just another American. And he dreads making a decision unless a lot of people say it is the right one. If something new comes along, he thinks, ignore it and it will go away.

I go higher up, to the man from the ministry. He has a college degree is from the States and he understands completely what I am saying.

"That is an excellent idea."

I think he will get it past Sultan Bahavri. *Inshallah*.

A lot of Saudis are conflicted about us. I was just walking through the hospital a few months ago and a guy came up to me –

"My mother's in here, she is sick." He explained in great detail.

"That's too bad. I'm sorry."

"Won't you take a look at her?"

"I'm not a doctor, I'm a paramedic."

"Yes," he said, "but you are American. The doctor they have there – she's an Asian."

"She's a Canadian, and a very fine doctor."

"Well" he said "I'd prefer if you would come and have a look."

I'm less qualified and he's asking me to attend his mother, but – the white face and blue eyes added to the fact I'm a man. They don't want Saudi doctors, they want western ones. The Saudi doctor who is now in charge of the Emergency Room at my old hospital, trained in Riyadh, and did a five-year residency in emergency medicine in Canada; he is perfectly competent and they will look right past him and demand a western doctor.

On the other hand years ago at the National Guard Hospital a nurse asked me to go and take this guy's blood pressure.

"– he doesn't want any woman to touch him. He's a *metawah.*"

I come into the room, here's this guy all in white, tall and very regal. I take his blood pressure.

"Are you a Christian?"

"Yeah."

"You will burn in hell. All Christians will burn in hell."

I take my blood pressure cuff off his arm and I hiss, "You need to read your Quran. The Quran tells Muslims to respect Christians and Jews and treat them like brothers."

I am not supposed even to have laid hands on a Quran. The book itself is very holy. If a patient asks for a Quran infidel staff are not allowed to touch one, so western nurses know they must wrap it in a pillow case or a cloth before they hand it over. And even Muslims are supposed to perform absolution by washing before touching it. Its words are the object of reverence.

So this man was annoyed.

The others said, "Oh! you shouldn't argue with him – he can cause a lot of trouble for you."

But he was full of self-righteousness where many Islamic scholars are tolerant, preferring to show kindness and lead by example. For a few, being a *metawah* is an ego thing. And those men are hypocrites: *maneefeq*, or two-faced. We have one in the hospital administration, and a more lying individual I never met in my life.

So while half Saudi Arabia respects us, the other half despises us, and sometimes these two emotions are mixed up in one individual.

The *Arab News* is the English-language daily we all read at the hospital and my favorite section is *Islam in Perspective*. I especially enjoyed a letter that a Saudi had allegedly written. Why, he asked, are Muslims forbidden to eat pork?

A cleric answers: *The swine is the most loathsome of creatures who wallows in his own excrement and eats feces and will invite other swine to have sexual relations with its mate and relish watching, and if you eat pork you will behave in a similar way.*

So I go to work knowing that half the hospital has read this and believed it. Yet I can drive out into the middle of nowhere, and if my car breaks down the first three or four Saudis who happen along will stop and help me. They will get their toolbox from the trunk and try and figure it out and if it needs a push they'll do it. They are very good that way.

We were in the desert exploring an old Turkish fort and I parked in the sand, and got stuck. It was 120°F and I could hardly touch the sand to scoop it away.

This little old Bedouin man trundles up in his pickup and climbs out.

The first thing he asks is, "Why did you park there?"

(That's sand. Everyone gets stuck. Which you are.)

If you live in the desert, you know these things. But he helped a lot and I was pouring sweat and guzzling water and pouring it over my head, it was so hot. I kept offering him water: he had not a bead of perspiration –

"No no," he said, "I'm fine."

Finally another guy in a four-wheel drive came by and wanted to help dig it out.

"No," I said, "just push, just push it with your bumper."

"But I'll scratch your car!"

"I don't care," I said, and he did it. I got out.

Unsurprisingly perhaps, there is endless tip-toeing around the fact that there are non-Muslims in the country at all. Ninety years ago, Gertrude Bell[17] nearly got lynched in Arabia for soiling it with her unveiled presence, and these extremists must still be placated. It follows that if there's anything hidden

---

17   In 1916, Gertrude Bell, a famous British diplomat was photographed with a young warlord, later King Abdul Aziz. She was dressed in First World War clothing – ladylike hat, long-waisted jacket, and long skirt – her face was uncovered.

under a rock, don't lift it; if you don't discuss anomalies they are not happening.

Which is why, when I was working for the Crown Prince and got six passport photos made for my visa, the Protocol Office at the Palace refused them. They told me I needed new ones. So I got some more made and the Protocol Officer handed me the original pictures in a Ziploc bag. They were cut in minute pieces, shredded –

"What was wrong with these?"

He looked embarrassed. "You were wearing a cross, Tom."

I'd got the pictures done at an airport booth in Thailand when I happened to be wearing a tiny crucifix around my neck. I'd forgotten about it and on photographs that size, you'd have needed a microscope to see it.

It's like *Birdsong*, the Sebastian Faulks book. On the front of the new British edition there is a First World War Tommy gun and a hill with a cross in the background. The cross (all it represents is a gravestone) is blacked out on every copy in every bookshop in Jeddah. Yet the book itself is not censored.

Sometimes it's like the whole of Saudi Arabia is suffering from some compulsive disorder. I suppose it's rooted in fear. Nobody discusses race, either. In Jeddah you will see people of all ethnic origins from black to Caucasian and they all claim to be Saudi Arabian, period.

If you say, "Oh, but originally, surely – you look Asiatic" – or Filipino, or Sudanese – it is an insult.

It is rare that a Saudi admits to being descended from anyone other than the original Arab followers of the Prophet, and yet less than fifty years ago there were still African slaves here. Sailors have settled in Jeddah and other ports for centuries, and pilgrims came for the *hajj* and stayed. One person did tell me that "well over a hundred years ago" his father came from Malaysia, for the *hajj*, and never went home. This person also told me that people from Riyadh feel themselves to be pure Arab, whereas the Jeddah Saudis are more mixed and therefore looked down upon.

Everybody in the Wahhabi version of Islam is supposed to be equal and yet some are self-evidently more equal than others. People are snobbish. Many wealthy Saudis affect to be appalled by the idea of sleeping in a tent, for instance. And poor ones defer to the rich all the time. The nicer your car the more ridiculous the place you can park it in. We have our own tow truck at the hospital car park, and a Porsche or a flashy Mercedes will stay while they haul away a Caprice or a Toyota.

All sorts of things are brushed under the rug: everything from ham sandwiches and crucifixes through to the sex trade and drug addiction and dishonesty. And there are yet more sins: money lending and insurance are considered contrary to Islamic teaching. This can be awkward if you need a loan, or if you run somebody over. But both eventualities are allowed for.

The banks get round the loan thing by giving you the money and charging for it, like rent, and the insurance predicament is resolved by either inaction, or blood money.

Inaction works simply enough. One day I was standing right next to the security guy on the hospital balcony, just talking, and this old Bedouin grinds his car into a space, in and out, he scratches a nice Lexus twice, gets out, never looks back and walks into the hospital.

Security ignored it. You bump, hit or run into other cars like it's a natural occurrence.

But if a kid ran out in front of my car and got hit and did not survive, I'd be escorted to the police station and a judge would order me to pay blood money to his family. Fault would not be the issue: I would be liable. For a girl I'd have to pay less than a boy. Depending on the kind of family the person came from, it's generally 100,000 riyals for the life of a male and 50,000 riyals for a female. That is, $30,000 or $15,000.

Recently car insurance has become available, from western insurers, and it covers you for a million riyals blood money. Theoretically it's still illegal, but they've found a loophole.

Third-world immigrants service this country invisibly, like a slave class. The King Faisal Hospital would deteriorate rapidly were it not for an army of people constantly mopping and cleaning and deodorizing. Wealthy Saudis almost literally do not see them; cleaners just don't register on their scale as people.

At the King Fahd (the National Guard Hospital), and both King Faisal Hospitals, special suites are reserved for the Crown Prince and the King. They are maintained and checked daily and always in a state of readiness. Here in Jeddah we have the King's own dedicated suite, ICU and emergency room kept empty all the time.

During one night shift, a Bedouin came in whose mother was being treated here. Now to occupy a room at this prestigious hospital the family must be exceedingly well heeled, but this guy walks into the regular bathroom, sees it's western style, and walks right out. Ahead he sees a door. In Arabic there is a notice –

EMERGENCY ROOM ONE: HIS MAJESTY KING
FAHD ONLY.

I guess he can't read. He opens the door, goes in and defecates on the floor.

In the trauma bay, I look across one day and there is a pediatric patient aged six and his mother, a Bedouin, is standing next to the bed. She lifts him up, stands behind him, unbuttons and lowers his breeches, holds his penis so that he can pee on the floor, pulls his pants back up, lays him back on the bed and sits back down.

In both cases, these people think that their mess will be cleared by invisible hands. All their lives, their dirt has been swept up by an immigrant worker.

A Saudi friend of mine came to live in the Bin Laden complex, where I live. I think it was the day he moved in that his driver was sitting outside late at night – it was a zillion degrees.

"There's no place for the driver to sleep," I said.

"No there isn't," my friend said. "But that's OK."

"But I've got a spare bedroom. Would he like that?"

"No! No that's not necessary at all. He'll sleep in the back seat of the car."

And he did. I took a soda out to him, and he was just settling down.

There are immigrants who don't have jobs. On the streets of Jeddah, there are Afghan children on every street corner selling trinkets or packages of gum. They will not leave you alone until you give them something. You're told not to tip them, because handlers get them into the country in gangs, keep them, and take the money. One kid at the service station, she is about seven and I always give her a few riyals. She has a father who mends shoes beautifully on the sidewalk with his tools. In three minutes he repaired a pair of Doc Martens for Nicola.

Some of the children are maimed. I don't know if that's from land mines, or because, as some Westerners say, their handlers do it to them. I rather doubt that anyone would cut their arm off, so that you can hand them a riyal. They are beautiful little children. Smart, and nice looking, though dirty, and they don't speak Arabic when they come, but they pick it up fast. They walk around selling things like water, which everybody wants, for a riyal, or Chiclets or plastic inflatables. How they keep the water cold, it must be in a block of ice in a bush – it's 130°F and they must just make a fraction off these things. But they are working, they have some dignity. Most times the Afghans try and sell something, where the Sudanese and the Somalis just hold out a hand.

This little kid at the gas station and her father the cobbler have probably been in the country a long time and have an official sponsor, because they are always there, whereas the beggars get rounded up sometimes and jailed. The idea is that they should go home, but without the fare they can't, and without relatives to feed them in jail, they go hungry.

Thanks to the willing underclass, the rest of us are cushioned from life's little grinds. In every other Ikea store I've been to in the world, you have to pick stuff up, and get things from the shelves. In Jeddah, a poor immigrant will get stuff for you, and push the trolley, and put it all on the conveyor, and fill the bags, and push it to the car, and accept your tip, which he needs because that's what he lives on.

At supermarkets it is the same. Near the checkout someone says, "Here! Here!"

And a man takes your full trolley and pushes it through the least crowded line, walks behind you to the car pushing it, and loads the trunk. For five riyals.

I remember in '93 how Saudization was going to see the back of all of us immigrants within five years. Here I am a decade later and the rule has not changed: no Saudi, no matter how poor, works on his own car. I have a toolbox and repair things and they are fascinated. In the compound I'll have the hood up and the spanners out and Saudis stand around and watch. They are amazed.

"Why are you doing it? How do you know how to do it?"

I tell them I like to do it. One of my ambulance drivers was so proud that his boss with his own hands fixed things.

"With his own hands!" he says. He boasts of my skill.

I bought shelves at Ikea and put them up, I installed a ceiling fan and dimmer switches and painted the hall, I like doing these things, in our apartment. And I stenciled the walls (Nicola made me paint over the stenciling, but we won't go there).

Saudis are mystified. "Why? Why Tom, why do you do this?"

25

Fertility Treatment for an Eleven Year Old

———

The other invisible workers are women. I admire the Bedouin for adapting to the desert, but I don't under-estimate the toughness of their women who bear child after child in the heat and dust. Also, their ingenuity. Somebody kept those *thobes* snowy white with hardly any water and those carpets beaten, somebody ground the spices and packed the bundles tight as an onion to lift onto the camels, and you can be sure it wasn't the men.

What Bedouin women contribute now is harder to say. Most of them still have hard lives and no education. They are powerless in any formal sense; Wahhabi elders in the political structure make sure of that. Within a family you may find powerful matriarchs or beloved wives. I asked my friend who fought in Afghanistan whether he'd take a second wife and he said no, he loved the one he had. Besides, if he so much as mentioned it she'd cut his balls off.

So there's a set-up recognizable to a Westerner. I'm not sure how common it is, though. The young wives in most families are subservient to the older women and some of them are harridans who can grind you down. Women don't generally work, once they are married, and Hannan, a newly married friend of Nicola, told her that the worst thing was being left alone all day with her husband's mother. She has been married for all of nine months now and is not yet pregnant. She worries obsessively about it and her mother-in-law drops heavy hints.

Infertility is a matter, not of God's will, but of blame. We had an eleven-year-old girl come in for fertility treatment in the IVF unit because she wasn't pregnant yet. She got treated, too. I thought I'd seen it all then, but I don't suppose I have.

So Hannan would not be discarded or divorced if she didn't have a baby, her father is too powerful for that, but should her husband choose to take a second wife she would be despised and treated with distain by his mother, his second fertile wife, and all the rest of the women who in an extended family set the tone of whatever debate there is.

I worked with the son of a General in the National Guard. This guy was an interpreter, and his sister had a master's degree in English literature and was a teacher. This girl loved her job, but the father felt it would be a good thing for the family to make an alliance with another Bedouin tribe. Married women are not expected to work. And he married her off to a young man who could not read or write.

"You're getting married next month."

She did not even know this man's name and her brother told me she cried for the whole month. Her career was over. It is unheard of to go against the family; you have no choice.

Like Saif, he's done well out at the palace since I left – maybe his paramedical skills are not honed razor sharp, but he's got a lot of contacts. He was seeing a western girl, but his father told him he was to marry his uncle's daughter. She was sixteen.

"But I haven't seen her since she was seven!"

"So? That's who you're marrying."

He has two children now.

"It's all right," he tells me. Both he, and this girl of sixteen, had been told what to do, and for him it has worked; but it is a first-cousin marriage.

The jobs open to Saudi girls are teaching and medicine. The nation requires women to teach girls and women to deliver babies. That's pretty much it, regardless of what you may read about attempts to encourage scientific education among Saudi women. The glass ceiling is set pretty low. Benazir Bhutto, a high-achieving woman, came and visited the Crown Prince and the Pakistani doctors were very proud, but I don't think the Saudis took her as seriously as they would a man; in the Wahhabi mind such a woman is an aberration.

My boss now is a woman, close to sixty years old, from the Philippines. She has a German passport and lived in Germany for many years. She has a huge knowledge of neo-natal, pediatric and adult intensive care. She has European and American nursing licenses. She speaks five languages, including Arabic, fluently, and has lived in Saudi Arabia for seventeen years. She has been an intensive care nurse and has years more experience of teaching than I have, but when the hospital wants someone to give a presentation or pitch an idea, they ask me, not her; a woman's views would not get respect.

This is how I get credit which would otherwise go to her. Part of my job, since the financial fiasco, is to bring money into the hospital, for instance, the contract that puts our ambulance service on call for the American Consulate. That was an easy sell because we are the only North American ambulance service in Jeddah. Another contract was made with Raytheon. They make Patriot missiles, and have an outpost in Jeddah. I trained ten of their staff in first aid, CPR and the use of the automatic defibrillator. I got them to use our ambulance service too, which was another easy sell.

And yet – Sultan Bahavri our boss insists that I must make these approaches, not the woman who is senior to me and more experienced. He sees no reason to believe that Westerners would accept the word of a woman, because he certainly wouldn't himself.

When there is a meeting with one of the Bin Mahfouz family (Khaled Bin Mahfouz is heavily implicated in the BCCI scandal, and the family runs one of the richest and biggest charitable organizations) it's me that goes. I have to see Mohamed Bin Mahfouz about assembling the jump kits they will donate for use at the *hajj*. A jump kit is a kit you can put over your shoulder and jump out with: you have IVs in it, a defibrillator, bandages, stethoscope – then it turns out they want life support training as well – and senior management bypass my woman boss and ask me to tell this charity what to put in the kit and give them the training. They assume that a woman or an Asian will not be listened to, and she is both.

She speaks fluent Tagalog, German, Arabic, English and Spanish. She has a sister in the States and she asks me – Can I get a job in America? American teaching hospitals would fall over themselves to give this woman a job. Spanish is the big language especially in Texas and California, and she worked with the American military and ran a nursing school.

If I don't know something, this is the person I ask. She is like my mentor, but they treat her like a housemaid and they kiss my ass.

She has learned to live with it and may feel bad about it. In Saudi she can save so much that now in the Philippines she would count as almost rich. I don't think she has a great life, but the older you get, I think the harder change becomes.

Maybe her assertiveness level is down too far from living here and internalizing the negative messages. But when she gets older she will have to go away.

I don't have any reason to think that most Saudi wives are ill-treated any more than most American ones. Some are certainly loved and cherished and protected and have very nice lives. But they have few rights and must rely on the good will of their husbands, and to the western mind that is unacceptable.

I've never seen any battered wives, but it seems there's nothing to prevent it[18]. The Quran permits men to beat their wives, just lightly and not on the face. In early 2004, in a move which broke the traditional taboo surrounding domestic violence, the international and Arab press widely reported the case of Saudi TV presenter, Rania Al Baz. Her husband Mohamed Al Fallata pinned her to the ground and repeatedly smashed her face into the marble floor. According to Rania, he only stopped to give her time to recite the *Shahadah* (Islamic profession of faith), "because," he said, "I am going to kill you." He dumped her unconscious and near death outside a local hospital. While she was in a coma, her father took photographs of her horrific injuries, which she later distributed to the press. Her husband argued she had disobeyed him and that the beating was justified.

At work, there is a gulf between western nurses and Saudi ones even though they get on well enough. They've got different taboos. As Nicola tells it, the Saudi women view her and the

---

18   On May 11, 2009, A Saudi judge, Hamad Al-Razine, tells a conference on domestic violence that a man has the right to slap a wife who spends money wastefully and that women are as much to blame as men for increased spousal abuse.

others as utter trollops. She might show them photographs in which she's at the beach wearing shorts and a tee-shirt (bearing in mind it's 130°F) and they'll say, "Why are you wearing that? That is not very modest."

And if they've seen a movie on DVD (there are no cinemas, they're forbidden) they'll say, "Do girls really do that?"

Nicola will say, "Well, some do...." and feel they are making a personal attack on her morals, which they are; they have internalized messages about propriety and expect her to have done the same. It is a repressive, unhappy way of looking at life, which can easily make the bravest woman feel ashamed of her own existence. Western women feel offended and claustrophobic and most I know get disillusioned after a while and disinclined to socialize with their Saudi counterparts. They'll get invited to a wedding (the women's section of course) but once they're there, they find themselves treated with disdain and suspicion. They could hang out at a beauty parlor making friends with the Saudi girls because that's where they like to go, but western girls generally feel impatient with beauty parlors. Also, I'm told that conversation somehow turns inexorably to the Quran after a while. And if they go shopping with a Saudi friend, they'll be in a mall and some man will say to the Saudi woman, "What are you doing with her?"

There is always this implication that western girls are a lower form of life.

Yet things that Nicola is quite prim about, Saudi girls take no notice of, such as men who kiss and hold hands at work. Men do routinely hold hands and greet each other with a kiss on each cheek and sometimes, extra specially, a kiss on the nose. Nicola will mutter about it being unprofessional, but to the Saudi girl she works with, Miriam, this is completely unremarkable.

Miriam's got a different set of hang-ups. The only time Nicola really interacts with Saudis outside work is when someone is having a leaving party. These are held at restaurants in the family section, because unmarried girls have to sit there. Everyone goes from the department, and occasionally a couple of the ward clerks, who are Saudis, will arrive. Miriam will not turn up, because she does not see it as appropriate to mix with Westerners and unmarried men.

On the other hand Hannan, the Saudi girl who is worried about not being pregnant yet – she used to work at the hospital before her marriage – would go. She'd get her driver to drop her around the corner from the restaurant, and phone later when she wanted to be picked up. Nobody must know she was attending anything with such potential for immorality as a leaving party.

If I go into Nicola's office sometimes I'm just in time to see Miriam diving out the other door in a panic to cover her hair and I call out, "We're all going to the beach tomorrow, Miriam, I'll swing by your house and pick you up. Get your beach gear"

But I'm just teasing. There would be major repercussions. It's sad because Miriam is desperate to learn how to dive, but she has to find a female instructor and a female beach. They are all family beaches, and if an unmarried girl goes diving she cannot be properly covered; women must wear nothing that might draw attention to their bodies and a wetsuit would be shocking.

Nicola and Bridget were once alarmed, far down underwater, by a huge black shape. It was a Saudi girl enjoying a dive, fully dressed in a wetsuit with her hair and face covered by a scarf and the *abayah* drifting eerily around her body.

Lebanese girls, aware that they should maintain some modesty, will wear long t-shirts and boys' swimmers on the beach. But to Saudi girls, they're just *sluts*.

Of course going to extremes to avoid any potential for immorality extends all the way to the top. Female participation in sports has long been a controversial issue in the kingdom, with physical education banned from public girls' schools and clerics issuing religious prohibitions on female participation in sports. Unhappy at the growing number of unlicensed female gyms, the Ministry of Municipal and Rural Affairs closed two in Jeddah and one in the city of Dammam. A woman who would abandon her husband and children to go to the gym must surely be "shameless". In a local newspaper, Sheikh Abdullah Al Maneea, a member of the official Supreme Council of Religious Scholars, writes "Football and basketball are sports that require a lot of movement and jumping," He goes on to suggest that the excessive movement may harm girls who are still virgins, by causing them to lose their virginity.

You do get rumblings of discontent about this exaggerated sense of propriety, but not under normal circumstances. On March 15, 2002, a girls' school in Mecca caught fire and the *metawah* would not let the girls out because they were not wearing their *abayahs*; and they would not let the firemen in because they were men. The emergency exits were chained shut to keep the girls safe. Fifteen girls burned to death and fifty were injured, and the *metawah*, still to this day, assert that they did the right thing. At that time some Saudis were quite outraged by this attitude and said so. But it takes a fire.

Western women are routinely intimidated by the behavior of men. I glanced out of the window at the hospital once, and saw three nurses waiting on the sidewalk below for a hospital bus to come and take them downtown to the shops. Unwisely, they had left their hair and faces uncovered. Parked on the far curb was a policeman, intently staring at them. I look down at them, look across at him, and he is behind the wheel with his pants down whacking off. Just the sight of three uncovered women was so erotic for him that he could not control himself.

Later on I ask one of the girls if she noticed a policeman parked near the bus stop.

"Funny you ask that," she says, "we were trying to ignore him because he just kept staring at us, we felt really uncomfortable."

If a man makes any kind of unwelcome advance to a woman in a public place, she is well within her rights to yell or even hit him, and if she is seen reacting in a way that is loud and aggressive, a group of Saudi men will surround him in no time and reprimand him. But most women are too intimidated by the general atmosphere to say anything.

Nicola's former boss is an attractive blonde diving enthusiast aged 52 whose partner, also an accomplished diver, is a huge German. Yet she can go to the quietest beach with him, and wear a wetsuit, and Saudi men will just proposition her, masturbate in front of her, apparently not intimidated by this guy at all because in their minds, if he lets his woman wear a wetsuit, he must think she's just worthless, and fair game.

I'd been going out with Nicola for a while when we were way on the outskirts of Jeddah, we'd just taken my Z3 for a ride with the top down along the sea shore, and we saw a young man trapping wild falcons for sale. He had one and I talked to him a bit and took some photos. He seemed like a nice young fellah, early twenties.

He and I go down to the beach and we are flying my kite. Nicola has taken her *abayah* off and is driving my car on the beach. She stops, talks to me, he comes up and asks her –

"Can I have a ride?"

"Sure," she says, "jump in."

Off they go and she comes back and drops him off.

"Come on, I want to go."

"OK."

We're in the car.

"Anything the matter?" I say. She is very quiet.

"He lifted up his *thobe*! He'd got a huge erection. And he was POINTING!"

The little bastard. I'd really thought he was a nice guy. But Saudi men are taught from infancy that western women are just whores.

In such an atmosphere, women have to plan and negotiate the simplest things, like getting around town. Me, I can just do it – I can walk, skateboard, ride a unicycle, drive, go in my friend's car, catch a town bus, hail a cab. Whatever. A woman of course is not permitted to ride anything with two wheels or drive a car. She cannot catch a town bus as they are only for men and nor, if she is unmarried, can she accept a lift from a man.

That leaves taxis. Women just walk along, and taxis will toot at them; but they gotta be choosy. There are a few Saudi-owned taxis with a registration number starting with 700 and they're unofficially warned off those because of the drawbacks outlined above. Unfortunately the 700 is displayed out of sight on the trunk. New nurses are told – "If he has a *thobe* and *ghutra*, avoid him. Bangladeshis and Indians are OK, but not Saudis."

We spend some of our time on the compound whining and being arrogant, like a lot of expats. Then there is gossip which is a lot more fun. The Irish girls are a favorite topic. They will tell you they are in Saudi to save up for their wedding and pretty soon you get them coyly admitting that they might consider a "final fling". And another, and another. Six or seven final flings later, they go home all weepy and sentimental for the wedding.

Then there are the men and women who come to Saudi having left their partner at home. For nearly all of them work in Saudi Arabia bobs up like a lifebelt offering release from a sinking relationship.

They don't all admit this to themselves, but Jim did. He had no trouble with it. He's a short bald Londoner, about forty, with two teenage children, and just a month before he left for Saudi he'd divorced their mother and married his pregnant girlfriend.

And he just hit the ground looking to get laid. In a hospital there are six or seven available women to every man, so within days he was seeing a Filipino girl. She would call all hours of day and night. This timid voice –

"Is Mr Jim there? Where is Mr Jim?"

He'd be mouthing "I'm not here – *not here*" and disappearing out the door.

He started going out with an English nurse named Sarah. At the same time he was sleeping with one of the female doctors. Pretty soon Sarah moved into his villa with him and three other men. This would not go down well if it was found out.

So Sarah lives with him for six months, until his new wife Marisa arrives. Musical chairs: Sarah moves out of the villa the morning Marisa gets off the plane. Marisa goes to live with

Jim and the baby in a married couple's apartment. Marisa turns out to be twenty years younger than Jim, and attractive, and of course their baby is only four months old. What a reunion. Oh darling I just can't say how much I've missed you –

The whole compound raises its eyebrows.

Sarah is now back in her single female accommodation and Marisa, the wife, gets an office job at the hospital. And everybody knows everything. Jim gets verbally disciplined several times, because he now sneaks out of work to go and spend time with Sarah. When Jim and Sarah get days off at the same time they rent a bungalow at the beach for the day, and stay there with the baby.

Sarah is heard to wail – "Oh this is my baby! Baby Alice!"

Once when she is blind drunk she is whimpering – "Jim should be my husband! Alice should be my baby!"

So you get these emotionally incontinent women attracted to their own destruction like iron filings to a magnet.

Rumor has it that Sarah has already been home for an abortion. Well, she now needs another and Jim gets emergency leave to take the same flight back to London. His caring attitude to Sarah is less romantic than you'd think; he wants to be sure that she does, in fact, get things fixed.

He tells his wife he's going on a two-day training course to Riyadh. She believes him.

Five or six people, independent of each other, have already told Marisa what is going on. Jim denies every word of it.

"They are jealous of us. That is the way they are, here. You don't know them, you know me. Look into my eyes. I am your husband."

So Sarah and Marisa continue to work together. Sarah has even been to Marisa's house for a drink. Jim is walking a fine line, because he is scared that Sarah will talk, and she is some demanding piece of work. One day she comes into the hospital flaunting a woman's Breitling watch. Odd, because that very day Jim turns up wearing a man's Breitling that matches it exactly.

Marisa doesn't comment. She doesn't have a watch.

You could say she is in denial.

She takes people aside and says, "What do you think? Would Jim cheat on me?"

Well, some don't say, because they don't want her to feel bad. But by now the whole hospital thinks she is just dumb, and she has forfeited all sympathy.

Sarah is the one crying for help. Around Sarah, there has to be drama, and the usual subject is a real or imagined pregnancy, which is her one hope of hooking Jim.

One night she calls the ambulance to pick her up. She is in her little villa drunk as a skunk. Blood everywhere. There is a self-inflicted vaginal bleed; she has tried to abort herself with a knitting needle. She thinks she's dying.

I'm saying, "You're all right, you're all right."

I start an IV on her – we bring her in to the emergency room. A western doctor sees her and knows she is drunk, but he is duty bound to consult an OBGYN doctor. This little female gynecologist comes who happens to be a Saudi and starts asking Sarah about her sexual history. Sarah refuses to co-operate. She's slurred, verging on aggressive.

"You have been drinking!"

She denies it.

"You are not co-operating. I shall have to page my consultant."

The consultant is a Saudi man. He can't do an internal examination even though there are chaperones and Sarah is past caring, but he decides at least he wants a blood alcohol test. We agree and they leave us alone to do it.

Bridget the Charge Nurse murmurs, "I'll sort this out, don't worry."

She sends one of the male nurses to a 24-hour chemist to get perfume and toothpaste and a toothbrush and they clean Sarah up, and we take some blood from Trevor who is my partner on the ambulance. He happens to have blood of the same type as Sarah, but he is sober and not pregnant, either.

The consultant lets Sarah sleep in the trauma bay and gives her painkillers. All of us, having covered up for her, have put our jobs on the line. The next day she doesn't even thank us and denies that any of this ever happened.

She then flies home. Within a few weeks she has called the recruitment agency and negotiated another contract, so that she can come back to Jim. She stays another year, and leaves, but a British paramedic has to work a certain number of days on a British ambulance to keep his license, and within a week Jim is talking Marisa into the idea that he needs to go back to England to do that.

She'll stay while he goes, of course.

26

The Exodus

———

We live in the Bin Laden compound. After September 11th I was particularly pleased; I thought this is the last place they are going to blow up.

The prettiest resort on the Red Sea is Sahia Beach, which is also owned by the Bin Laden family, and because I live where I do, I have a free pass to it. Normally it would cost $7,000 a year in membership. It's used by lots of Lebanese, some rich Saudis, and a few Westerners. There are juice bars, terraced swimming pools, luxuriant gardens and a gymnasium. The gravel beach is covered with a clean thick layer of imported white sand, and there are beach umbrellas and a little man bringing you non-alcoholic drinks.

Beaches are segregated because of the way Saudi women must remain covered. Western beaches are shielded from the eyes of Saudi men, and there are security guards to discourage snoopers.

Most times we just go diving and explore the countryside. Diving, you have to pick your spot, and we like to dive off boats out to sea. Saudis tend to dive with spear guns, hunting fish. A woman who works at the hospital was shot in the leg by a spear gun. They have a kind of arrow and the wings spread making it extremely difficult to pull out. Westerners are environmental divers mostly, so the two camps don't care to dive around each other. There are occasional problems with sharks – we saw a barracuda once – but much more serious is the pollution. The Westerners do worry a lot about the Red Sea.

The Geological Society had an infra-red photo of pollution around Jeddah which went from green (unpolluted) way out from the coast, changing to red (polluted) the closer you got to Jeddah, and off Jeddah proper it was black (extremely polluted). You find oil barrels dumped, bottles of Esso Premium oil lobbed into the sea, patio furniture, deck chairs.... if you walk close to any inhabited area the beach is polluted with water bottles and garbage, and the other day we found syringes and other medical waste.

Then there is building work, palaces for rich people disrupting everything, so you can't see much underwater because of the silt. The silt falls over the coral and chokes it. All the coral reefs either side of Jeddah are dying.

Sewage pollutes the sea as well. There is a treatment plant that deals with effluent from the new villas, with their flush toilets and showers. Most places have septic tanks that have to be emptied. The tanker drivers go on strike from time to time – I believe they're paid by the load, the more they pump the more they earn – none of them, of course, are Saudis. If the sewage starts overflowing then mosquitoes get attracted to it and you get outbreaks of hemorrhagic fever, dengue, from bites. Patients bleed from every orifice. It's not as unavoidably fatal as Ebola, but you can die of it.

The sewage truck drivers have to pay to access the dump, so most of the sewage is disposed of straight into the sea, or dumped as fertilizer on local farms.

We've got this book, *Desert Treks around Jeddah*. We like to get away from the compound and into the countryside.

There's no tourist industry here, just the annual flood of incomers for the *hajj*, and all year round many interesting places are deserted.

All the way down along the coast from Syria, at one-day camel ride intervals are the ruins of Turkish forts. When Arabia was part of the Ottoman Empire these were a long line of defense. You'll see a cliff, a hundred feet high, with massive blocks of rubble that have fallen down, and a fort on top. There are sometimes watchtowers thirty or forty feet high, with walls between that can be patrolled along the top.

There is one fort that King Abdul Aziz, in his years of prosperity, converted into a hunting lodge (at that time there were still desert gazelle left to hunt). He had the walls plastered smooth and extended, and since he used the place right up to the year he died, it is probably the best preserved. The *wadi* bed nearby is dry most of the year, and that's where he would land the plane the Americans gave him.

There are lots of rooms and extraordinary exposed brickwork forming spirals, round and round – like the inside of a hive; I guess it is the kind of skilled work that is used in building the domes of mosques. The rooms are about twelve feet high, with a wide base stepped out like footings to make the building more stable, and you can enter the old *majlis* hall and see the throne, carved out of marble, where King Abdul Aziz sat, with benches for his aides either side of him.

There was a wooden roof when he was there, but now it's mostly open to the sky, and there is some Arabic graffiti spray-painted.

Right beside the fort is the village used by his servants. Mud brick houses with palm-tree supports for the roofs.

There are old cars lying about; I saw a '52 Dodge Pickup and I guess that dates the departure of the last hunting party.

The only thing that is in amazingly good shape is the mosque, particularly the minaret. I climbed up the narrow winding staircase inside it. It is quite claustrophobic and dark, and then you come out high up and stare down at the village and the miles and miles of sand and scrub. Normally I would never, ever, get to climb inside one of those.

It is as if he died yesterday, and everyone suddenly left. All those people working for him, and then he's gone, and they're gone too, to find work elsewhere.

The continuing influence of King Abdul Aziz is what it all comes back to. He was so strong, and so loyal to the Wahhabi way – which had brought his people so much advantage – that everyone admired him. They were used to following a leader, and he was stern but principled.

His way of thinking still inspires the Crown Prince and the other elderly Sauds. Even Prince Naif who appears to be genuinely horrified by the way things have got out of hand, and now blames anything he can't attribute to a Jewish conspiracy on the Muslim Brotherhood.

Since 9/11 the Saudi government has been made well aware that from beneath their cover as "charitable organizations" based in Saudi Arabia, Wahhabi fanatics have built support through Pakistan to Malaysia and the Far East. The House of Saud has belatedly woken up to the fact that these guys are out of control, and the need to do something about it.

A *metawah* wrote on a popular Islamic web-site, "I'd like to say that the overwhelming majority of my fellow Saudis totally condemn terrorism. Sadly that is just not true. The majority applaud any action that discomforts the royal family whom we perceive to be unreliable in religious terms, and to be too friendly with the US. So we support any action against them, regardless of who dies. And I see this support for terrorists all around me, in overt celebrations, the smiling jokes among friends and the victory fist punched in the air."

I had been in Saudi Arabia through the car bomb attack on the National Guard in November 1995, and I had watched CNN in horror as they recovered the bodies of the American soldiers after the truck bombing of the Al-Khobar towers in June 1996. These events came and went and soon everything returned to normal, or as normal as things could be in the Magic Kingdom. But there was a subtle change going on, an almost undetectable undercurrent. I could feel it. I just couldn't seem to put my finger on it. Maybe it was the old Saudi men in the dusty souks that I loved to explore were not so quick with their friendly smiles, or invitation to sit and have tea, or the occasional "FUCK YOU AMERIKI" yelled at me from the passing cars of young Saudi boys. Whatever it was, I don't think anyone could have looked through their crystal ball and seen the freight train that was barreling down on us all. Not just at little ole me, or at Saudi for that matter, but at the entire world as we knew it.

Events moved fast after 9/11. I remember thinking to myself, if Saudi and none of the other Gulf counties are worried about these Weapons of Mass Destruction, then why are George W. and his buddies pushing so hard to invade Iraq? Maybe they know something no one else knows. I was mystified. I think the rest of the world was too.

We expats in Saudi held our breath, when on March 20, 2003, the United States and its coalition partners launched the invasion of Iraq. Then we watched amazed twenty-three days later as President George W. Bush, swathed in military garb, stood on the deck of that aircraft carrier and boldly announced, "Mission Accomplished"

In just twenty-three short days the fifth largest standing army in the world was defeated and Saddam and his sons were on the run, but for those of us living in Saudi things had only just begun.

It didn't take long.

On the night of May 12, 2003 terrorists simultaneously hit three western housing compounds; exploding car bombs they killed 35 people and wounded over 200. One of the compounds attacked was the US Vinnell compound. Those tasked with training the Saudi National Guard, and the same employer whose job offer I had turned down several years before.

Al-Qaeda was alive and well, and living in Saudi Arabia. Gone was the talk of western alcohol barons blowing up their competition in fictitious turf wars. This was the real deal and the Saudi government and Prince Naif finally had to admit it.

In November an attack on another compound in Riyadh killed 17 people. The compound was full of Lebanese Arabs, and initially seemed an unlikely target. But it had been occupied by an American company the year before. The people there thought they were safe. They were not infidels or American, they were fellow Muslims, living, and working, and minding their own business.

The rest of the year brought an almost daily series of shootouts between militants and police. Stress levels increased;

there were security checkpoints in the streets and on every corner. My trips to the *souq* decreased, it seemed best to stay at home and lay low.

The United States ordered all non-essential government personnel and their dependents to leave Saudi Arabia. The US government could no longer assure their safety, or ours, for that matter.

Why I stayed is hard to say. I fondly remembered camping with the Bedouin in the desert. Their generous spirit and kind hospitality. Watching them hunt with the falcons. Exploring the countryside in my 4×4. Following the route of the Hajaz railway in the western province of the country. Seeing ancient Dedans tombs carved in the cliff face, or the 2,000 year old Nabatean tombs of Madain Saleh[19].

To me it was all an adventure. These kinds of places did not exist in California. Saudi is a fascinating place. If I just laid low maybe it would all just blow over.

After the last bombing, all western compounds were now guarded by the Saudi military. New cement barricades went up around the perimeter of the housing complex. We had three Saudi soldiers tasked with checking all vehicles going in and out. They seemed pretty unenthusiastic when it came to our defense.

I once pulled up to the checkpoint and showed my ID, and the soldier pointed his machine gun right at my chest. I grabbed the barrel and pushed it away. He gave me a bashful apology. I don't think he meant to do it. He was just

---

19   On February 26, 2007, four French men were shot execution style in front of their female family members and children while parked along side the road. They were on their way back from Madain Saleh. The same route I'd traveled in 2003.

being careless. His buddy sitting up on the Hummer in charge of the 50 caliber machine gun was protected from the glaring sun by a very brightly colored beach umbrella. I often saw him fast asleep slumped against the gun. I had no allusions about our protection if the compound was attacked.

2004 brought little improvement. On May 22, a German Chef, named Herman Dengl, was shot and killed as he left a Riyadh bookstore. On June 6, Simon Cumbers an Irish cameraman for the BBC was shot and killed while filming in an area south of Riyadh. Reporter Frank Gardner was shot in the head in the same incident, but miraculously survived.

Things went from bad to worse.

A month later, Robert Jacobs was followed home, and shot and killed in the driveway of his Villa in Riyadh. It was all filmed and later posted on the internet. I can still vividly hear his screams of "Wait, Wait! No... No..." as he was shot multiple times. In the background chanting glorifying *Jihad*, or holy war, can be heard. The video described the victim as "American Jew Robert Jacob, who worked for the spy group Vinnell."

The following month terrorists attacked two compounds in Al-Khobar on the east coast. They took more than 50 hostages killing 22 of them. They demanded to know whether the hostages were Christian or Muslim. If you gave the wrong answer you had your throat slit, or received a bullet to the head. The first victim was Briton, Michael Hamilton; he was shot in his car outside the compound. The terrorists tied his body to the back of the car and dragged it through the streets.

The compound was quickly surrounded by police and military. The Saudi manager of the compound begged them to enter, but they refused. The terrorists unconcerned by the growing military presence roamed the compound unchallenged and killed Westerners at will. They were so relaxed in fact that they had the Philippine kitchen staff cook them a meal in the restaurant. The Italian chef had his throat slit along with the German Maitre.

When night fell the killers got in a car and drove away. Remember that hundreds of police, fire fighters, military, and reporters were surrounding the housing complex. The Saudi security forces waited until dawn, when the news cameras had best light, to stage a phony rescue. I clearly remember the TV footage as the helicopter hovered over the Oasis hotel and black clad Saudi Special Forces repelled onto the roof. The sounds of flash grenades could be heard, as they so bravely rescued the hostages. President Bill Clinton called Crown Prince Abdullah and made a public statement congratulating the work of the Saudi forces.

It was all a farce. I attended an embassy wardens meeting shortly after the attack. The Ambassador, who swore he would deny it if we mentioned it in public said, "The *only* way they could have escaped is with the complicity of Saudi security forces."

This same type of collusion and apathy prevailed in other attacks throughout the kingdom.

On June 18, 2004, American Paul Johnson was beheaded by terrorists[20]. Again the gruesome murder was posted on the internet for all to see. He was stopped at a fake police check point in Riyadh and abducted. The kidnappers had official uniforms and a police car. Collusion with government officials was suspected; most of the weapons found were direct stock

---

20   The act of beheading non-muslim captives dates back to Prophet Mohamed's time, when he ordered the beheading of 700 men of the Jewish Banu Qurayza tribe of Medina for plotting against him.

from the Military National Guard. Johnson's body was found a week later. The following month, Saudi security officials found his head in a refrigerator in a villa in Riyadh.

The carnage just kept coming. I didn't know who to trust anymore.

In August another Westerner, Tony Christopher, was shot dead while working at his desk in Riyadh. They just walked up and shot him and left. How did they know he was there? Someone had to inform them a Westerner was working there. I didn't feel safe anymore. I just needed one of my Saudi friends to tell the wrong person he worked with an American, and then I would be an easy target. Paranoia was setting in and the constant stress never seemed to let up. I have always been a pretty laid back and prone not to over obsess about things. But I was worried like never before.

In September a British man, Edward Muirhead-Smith, who worked for Marconi was shot to death in his car outside a supermarket in Riyadh. Then ten days later another Westerner, Laurent Barbot, was shot and killed while sitting in his car at a red light in Jeddah. The attack in Jeddah was too close to home. It was becoming increasingly difficult to shrug off what was happening all around me.

Then in December terrorists attacked the American consulate in Jeddah, killing five employees. Now this was where I used to go and have drinks at parties on the weekends. I played poker and went diving with the young American Marines who were tasked with protecting the staff there. From my old apartment I could look down at the American flag waving over the consulate grounds. This was my backyard. I'd had enough.

Stress is a funny thing. You don't realize how badly you're affected until you're out of the situation. There wasn't an over abundance of crisis counselors available to us in Saudi. At the end of 2004, I boarded a plane and left Saudi Arabia for good. I looked down for the last time at this vast desert kingdom from my vantage point at 35,000 feet. There was a lump in my throat. I was saying goodbye to a country that I had spent the better part of a decade in. A country with which I was still deep in a love-hate relationship. The world changed after 9/11, and whether George W. Bush, or the US government want to admit it, Saudi Arabia was at the heart of it all.

Glossary

Abayah	A full-length black outer garment worn by Saudi women to preserve their modesty.
Al-Saud	The ruling family of Saudi Arabia.
Arghal	Braded black piece of rope used by Saudi men to hold the headdress in place.
Bakshish	A bribe or kickback.
Bedouin	A predominantly desert-dwelling Arab ethnic group (previously nomadic, presently settled).
Djinn	A spirit in Muslim mythology who could assume human or animal form and influence man by supernatural powers.
Ghutra	Traditionally a red checkered headdress worn by Saudi men.
Hajj	The pilgrimage to Mecca that every Muslim must make once in a life time.
Halal	An object or action permissible according to Islamic law. Widely used to designate meat from animals slaughtered according to Islamic law.

Hijab	The headscarf worn by Muslim women, sometimes including a veil that covers the face except for the eyes.
Inshallah	God willing.
Kaaba	Cuboidal building in Mecca, and Islam's most sacred site.
Kiswah	The black and gold cloth that covers the Kaaba.
Majlis	A meeting or sitting room for receiving guests.
Mecca	City in west Saudi Arabia, the holiest city in Islam.
Metawah	Also known as the morals police. Men who seek out and arrest or punish those who they deem are not abiding by Saudi religious law.
Quran	Central religious text of Islam. Considered by Muslims to be the final revelation of God to mankind.
Saluki	Oldest know breed of domesticated dog. A speedy hunting dog, often used in tandem with falcons.
Shahadah	The Islamic profession of faith and the most important of the five pillars of Islam (There is no God but Allah, and Mohamed is his prophet).
Sharia	The body of Islamic religious law. The term means "the way".
Shisha	An oriental tobacco pipe with a long flexible tube connected to a container where the smoke is cooled by passing through water.

Sidiqi	Means "friend" in Arabic. This term is also used as a name for home made alcohol that is close to 200 proof and is highly flammable.
Souq	A market, or part of a market, in an Arab city.
Thobe	A long white shirt-like dress that is traditionally worn by Saudi men.
Ulema	A body of Muslim scholars or religious leaders.
Wadi	A valley, or dry river bed.
Wahhabi	Ultra-conservative form of Sunni Islam, attributed to Mohamed ibn Abd-Al-Wahhab an 18th century scholar.
Wassta	A persons connections or influence.

Made in the USA
Lexington, KY
24 July 2013